The
New
ITALIAN
COOKING

By Margaret and G. Franco Romagnoli

The Romagnolis' Table
The Romagnolis' Meatless Cookbook
The New Italian Cooking

The New

ITALIAN COOKING

*by Margaret and
G. Franco Romagnoli*

An Atlantic Monthly Press Book
Little, Brown and Company
Boston — Toronto

Second Printing

Library of Congress Cataloging in Publication Data
Romagnoli, Margaret.
    The new Italian cooking.
    "An Atlantic Monthly Press book."
    Includes index.
    1. Cookery, Italian.   I. Romagnoli, G. Franco,
joint author. II. Title.
TX723.R539   641.5945   80-16055
ISBN 0-316-75565-6

ATLANTIC–LITTLE, BROWN BOOKS
ARE PUBLISHED BY
LITTLE, BROWN AND COMPANY
IN ASSOCIATION WITH
THE ATLANTIC MONTHLY PRESS

Designed by Janis Capone

*Published simultaneously in Canada
by Little, Brown & Company (Canada) Limited*

PRINTED IN THE UNITED STATES OF AMERICA

For
Jane in Gloucester
and
Mirella in Rome

Contents

Introduction   ix

Basic Procedures   1

    Flavorings, Herbs, and
      Ingredients/ *Aromi,*
      spezie, ed ingre-
      dienti   3

    Weights, Measures, and
      Temperatures   19

    Equipment/
    Batteria di cucina   22

    Batters, Butters, Basic
      Sauces, and Broths/
    Pastelle, burri, salse, e
      brodi   25

Appetizers
Antipasti   49

First Courses
Primi piatti   77

    Soups/*Minestre*   81

    Pasta   91

    Rice/*Riso*   134

Second Courses
Secondi piatti   153

    Beef and Veal/*Manzo e
      vitello*   157

    Pork/*Maiale*   171

    Lamb/*Agnello*   176

    Poultry/*Pollame*   185

    Omelets/*Frittate*   214

    Seafood/*Pesce*   220

    Vegetables and
      Salads/*Verdure ed in-
      salate*   255

Desserts
Dolci   277

    Ice Cream, Ices, and
      Fruit/*Gelati, sorbetti,
      e frutta*   280

    Cakes and Pastry   295

    Cookies   325

On Italian Wines   333

Index   341

Contents

Introduction

When put to the task, we can produce no simple definition of today's Italian cookery. We could say that it follows the old or classic cuisine but, since they coexist, the question arises as to where to draw the line of demarcation between the old and the new.

An attempt to break away from the rigid norms of classic Italian cuisine was made in the early thirties by Filippo Marinetti, poet and founder of the Cucina Futurista. He proposed dishes that did away with the usual combinations of tastes and textures but used extravagant ingredients which, to say the least, clashed absurdly with each other. His intentions were good, perhaps; but he made the mistake of suggesting that Italians abolish pasta and that was that. His attempt to create a new cuisine failed and the Cucina Futurista never took off.

It is impossible to find an exact birth date, but certain symptoms of a new style of cooking began to appear in Italy in the fifties. The trauma of World War II was wearing off, the economy prospering, and a new sense of freedom, a doing away with the old, pervaded Italian life. Regionalism and provincialism, so influential in nursing old traditions, were beginning to crumble under the influences of freer travel, radio, TV, and print. For better or for worse, the patriarchal structure of the family weakened: the young, while still having to share the family roof, began to have their say and women assumed an active new role away from the hearth. It was a new life-style, conducive to experimentation in all cultural aspects. All of this reflects on Italian cooking today. Nonetheless, the new cuisine is not revolutionary, even if in the eyes of Pellegrino Artusi, the Italian cooking guru of the beginning of this century, it would appear so. But then, any one of his suggested menus would seem preposterous today, especially in its disregard of calories and nutritional balance.

The new style begins in suggesting subtle changes in the classic, adapting to new ingredients, new methods, new implements.

Italy, historically open to foreign influence, is now more than ever exposed to fast, more direct international contacts. Modern travel and commerce have introduced foods once truly foreign to the Italian kitchen. But, as in the past, they come to the table with a definite Italian accent. Would you believe Chili con Carne, Roman Style? Or Corned Beef and Cabbage, Italian Style?

In the sixties, frozen and prepared ingredients began to appear in quantity in Italian stores and kitchens. As supermarkets took over corner groceries, name brands became popular, many offering shortcuts in cooking. Of course, not all modern Italian food is fast, but much of it considers the exigencies of today, adapts to the new (smaller) family size and the fashions and necessities of the single person.

All the above makes the new cookery fit right into contemporary trends in the United States. Nearly fifty-two percent of all American households are composed of only two members; in a beautiful blending of the language, more "singles" are living "together" than ever.

We, and many friends of ours, have found ourselves (with a little bruise to our egos) to be part of a statistic: formerly dedicated shoppers and cooks for six, we now shop and cook for only two. It is, as the saying goes, a new ball game. It requires retraining in shopping and in cooking, as well as knowledge of ways to recycle or freeze some unavoidable leftovers. The latter is especially a recent problem for us: when we had four young mouths at table (and their many friends, grouped under the friendly name of "Jaws") we did not know the problem existed.

Even our reliable kitchen equipment is becoming obsolete. Fortunately, the kitchenware industry has kept abreast of the new trend. Every day new utensils appear on the market, built, like the famous bicycle, just for two.

We have not disposed of our outsized pots and pans, however. We find ourselves following another trend: the elegant large party, or in the words of our young "Jaws," the Bash.

Nor have we closed our eyes to the classic cuisine of yesterday. For those who wish to pursue traditional recipes we suggest you look at our earlier two books: *The Romagnolis' Table* has over 200 of our family recipes (including ones most frequently asked for by our TV viewers) and

The Romagnolis' Meatless Cookbook has nearly 250 recipes based on Italy's famous *cucina di magro,* those exquisite dishes invented to fill the order of the Roman Catholic Church to refrain from eating meat on Fridays, during Lent, and on other prescribed days. It has a host of meatless pasta dishes as well as many from Italy's traditional fish cookery.

Another trend we do appreciate is that a greater variety of Italian wines is being exported. Not too long ago, those commonly known in this country could be counted on the fingers of one hand. To talk of the many others was purely academic, since they were rarely available. And when they were, their quality and taste were somewhat removed from what they should have been, and thus seldom were to be recommended. Thanks to better international trade and Americans' growing fondness for wine, Italian wines are increasingly in evidence. Thanks also to self-imposed rules, Italian producers are applying higher standards for national as well as export trade. The above is also true of Italian cheeses. With a touch of chauvinism we can say that Italian cheese and wine can compete with and stand up to the best that are produced and that we simply rejoice in their availability.

Basic Procedures

Flavorings, Herbs, and Ingredients

Aromi, spezie, ed ingredienti

The first thing that comes to mind when we think of flavoring an Italian sauce or soup is the word *battuto,* which literally means "beaten." The *battuto,* with its suggestion of the sound of a sharp knife beating and chopping down through a neat little pile of *aromi,* over and over again, is the very fine mince prepared at the start of the recipe, to cook in olive oil or butter.

The *battuto* or mince is the first step and creates the first taste. It is usually made with celery, carrot, onion, and parsley, and frequently added to these are other herbs and lean-and-fat pork.

Whenever possible we use fresh herbs, as the dried herbs tend either to become rather sharp with their drying or, when left too long on a shelf, taste like old grass cuttings. If you have to rely on dried herbs, then, buy in small quantities and check the aroma before using. Commercially freeze-dried parsley and chives, however, at least when newly opened, work almost as well as fresh herbs.

Italian flavorings and ingredients are almost innumerable. The ones we've listed below include a few of the most commonly used, a few substitutes and new ideas which come to mind for the new cook or for the busy cook, and a few essential ingredients which call for explanation or comment. They are in alphabetical order.

Anchovies: a favorite component of *antipasto,* they are also a marvelous flavoring. Put up in olive oil or salt, anchovies are used in salad dressing as well as part of many sauces. The ones packed in salt are better for these purposes and are usually found in specialty shops or Italian groceries. They should be cleaned under running water, skinned (the skin falls away at a touch), and boned, a simple business of separating the filets with your fingers and slipping out the backbone whole. Contrary to what one might think (if one has never used anchovies as a flavor) this kind of seasoning does not leave a fishy taste but a delightful, slightly salty accent. If you can't find the anchovies in salt, the ones put up in oil are quite acceptable — and they should simply be drained before use. When available, anchovy paste (not pâté) is a quick source of anchovy flavor. Anchovies can sometimes be substituted by capers.

Artichokes appear in every course of an Italian meal. They are an extremely versatile vegetable, the preparation of which is much more simple than many realize. Briefly the steps are: snap off the outside green leaves until you reach a layer that ranges in color from pale yellow at the base to green at the top. With a sharp knife cut off ¼ to ⅓ of the tops of the leaves. Peel the stem by removing the dark outer skin, leaving only the inner, almost white, flesh. Cut off and discard about ⅛ of an inch of the bottom of the stem.

Pare around the remains of the snapped-off leaves, discarding the toughest of the green and saving as much of the white as you can.

Rub the prepared artichoke with lemon or soak it in water acidulated with lemon juice to prevent the discoloring of the artichoke. If stuffing whole artichokes, you can pull the leaves away from the center and scoop out the thistley choke clinging to the heart. A grapefruit spoon or a sharp melon baller or a demitasse spoon is good for this.

If using artichokes halved, the choke is easily cut out with a paring knife.

If your recipe calls for artichoke wedges, cut the trimmed artichoke in half, then in quarters, then each quarter in as many wedges as you wish according to the thickness desired. In cooking artichokes, use either stainless steel or enameled pans: aluminum and iron utensils will further change the already fragile color of artichokes.

If boiling artichokes, use abundant boiling water with 1 teaspoon salt per quart of water and the rind of the lemon, the juice of which you used in the cold water during preparation of the artichokes. An artichoke is cooked in about 10 minutes or when the heart is tender to the tines of a cooking fork or a cake tester.

Basil, an annual in most herb gardens, is now found in some farm markets (our own, thank heavens!) year round and is imported fresh from California by many restaurateurs. Its most common uses are with tomatoes, in sauce, and in salads. Its special use is in making *pesto* (pages

36 to 39), the Genoese sauce. Dried basil may be substituted for fresh in an emergency, but with caution, and never for *pesto*. Fresh basil may be home-packed in olive oil to retain its flavor over the winter. To freeze fresh basil, mash, pop into plastic sandwich bag, seal, store in the freezer, and enjoy on a winter's day even if the color is gone.

Bouillon Cubes are used frequently in the modern Italian kitchen in place of home-cooked broths. They can be extremely helpful in last-minute cooking decisions as a fill-in flavor, an accent to a sauce. We prefer the Swiss bouillon cube to the American because of its larger size and more delicate flavor, and because it is more moist and thus can be broken easily. If you substitute American bouillon cubes, use with caution: they can be very salty.

Bread: there are many varieties of Italian bread, and all of them should be crusty on the outside, firm on the inside. Avoid the squashy versions some supermarkets sell. For any recipe in this book that calls for bread, slices of firm Italian bread are recommended over American bread. A substitute could be *pane a cassetta* or top quality sandwich bread, which is more firm and less sweet than the average American bread. Crustless day-old Italian bread is frequently moistened in milk, water, wine, or vinegar, shredded, and used to give body to sauces or to lighten mixtures of meats.

Bread Crumbs, unseasoned, are widely used in Italian cooking for breading and for giving body to stuffings, sauces, and soups. Sometimes bread crumbs are toasted and used with pasta in place of cheese. Commercially packaged bread crumbs are sometimes labeled "Italian Style" or "Italian Seasoned" and/or "Toasted" and are sometimes too finely grated, any one of which is bad news. Look for the unseasoned, not too fine; or, even better, make your own bread crumbs. Unseasoned bread crumbs should be made with dried-out (either naturally or in a low oven) Italian or French bread. Leftover bread is good for this: once it is dried and rock hard, grate it and store it in closed containers. If you use a food processor for the grating, be careful not to pulverize the bread.

Butter in the Italian kitchen is unsalted and, therefore, we are most familiar with it, prefer it, use it constantly, and have written all the recipes in this book to call for unsalted butter. It gives the cook more leeway. If you don't have unsalted butter, however, just adjust the recipe's salt accordingly and don't fret.

Capers are the flower buds of a Mediterranean plant which thrives on old ruins; we've seen them in Roman amphitheaters and clinging to Greek temples in Sicily. We use them in sauces for their distinct flavor. Capers are packed both in salt and in vinegar. If your specialty store carries good, plump Italian salted capers (some either get left too long in the open can or were miserable to begin with), they are to be preferred to the tiny vinegary ones. Again, it depends on the brand. Whether you are using salt-packed or vinegar-packed capers, soak them for 5 to 10 minutes in cold running water (or change the water a couple of times) and drain. Capers may be substituted for anchovies to flavor a dish if you wish.

Cloves are used particularly as an aromatic accent in meat sauces and long-cooking meat dishes. Cloves should be used with discretion, since they can be overpowering.

Egg Substitutes: for those who love egg pasta but are not allowed to eat eggs, we recommend the frozen egg substitute for making homemade pasta. Powdered egg substitute makes fine thin omelets and works well in *crespelle* (pages 132 to 133). When combined with egg whites, the powdered substitute is good for use in vegetable casseroles.

Egg Whites: when you are faced with one or more extra egg whites, freeze them in small, dated containers. They will keep up to a year and can be used frozen to clarify broth, thawed to make meringues (pages 325 to 329), or thawed and mixed with egg substitutes to glorify an omelet or bind a casserole.

Flour in the recipes in this book, unless otherwise specified, is all-purpose unbleached flour. All-purpose unbleached flours have a higher percentage of durum wheat flour than others and thus more gluten and better rising capabilities.

Garlic is a flavor people go to battle over, and all we can say is, "handle with care." Contrary to what many Americans think, garlic is used sparingly in most Italian dishes. Most of the time the clove is sautéed, whole or halved, and then removed from the oil or sauce, having completed its flavoring duty. Sometimes it is minced, and when so it should be very finely minced, not chopped haphazardly. If a soup calls for a whole clove during cooking, skewer it with a wooden pick so that the clove can easily be removed at the end of cooking. Finally, never use a shriveled, darkened clove of garlic; it is just too bitter and old.

Lemons: one of our friends has pointed out that Italian cookery seems to use an inordinate amount of lemon rind and lemon juice. We use lemon rinds in preference to lemon extract, except in dire emergencies. And to keep a supply on hand we freeze the rinds of freshly squeezed lemons: just slip them in a plastic sandwich bag and seal. Frozen rinds are easy to grate, though cooooold, and they are a quick source of zest of lemon. Grated lemon rind may be substituted for juice in some cases, such as with thin slices of turkey breast (pages 193 to 194).

Marjoram and Oregano are cousin herbs, almost interchangeable if used fresh from the garden. Dried, marjoram is the more delicate herb, and oregano the more definite. Dried oregano should be used sparingly since it can be sharp in an overdose. Like all dried herbs, these two deteriorate in long shelf stays and thus we do not recommend buying them in those huge jars — unless, of course, you are feeding an army or a host of young "Jaws."

Mozzarella is a soft, moist cow's milk cheese. Originally it was made from the milk of the water buffalo, which in Italy has gone the way of the Great Plains buffalo in America. It is used in cooking for its grand melting property. Fresh *mozzarella,* where specified, is a must and a far more subtle cheese than that found in supermarkets.

Mushrooms: Italy is blessed with an enormous variety of wild mushrooms. Gathering them in the spring or fall is mostly a family affair, yet some quantity and variety reach the local markets. To our knowledge no fresh Italian mushrooms show up on the American market.

Dried mushrooms, *funghi secchi,* are varieties especially chosen for drying and marketing both in Italy and around the world. The types most frequently used are *ovoli* or *porcini;* with an incomparable flavor and aroma, they are one of Italy's true delicacies. Italian specialty shops carry them and they are quite expensive. But a few go a long way, and even fewer will jazz up the flavor of fresh mushrooms. *Funghi secchi* must be soaked in lukewarm water to cover for about 30 minutes, lifted out, and pressed dry gently with paper toweling. The soaking water, filtered through double cheesecloth, adds additional mushroom flavor to any dish.

Nutmeg holds a special place in Italian flavorings. It is an historical holdover from the time when Italy, especially Venice, was a center of the spice trade. We buy whole nutmegs, which are roughly the size and shape of pecans, and grate at the time of use. Freshly grated nutmeg is much more flavorful and aromatic than commercially powdered nutmeg and yet one teaspoon of freshly grated nutmeg is roughly equivalent to ½ teaspoon canned, which is very dry and has settled considerably in its package.

Olive Oil: quite frankly, there is no equal to genuine extra virgin Italian olive oil, which is hard to find in the U.S. What you can get is good virgin olive oil, and we can recommend it. Its flavor is light but definite, it is more viscous than vegetable oil. (If the oil you have on hand is strong tasting, get rid of it. Bitter olive oil doesn't deserve the name olive and yet it is sold around the country.) To make a wise choice you may wish to try buying a small bottle of each of several brands of virgin olive oil and tasting each on a morsel of bread.

If you must or wish to substitute other oils for virgin olive oil, the taste will differ. Mild tasting vegetable oils can be used if necessary in mayonnaise, where the lemon juice takes over the major flavoring process. Safflower oil also could be substituted for olive if necessary, but never for frying.

In today's Italian cooking, an increased use of vegetable and peanut oils is part of the new influence of international cooking and modern dietary trends, and these oils are actually preferred for frying. But as long as no one forces us to leave olive oil alone, we'll go on using it, a gentle flavor for our salads, fish, and vegetables. *Viva!*

Oregano: see Marjoram.

Pancetta is Italian bacon, cured but not smoked. It comes rolled in a tight roll, and you should be able to find good *pancetta* in any reputable Italian *salumeria*. Like American bacon, however, *pancetta* can sometimes be too fatty; it can also take on a disagreeable taste if it doesn't get consumed (sold) at a steady rate. Beware, and don't be disappointed.

Some cooks substitute thick-sliced smoked bacon for *pancetta,* but we find that top-quality, very lean salt pork is closer to the taste of good *pancetta.* It looks like lean slab bacon and, like *pancetta,* it is unsmoked. Some brands of salt pork are too salty even if they are nicely lean. This is easily corrected by blanching the pork briefly in boiling water, draining it thoroughly, and then proceeding.

Parmesan Cheese is universally recognized as the best of the *grana* cheese (*formaggio grana*) of Northern Italy. It is made from skimmed cow's milk and should be aged at least two years. Like good wine it improves with age.

Good imported parmesan can be used as a table cheese as well as freshly grated to grace a dish of pasta or *risotto* or soup. American Parmesan does its job adequately too, especially if the cheese is to be incorporated in a casserole and is not a major flavoring. Just beware, lest it has been sitting on a shelf too long and has become so dried out as to resemble salted sawdust.

Parsley, available all year round in most markets, is used in Italian dishes as an ingredient more than a decoration. Rarely do you find a bunch of parsley decorating a dish on the Italian table. Italian parsley is flat-leafed and is more fragrant than the curly-leafed parsley. Curly parsley can be substituted for Italian when that is not available, but do use a bit of the tender stem when a mince is called for: it adds flavor.

Pecorino **Cheese,** frequently called "Romano" in the U.S., is made from the milk of the ewe (*pecora*). It is a hard cheese with a tight grain and a sharp flavor. *Pecorino* is made in various regions of Italy, but the *pecorino* made in the Roman region is known as the best of all.

American *pecorino*, or American Romano, is sharper than the imported, especially when sold already grated. So, use it with discretion.

Pepper for seasoning should be freshly ground, if possible. Like nutmeg, the freshly ground has a finer flavor than that which has been ground and packaged commercially. In this book, black pepper is always called for *unless* white is specified.

Prosciutto, either raw (*crudo*) or cooked (*cotto*), is cured unsmoked ham. It should be a deep pink, moist, well veined, with a rim of light sweet fat, tasty but not salty. It is hard to find the real thing in the U.S. Italian *prosciutti* are barred from import in the U.S., so the imported ones are from Switzerland. They are not bad, but they aren't Italian. Most American-made *prosciutto* is cured with nitrites and hence is drier and more salty than Italian *prosciutto*.

At long last, however, the Italian method of aging, curing under salt at the right temperature, is being used in one factory in the U.S.: Daniele in Pascoag, Rhode Island. The Daniele people set up the plant in 1976 and their *prosciutto* is beginning to make headway in Italian specialty shops and topnotch restaurants. Their process is exactly the same as that used in San Daniele, Italy, home of the sweetest of *prosciutti*.

If the *prosciutto* in your market doesn't measure up to qualifications you can try a substitute: Polish (style) ham or country-smoked Virginia. We suppose that sounds like heresy, but to tell the truth we'd rather offer a good substitute than go without a favorite dish when the appetite calls.

If *prosciutto* is to be used in whole slices, be sure to have it cut lengthwise, parallel to the bone (or to the place where the bone once was), neither thick nor paper-thin. If it is to be used diced in a dish such as *risotto*, or minced in a *battuto*, you can get the less lovely looking but equally good tasting cuts nearest the bone or at the end of the *prosciutto*. And if you like soup, ask the clerk if you can have, or buy, the *prosciutto* bone when it is down to its last snippets: with lentils, as in Lentil and Sausage Soup (83), or in Pasta and Bean Soup (86 to 88), or with dried peas its flavor is incomparable.

Red Pepper (*peperoncino*) is hot pepper and is usually sold whole in Italy, crushed in America. It is used to flavor olive oil in hot sauces. We prefer the traditional Italian form, the whole dried pod, which can be seeded and then cooked briefly in olive oil before being discarded for good. Tabasco and hot pepper sauce, however, have infiltrated the new cooking in Italy and are being used more and more in place of the seeded pod. When added to hot olive oil, Tabasco or hot pepper sauce skitters like mad; so if you use one of these be sure to wait and add it after a few more elements have gone into the pan.

We do not recommend the crushed red pepper, as it isn't easy to remove from any oil and thus tends to overcook and become bitter rather than hot. Chinese and Italian specialty shops carry the whole, dried peppers.

Rice: for years we have recommended American long-grain rice in place of Italian imported rice because it cooks up well and quickly and holds its shape and because not everyone can rush out to a specialty store and find the imported *Arborio*. However, in our peregrinations doing cooking lessons around the country, we have found a simply marvelous fat-kernelled, long-grain rice from Arkansas. We feel that if you can find it, labeled "extra-long-grain" or "extra-long-grain-enriched" (one brand name is Chefway), you should try it for *risotto*. (See pages 134 to 137, the introduction to the rice section.)

Ricotta is a soft, spoonable, unsalted ewe's milk cheese. It is to be kept refrigerated and consumed fresh, and it is used in pasta, rice, and desserts.

Rosemary is such a favorite of ours with pork, lamb, fish, and poultry that we cannot conceive of cooking without it and hence even in cold New England we keep a pot going in a sunny window all winter long. The rosemary leaves look like fat, flat pine needles and have a slightly resinous aroma. A twig of fresh rosemary can flavor any dish and be removed easily. Dried rosemary, if not too long in the pantry, can be substituted for fresh, but is not easy to remove after cooking. For this reason, some prefer to wrap the rosemary in kitchen cheesecloth. If you have never tried fresh rosemary, we urge anyone who can to buy a plant and experiment. It may be a conversion.

Saffron, a spice derived from the pistils of the saffron crocus, is an essential of *risotto alla milanese* (page 143) and is used both for coloring and flavoring. It is quite expensive and is sold by fractions of grams in packets, in a powdered or natural form. We prefer the powdered Italian saffron, as its increased availability and sales give you a fresher product than the natural dried pistils. The dried pistils should be crumbled and dissolved in 2 tablespoons of warm liquid before being added to your dish.

Sage is another old favorite and familiar to most American cooks for use with sausage and pork and poultry. It is a very pretty and hardy perennial, which we keep in the garden all year round. Sage is used with trout, turkey, veal (the famous *saltimbocca,* page 193), and other meat dishes. We prefer fresh sage, but if you use the dried, use it sparingly. Dried ground sage is very pungent, so beware. Dried whole leaf sage is not bad at all, if not too old, and you can crumble it at the moment of cooking.

Tomatoes: as everyone who has ever eaten Italian food knows, the tomato is one of the country's favorite ingredients. Most Italian recipes, however, use far smaller quantities of tomatoes than many Americans presume.

In sauces, soups, salads, as a vegetable stuffed or in juice any time of the day, the tomato is prized. Its flavor depends on the soil it is grown in, the time it was picked, the manner in which it was canned, and the variety of the tomato plant.

Campania, or the Naples region, is famous for its San Marzano plum tomatoes, meaty, pear-shaped tomatoes which boil down perfectly for sauce. You can get them in American markets, in cans, seasoned with salt and a basil leaf. You can also get canned California plum tomatoes seasoned with basil. Some American plum tomatoes, however, are put up with added tomato puree, and that's the rub. Tomato puree seems almost as concentrated as tomato paste, tending to add a sharp acid taste to the tomato. This can be controlled by the addition of a pinch or two of sugar. To tell the truth, some of the imported San Marzano as well as some of the Californian cans we've opened were far from the plump fruit we expected. So we take a rational route: pick a can of Californian or other American-grown plum tomatoes, labeled Italian style and/or pear-shaped; open; taste; and, if the tomatoes are sharp, adjust with a quarter teaspoon of sugar per pound. Taste again as the sauce is cooking, and, if it is still too sharp, add a bit more sugar.

We do not recommend the ground tomatoes canned with tomato puree. They are just too tomatoey.

Of course, fresh, sun-ripened plum tomatoes are the first choice when in season. If they are very ripe, all they need is a good wash and the skins slip off in your hands. If they are less than ripe or ripened off the vine, we let them sit in a sunny spot for a few days and then we blanch them in boiling water for a few seconds and the skins peel off with no effort. Ripe plum tomatoes can be cut in wedges and passed through a food mill for seeding, but the traditional way is to squeeze with the palm of the hand against the side of a colander or sieve.

There is another substitute for plum tomatoes, which simmers down well and gives a fresh taste to a good sauce: canned pure tomato juice. While not as thick when simmered, it closely resembles in taste plum tomatoes which have been put through a food mill or seeded and spun in a food processor. We first tried it during some minor emergency that had to do with appetite: "I'm dying for a dish of pasta with tomato and basil." Check out brands in your local store, taste them, compare the taste to that of fresh plum tomatoes, and choose.

Tomato Paste is a concentrate, and a little goes a very, very long way. A teaspoon in vegetable soup adds just the right amount of accent, whereas a can of tomato paste in a sauce will kill the flavors of the other ingredients. In short: use it sparingly. An opened can may be divided into teaspoon quantities and stored in your freezer, with foil to separate the teaspoonful.

Tuna in Italy is packed in olive oil. The best is from the belly — *ventresca* — of the fish and is a dark color. In the U.S., we buy Italian-style tuna, also dark, also packed in olive oil. A substitute can be found in American so-called light tuna packed in vegetable oil, but it is not quite as good.

Weights, Measures, and Temperatures

It is a bit ironic for the two of us, whose cooking roots rest in Italy, to find ourselves tackling again the weights and measures problem. Margaret, brought up with ounces and pints, had to familiarize herself with grams and liters to make sense of what was going on in the Roman kitchen. Almost as soon as she could call solids and liquids in their metric terms, our move from Rome to Boston forced Franco to put the whole process in reverse and learn how many ounces make a kilo. It took some time, but finally the knowledge of the two systems came in handy while we assembled our first cookbook (*The Romagnolis' Table*) and translated our collected Italian recipes from the metric to the American system. Now we are at it again and we will abide by the coming law of the land: our weights and measures will go down in grams, kilos, liters, and degrees Celsius.

But, for practical measuring units in the kitchen, we shall retain the spoons and cups where reasonable. A tablespoon of butter (you can, if you prefer, call it an ounce or 28.3495 grams) is still a tablespoon of butter. A cup of milk (¼ of a quart or 0.236 of a liter) is still a cup of milk and much more appealing and less confusing than having to deal with 236 milliliters or 227 grams. Convinced as we are that in family cooking a sturdy kitchen scale with both grams and ounces on its face, helped by good sense, is more important than a pharmacist's scale, we will give both measures to the closest approximation. We will say, for example, that 2 ounces is equal to 60 grams, instead of 57.7 grams, and dare anybody to spot the added 3.3 grams from the final dish.

Temperatures

Celsius	British Ovens	Fahrenheit	
−18		0	
−12		10	
− 9		15	
0		32	freezing point of water
13		55	Refrigeration; wine storage
18		65	Room temperature
27		80	Bread-rising temperature
40 to 46		105 to 115	Water or milk temperature for dissolving dry powdered yeast
49 to 54		120 to 130	Water or milk temperature for cake yeast; interior temperature for rare beef

Celsius	British Ovens		Fahrenheit	
60			140	Interior temperature for rare beef, pink lamb, cooked ham
71			160	Interior temperature for medium rare beef, ham
77			170	Interior temperature for veal, pork, well-done beef
85			185	Interior temperature for roast chicken
93			200	For warming bread
100			212	Boiling water
	Mark ¼	(241° F.)		
120			250	Baking meringues
	Mark ½	(266° F.)		
	Mark 1	(290° F.)		
163	Mark 2	(325° F.)	325	
177	Mark 3	(350° F.)	350	Moderate oven, baking cakes
190	Mark 4	(375° F.)	375	Roasting chickens
200	Mark 5	(400° F.)	400	Hot oven for roasting New Zealand lamb
220	Mark 6	(425° F.)	425	Hot oven, baking puff pastries
230	Mark 7	(450° F.)	450	
246			475	
260			500	

Equipment

Batteria di cucina

Good equipment, like a good friend, will stand the test of time. Traditional Italian pots, pans, and knives are little different from those used in other cuisines. Almost everything in Italian cookery, with the exception of homemade pasta, can be accomplished within the boundaries of the standard *batteria di cucina,* basic kitchen tools. If you are a dedicated potwatcher or someone who takes real pleasure (as we do) in the mechanics of cooking, from mincing to stirring, then all the new gadgetry will hardly be relevant to you. On the other hand, if you consider some of these mechanics a bore, or if your time is limited, some of the latest utensils can be a boon.

Trying to keep up with all the latest developments in housewares is rather mind-boggling, and we do not pretend to have tried every modern item. But we do enjoy some of the new things, and we would like to put in a word or two about them in the hope that this will help you choose and speed you on your way.

The Food Processor does all that a blender does, plus slicing, shredding, grating, cutting, chopping, mincing, and making dough. It has for the most part replaced our *mezza luna* (half-moon chopper) and our favorite chopping knife. It takes little time to master and as far as we can tell presents only two hazards: in mincing onions, you have to use the on/off technique as briefly as possible or you will end up with mush and, in making doughs or creams with butter and eggs, if you process too long, the dough gets too warm for its own good.

The Pasta Machine, manual or electric, does some of the kneading of pasta dough, all of the rolling, and most of the cutting of homemade pasta. By eliminating the need of both a large board or counter for rolling out the pasta and the large, long Italian rolling pin, it saves not only time but space. Two pasta machines have made their appearance on the market: they could be called the ultimate in pasta making. Both mix the ingredients. One extrudes the dough in a variety of shapes; the other rolls the dough, and that we prefer because rolled egg pasta is better than extruded pasta.

The Pasta Pot with its own close-fitting removable colander is important for those who make a lot of pasta. It eliminates the traveling from stove to sink, the pouring of the pasta into a conventional colander, and the inevitable steam bath that operation involves. It also saves the cooking water, which is a great help if you need to cook more than one batch of pasta. The stainless-steel pasta colander-pot can also be used as a steamer or stock pot.

The Pressure Cooker is an old utensil recently updated for the modern kitchen. A host of safety devices have erased fears of explosions and of food-splattered kitchen ceilings. The electric ones equipped with thermostats are practically foolproof and are great energy and time savers. Pressure cookers come in various sizes and are calibrated for 10 or 15 pounds of pressure per square inch. They totally free your hands to do something else in the kitchen, cook food much faster than the conventional method, and, most importantly, enhance the taste of the food. There are several makes on the market, and each has a time-pressure cooking chart for a variety of foods. We used a six-quart, 15-pound Presto pressure cooker in our own experiments and cut some of the recommended times back to suit our recipes and protect textures. If making dishes using tomatoes, it is best to use the new pressure cookers with special coated linings, since aluminum and tomatoes do not mix.

Batters, Butters, Basic Sauces, and Broths

Pastelle, burri,
salse, e brodi

Certain basic recipes are used in the preparation of many Italian dishes. For easy reference, we have put the most important ones together here alphabetically. Also, we have offered versions adapted to the new food equipment in as many cases as we thought fruitful; in other cases a whisk or a mortar and pestle or a good sharp knife will be just as quick and effective as any modern machine.

Batters
pastelle

When a recipe calls for deep frying, Italian cookery has two traditional *pastelle*, batters, both put to quite different uses.

Batter I (Yeast)
pastella con lievito

Batter I is a yeast batter, especially crisp, and a must for salt cod filets or for meats or vegetables sturdy enough to withstand a double frying process. It starts as a soft bread dough, rises in an hour, and can be held in the refrigerator for 24 hours.

1 square compressed yeast (or 1 tablespoon Brewer's or 1 packet active dry yeast)

1 ¼ cups warm water

1 ½ cups all-purpose unbleached flour

½ teaspoon salt

If you are using compressed yeast (Brewer's yeast purchased at a bakery is the best), dissolve it in 49° to 54° C (120° to 130° F) warm water. If you are using dry yeast, dissolve it in 40° to 60° C (105° to 115° F) warm water.

Stir with a fork to break up the yeast. Sprinkle in the flour and beat with a fork until all the flour is absorbed and the mixture is smooth. Let rise in a warm place for at least an hour. It will become light and bubbly and will fill a one-quart bowl to the brim. Sprinkle in the salt, and stir well.

The batter may be used the minute it is well risen, or you may keep it in the refrigerator for 24 hours.

For a less thick batter, you may dilute with ¼ cup water after rising; but do try it thick at least once.

To use yeast batter: fill two saucepans (two-quart size is a good measure) each about half full of vegetable frying oil. Heat the oil in the first pan to 163° C (325° F) and that in the second pan to 193° C (380° F).

The batter will resist coating whatever is to be fried, but with the use of two sets of forks or tongs you can prevail, and the work proceeds simply. Use one set of forks or tongs to dip the food in the batter and then into the first pan of oil, returning those tongs to the batter. When the coated food rises to the top of the oil, and the batter is puffed and beginning to harden, use the second pair of tongs or forks to transfer it to the second and hotter pan of oil. Fry, turning the piece from side to side, until a deep, golden brown. Remove to drain on paper toweling.

Basic Procedures

Continue with the rest of the pieces. Pans hold about three to four pieces of vegetable or two fish filets at a time. The first frying takes less time than the second.

Of course you may find using a frying basket to your advantage, especially in the hotter of the two pots, but the forks work well. It takes about 15 minutes to batter, fry, and fry a second time a pound of vegetable. The pieces come out all puffed up, rather like lopsided popovers. Sprinkle with salt and enjoy.

Batter II (Egg)
pastella semplice

Batter II is based on eggs, is lighter than the yeast batter, and is suited for more delicate foods (such as zucchini or mozzarella). It is easily cut in half for a small batch for two or doubled for a larger group.

2 large eggs
1 ½ tablespoons olive oil
⅔ cup warm water
½ teaspoon salt
¾ cup all-purpose un-
   bleached flour

With a wire whisk, beat the eggs, oil, water, and salt until smooth and thoroughly mixed. Sprinkle the flour slowly into the egg mixture, whisking constantly. Continue to work with the whisk for 2 to 3 minutes, or until the mixture is the consistency of a pancake batter.

Let stand ½ hour before using. Or you may let the batter stay in the refrigerator up to 3 hours. After letting it stand, reconstitute it with a good whisking before using. This makes 1½ cups batter, enough for 1 pound vegetables.

Butters

burri

As in many cuisines, Italian cookery carries the rule "dot with butter" just a bit further by mixing the butter with herbs before it is time to dot anything.

Butters can be mashed up with a fork on a small cutting board, mixed with herbs, and reformed into easy-to-cut shapes.

Some, but not many, pan liquids are thickened at the last minute with a bit of butter worked with flour, *beurre manié* in French, *burro maneggiato* in Italian (page 29).

Herbed Butter for Fish

burro saporito per pesce

2 tablespoons unsalted butter, softened
¼ teaspoon crumbled rosemary leaves
¼ teaspoon dried tarragon
1 sprig Italian parsley
¼ teaspoon Dijon mustard
½ teaspoon lemon juice
dash of salt
abundant freshly ground pepper

Mash the butter with a fork. Mince together the herbs and mustard, and mash them into the butter. Sprinkle with lemon juice, salt, and pepper, and mix well. Spread half the mixture on the upper part of a fish filet before broiling. When you turn the fish, spread the remaining butter and continue cooking.

This amount of butter is sufficient for two ample servings of fish, one large steak, or filet, weighing approximately one pound. Multiply according to the number of servings needed.

Caper Butter for Fish

burro ai caperi

6 tablespoons unsalted butter
2 tablespoons capers, rinsed, drained, and chopped
juice of ½ lemon
¼ teaspoon salt, or to taste
white pepper to taste

Clarify the butter by melting it over low heat and skimming off the froth. Add the capers, lemon juice, and salt and pepper to taste. When the fish is done, pour hot butter sauce over each serving or over the entire fish. For 4 portions of fish.

Parsley Butter

burro verde

6 tablespoons unsalted
  butter
3 tablespoons coarsely
  chopped Italian parsley
juice of ½ lemon
¼ teaspoon salt, or to taste
white pepper to taste

Proceed exactly as with caper butter (above).
For 4 portions of fish.

Floured Butter

burro maneggiato

1 tablespoon all-purpose
  unbleached flour
1 tablespoon unsalted butter

Mash the flour into the butter with a fork. You
can use this amount to turn 1 cup of hot liquid
(chicken broth, beef broth, etc.) into a thin
sauce in 4 minutes, stirring gently over moderate heat.

One and a half tablespoons each of flour and
butter will turn 1 cup of hot liquid into a medium-thick sauce; 2 tablespoons each of flour
and butter will turn 1 cup liquid into a thick
sauce.

Basic Sauces

salse

Mayonnaise

maionese

1 egg yolk at room tem-
  perature
¼ teaspoon salt, or to taste
¾ cup olive oil
juice of ½ lemon
white pepper (optional)

No Italian kitchen is complete without its small bowl and whisk or spoon to make hand-whipped mayonnaise. But there have been conversions lately among those pressed for time. First the blender came into use, and now there is the food processor, which takes as little time as 2 minutes to turn out 1½ cups mayonnaise. We include all three versions here. Try them and choose.

Homemade mayonnaise easily keeps a week in the refrigerator. It should be covered with plastic wrap, placed directly on the surface to prevent a slight hardening of its top.

Handmade Mayonnaise

The main thing to remember in making hand-made mayonnaise is the steady, nonstop whisking (or stirring constantly with a spoon), always in the same direction.

Place the egg yolk in a small bowl. Add the salt. Whisk gently and steadily and add a drop or two of oil. Continue whisking and, when the oil is amalgamated, add a few more drops of oil.

When half the oil has been incorporated in the mixture, you have the look and feel of mayonnaise. Add a few drops of lemon juice, and continue whisking. The mixture will thin a bit with the addition of the lemon, but you can control that by adding more oil. Alternate back and forth, stirring or whisking steadily, until both lemon and oil are used up. Taste for salt, stir in the pepper if you wish, and you have mayonnaise in the purest sense of the word. Yields 1 cup.

If the mayonnaise curdles, you can start over: place a second egg yolk in a second bowl and whisk it well. Add a teaspoon of the curdled mixture while steadily whisking. When the new mayonnaise is well amalgamated, add more of the curdled stuff until it is all incorporated. Then continue, steadily adding lemon and oil until the mayonnaise is finished.

Blender Mayonnaise

1 whole large egg at room temperature
juice of ½ lemon
¼ teaspoon salt
⅛ teaspoon white pepper
¾ cup olive oil

Break the egg into the blender. Add the lemon juice, salt, pepper, and 3 tablespoons of the olive oil. Blend until the mixture is thick. Keep the blender going, and add the remaining oil in a slow, steady stream. If a small bubble of oil forms on the top of the mayonnaise, stop adding oil but keep blending until the bubble disappears. Then, continue pouring in the remaining oil, and blend a moment more. Makes approximately 1 cup.

Food-Processor Mayonnaise
If you like a thick mayonnaise for use in *insalata russa* (page 64) or with hard-cooked eggs, the recipe below will suit your needs. If you like a more pourable mayonnaise for use over fish or cold meat, cut back on the oil by about ¼ cup. And, if this is your first turn with food-processor mayonnaise, do not hesitate to stop the machine and test for consistency as you go along.

1 whole large egg at room
temperature
¼ teaspoon salt
¼ teaspoon dry mustard
(optional)
⅛ teaspoon white pepper
1 cup olive oil
juice of 1 lemon (approximate)

Crack the egg into the food-processor bowl. Add the salt, mustard, and pepper. Process on/off once. Add ¼ cup of oil, and process until the mixture starts to thicken (about 10 seconds). Slowly pour ½ cup more oil through the tube, processing as you pour, and continue until the mixture is stiff. Let the machine run, and add half the lemon juice, then the last of the oil. Taste, and adjust the seasonings as you please. Add more lemon juice according to the consistency and flavor needed. Makes 1½ cups.

Green Sauce

salsa verde

Traditionally, *salsa verde* is made with a mortar and pestle and is served with the classic *bollito misto* (mixed boiled beef, chicken, sausage, and tongue). It is such a perfect condiment for so many dishes that it belongs in any compendium of Italian recipes. You can use it to dress fish as well as meat, spoon it over sliced, ripe, salad tomatoes, or serve it with Italian tuna.

Salsa verde stores well in the refrigerator for days, but should be brought back to room temperature and stirred thoroughly before serving.

We do not recommend using a blender to make this sauce, but we have found that if you use a food processor and control the mincing of the parsley and garlic you can achieve a very presentable sauce in practically no time. So we give here both traditional and processor *salsa verde* recipes.

Handmade *Salsa Verde*

2 cups Italian parsley leaves with a bit of tender stem

2 tablespoons capers, rinsed and drained

1 garlic clove, peeled, cut in quarters

3 flat anchovy filets, cut in half

½ cup olive oil

⅜ cup wine vinegar or juice of 1 ½ lemons if serving with fish

salt (optional)

Place the parsley, capers, garlic, and anchovies on a chopping board, and mince finely. Put the mince in a mortar, and grind it to a paste.

Add the olive oil, 1 tablespoon at a time, and continue working with the pestle. When a thick paste has been achieved, start adding the vinegar or lemon juice slowly. Add only as much as needed to make a spoonable sauce. Taste for salt, and adjust as you please. Makes about 1½ cups.

Food-Processor *Salsa Verde*

The ingredients are the same.

Put the parsley, capers, garlic, and anchovies in the bowl of the food processor. Process on/off 4 to 5 times to obtain a fine mince (not a mush).

With the machine running, add half the oil through the tube. Scrape down the sides of the processor bowl, add the last of the oil and the vinegar or lemon juice. Taste for salt, and adjust if needed. Makes about 1¼ cups sauce.

Bolognese Meat Sauce

ragù alla bolognese

1 slice lean *pancetta* or salt pork

½ carrot, peeled

1 small onion, peeled

½ celery stalk with leaves, washed

3 tablespoons olive oil

giblets of 1 chicken

340 grams (¾ pound) lean beef, or mixed veal, pork, and beef

½ cup dry red wine

3 cups peeled plum tomatoes, processed or put through a food mill

2 teaspoons tomato paste dissolved in ¼ cup water

2 teaspoons salt, or to taste

freshly ground pepper

This is a simple sauce with a rich taste for use in *risotti, lasagne,* and pasta dishes using either homemade *pasta all'uovo* or commercial pasta. (If you have a pressure cooker, the sauce cooks in 15 minutes once the pressure is up to 15 pounds. If using a regular saucepan on top of the stove, simmer the sauce for 3 hours, stirring from time to time.)

Ragù may be used the day it is made, or it can be kept in the refrigerator for 3 to 4 days. It also freezes well and, if freezing it, you may want to use containers the right size for the eventual use of 1, 2, or 4 servings.

Cut the *pancetta* or salt pork in small pieces and put them with the carrot, onion, and celery. Process or mince until a fine paste has been achieved.

Sauté the mince until golden in the olive oil in a heavy pan or open pressure cooker.

Trim the chicken liver and heart. Skin the gizzard. Place the giblets and the meat(s) together and either process on/off until finely minced or send through a meat grinder.

Add the meats to the *battuto* in the pan and brown them thoroughly. With a wooden spoon, break up any little clumps of meat that tend to cling together. When the meats are browned, add the wine and let it evaporate. (Romans use dry white wine, but the Bolognese tradition holds to red.)

Add the tomatoes, tomato paste, salt, and pepper. Bring to a boil, stir, cover, and cook according to the pan you are using: 15 minutes at a 15-pound pressure or 3 hours in a saucepan. In long cooking, stir occasionally and cook, uncovered, the last hour to reduce the liquids.

This *ragù* serves 4 with *fettuccine* or *spaghetti* or in *risotto*. Always serve with a sprinkling of freshly grated Parmesan cheese.

Pesto

Pesto sauce is to Italian cooking what the Holy Grail is to medieval legend. Pure *pesto* hails from Genoa, the Grail from Jerusalem. Just as the Grail was revealed only to the purest of knights, legend also has it that the real *pesto* has been tasted only by the purest of gourmets. And only Genoese gourmets at that.

In our years of research, we have encountered so many real *pesti,* all delightful (though some even more than others), that we have come to the conclusion that real *pesto* is the *pesto* on the plate.

Pesto is a mixture of the flavors of fresh basil (purists use only basil from the Genoese riviera), garlic, olive oil (only *Ligurian* olive oil for purists), Parmesan and *pecorino* cheeses (the latter only from Sardinia), and pine nuts (defenders of the holiest of *pesti* allow this modern, and welcome, addition). Some experienced chefs, naturally owners of the real secret, add a few leaves of spinach to the basil, others a few sprigs of parsley. Still others use a mixture of pine nuts and walnuts. And there are some who add butter to the oil. All agree, nonetheless, that real *pesto* should be made with a mortar and pestle — as its name signifies. We agree, even if we do not insist that the mortar be of Carrara marble and the pestle of Ligurian basswood.

Where is the truth about *pesto* then? Perhaps, like the true Grail, it is in the song of the poet. True *pesto* is in the taste of the maker. After a few trials, you will discover the proportions of the ingredients most suitable to your own taste. Then you, too, will be the owner and defender of a real *pesto*.

There is, however, one unalterable rule: use only fresh basil leaves and good olive oil. It is also helpful to know that basil grown in a garden in the summer is far more aromatic than that grown in a greenhouse. Freshly grated cheeses, whenever possible, are also better than those grated and packaged commercially. Lightly toast the nuts if they are too fresh and too oily; otherwise they tend to paste up and not mix well.

At the risk of courting heresy, we have to admit that *pesto* can be made in a food processor or a blender; but the action is so fast that it is apt to lead to homogenized paste. So you must act quickly before the texture of the sauce is ruined. We recommend that you start by making *pesto* in a mortar and then experiment with the machines. Recipes for 3 variations, one for each mentioned, follow.

Mortar and Pestle *Pesto*

2 cups loosely packed fresh basil leaves

2 medium garlic cloves

1 teaspoon salt

85 grams (3 ounces) pine nuts, lightly toasted

1 tablespoon grated Parmesan cheese

1 tablespoon grated *Romano pecorino*) cheese

¾ to 1 cup olive oil

Place the basil, garlic, and salt in a mound on a chopping board, and chop finely. Spread the pine nuts out on the board and crush them with a rolling pin or a heavy meat pounder. Add the nuts to the chopped basil and garlic, and chop some more.

Put the basil-garlic-nut mixture into a mortar (ceramic, marble, or wood) and pound and grind the mixture with the pestle until the natural juices of the herbs and nuts begin to form a thick paste. Add the cheeses, and continue working with the pestle until the whole mixture seems well amalgamated.

Add the oil slowly, about a tablespoon at a time, and continue to work with the pestle. Stop adding oil when the nut-herb mixture has combined to make a thick sauce. This point will sometimes be reached before you have added all the oil. It depends on how moist the herbs and nuts were in the first place. For approximately 8 pasta servings, at 2 tablespoons each.

Blender *Pesto*

2 cups loosely packed fresh basil leaves

2 medium garlic cloves, peeled

1 teaspoon salt

¾ cup olive oil

85 grams (3 ounces) pine nuts

100 grams (3½ ounces) *Romano pecorino* cheese

Coarsely chop the basil, garlic, and salt together and put the mixture in a blender. Add half the olive oil, and blend briefly at low speed until the herbs are minced. Add the cheese, and blend at medium speed until everything is well amalgamated but not pureed. Stop blending a couple of times, and scrape the mince from the sides of the blender.

Scrape the mixture into a small bowl. Beat in by hand as much of the remaining oil as needed to make a thick sauce. For 6 to 8 servings.

Food-Processor *Pesto*

2 cups loosely packed fresh basil leaves

leaves of 5 sprigs of parsley

1 teaspoon coarse salt

3 medium garlic cloves, peeled and cut in half

2 tablespoons pine nuts, lightly toasted

2 tablespoons chopped walnut meats, lightly toasted

1 tablespoon grated *Romano pecorino* cheese

1 tablespoon grated Parmesan cheese

½ to ¾ cup olive oil

Place everything but the olive oil in the processor bowl with the steel knife in place. Process on/off briefly until all the ingredients form a very fine mince. Slowly add the pine nuts and olive oil through the tube, continuing to process as you do so. Scrape the sides of the bowl with a rubber spatula, and stop processing when you have the consistency of a thick sauce. For approximately 8 servings.

Naturally, you may use as much *pesto* as you wish with *spaghetti, linguine,* or even *fettuccine.* But, being a thick sauce, it is very stiff if chilled between making and serving. So we recommend serving it at room temperature, spooning it on individual portions of pasta to which you should add either a tablespoon of unsalted butter or a tablespoon of the boiling pasta water. Toss, and you may begin to eat.

For extra flavor, use a dollop of *pesto* in *minestrone* or soups, with boiled meats, or with poached fish.

To conserve *pesto,* put it in a jar with a tight lid, but before you seal it, make sure a thin film of oil has formed on top of the sauce. If it hasn't, add a few drops of oil. Keep refrigerated until time to use, and then bring it to room temperature.

Pesto may be frozen if made without the cheese. Add cheese to thawed *pesto,* and work well.

Tomato Sauce

salsa di pomodoro

1 small carrot, peeled
1 celery stalk, washed
1 small onion, peeled
3 sprigs Italian parsley
3 fresh basil leaves
3 tablespoons olive oil
3 cups peeled plum tomatoes
1 teaspoon salt, or to taste
¼ teaspoon sugar (optional, depending on tomato flavor)

Mince the carrot, celery, onion, parsley, and basil by hand or process on/off a few times.

Sauté the mince in the olive oil until golden in a saucepan or an open pressure cooker. Add the tomatoes and salt, stir, and cover. If using a conventional pan, bring to a boil, lower the heat, and simmer 30 minutes, stirring occasionally. Taste, and adjust the seasonings as necessary.

If using a pressure cooker, bring up to a 15-pound pressure and cook 5 minutes. Stir, and taste the sauce. Adjust the seasonings as necessary, and simmer for approximately 10 minutes, uncovered, to reach sauce consistency thick enough to coat a spoon. For 4 to 6 servings.

Tomato and Basil Sauce

salsa di pomodoro e basilico

6 tablespoons unsalted butter
2 cups canned peeled plum tomatoes, fresh, processed, or put through a food mill
6 fresh basil leaves, or ¾ to 1 teaspoon dried basil leaves
1 teaspoon salt, or to taste

Melt the butter in a sauté or frying pan over medium heat. Add the tomatoes. Break the basil leaves into the pan, and add salt.

When the sauce boils, lower the heat to simmer. Cook about 20 minutes, stirring occasionally, until the liquid has boiled down a bit, the color darkened, and the sauce thickened enough to coat a spoon. Taste for seasonings, and adjust to please. For approximately 4 servings of pasta.

White Sauce
besciamella/balsamella

Some food historians say the butter-flour-milk white sauce started in northern Italy as *balsamella*. The French claim it for their own, having named it after Louis de Béchamel, Lord Steward at the court of Louis XIV. The English-speaking world simply calls it white sauce. It is a sauce with very few secrets. Its only difficulty has always been undercooking, which results in a pasty-floury taste, heavy enough to ruin any dish it dresses. Beginners sometimes find it difficult to make it lump-free, in which case we advise using the American, quick-mixing flour.

Besciamella comes in light, medium, and thick versions, depending on the use to which it will be put. Chicken broth is substituted for the milk when *besciamella* is to be paired with poultry. When used with fish, the milk is replaced by fish broth. In these last two cases, the sauces are called more properly *salse vellutate.*

The seasonings are usually salt, pepper, and freshly grated nutmeg. They can be varied by the addition of either grated Parmesan cheese, minced parsley, cream, or mustard, depending on the sauce's final use, be it with *cannelloni,* fish, *gnocchi, lasagne, timballi,* or vegetables.

If you make a *besciamella* and do not use it right away, let it cool in its pan a few minutes, and then place a piece of plastic wrap directly on the surface to prevent a skin from forming on its top as it cools further. *Besciamella* can stay in the refrigerator for hours, but it must be reheated to regain proper saucelike consistency, unless it is to be used in layering casseroles or *lasagne.*

If you wish to keep *besciamella* warm for a while before using, place it in a double boiler with a tablespoon butter on top of the sauce or stir it from time to time to prevent a skin from forming.

4 tablespoons unsalted
  butter
6 tablespoons flour
2 cups milk
½ teaspoon freshly grated
  nutmeg, or ¼ teaspoon
  commercially grated
½ teaspoon salt
⅛ to ¼ teaspoon white
  pepper, according to
  taste

In a heavy two-quart saucepan, melt the butter over low heat. Add the flour to the butter all at once, and stir rapidly with a whisk. Continue stirring until all the flour has absorbed the butter and the mixture is smooth and has cooked at least 1 minute.

Meanwhile, in a one-quart saucepan, heat the milk until scalding. Add the hot milk to the butter-flour pan in a slow, steady stream, stirring as you add. Continue stirring, and raise the heat to medium for 3 minutes. Remove from heat, stir in the seasonings, return to the stove, and stir over low heat for 3 minutes or until the sauce has a very smooth consistency and no longer tastes of uncooked flour. Makes 2½ cups of medium-thick *besciamella*.

To make a lighter *besciamella*, use only 4 tablespoons of flour. A thicker *besciamella* calls for 7 to 8 tablespoons of flour, depending on your taste.

Broths
brodi

The broth recipes we give here are all adapted for preparation in a six-quart, 15-pound pressure cooker. Conventional broth recipes abound — by using a modern pressure cooker, one can make broth in 45 minutes to an hour, instead of 2 to 3 hours, without losing or damaging the old-fashioned, genuine taste of broth. Pressure-cooked broth can be used by itself, to make *risotti,* to make other soups, or as a light stock for main dishes. Broth can be frozen the moment it cools off, or it may be kept in the refrigerator up to 3 days.

Beef Broth
brodo di carne

675 grams (1 ½ pounds) marrow bone

450 to 675 grams (1 to 1 ½ pounds) lean beef (chuck, shin bone, bottom round)

1 ½ stalks celery with leaves, washed

2 carrots, scrubbed

1 medium onion, peeled

4 teaspoons salt

6 peppercorns

1 small bay leaf

1 teaspoon dried tarragon

3 tablespoons thick tomato juice, or 2 peeled plum tomatoes

2½ quarts cold water (approximate)

Put the bones and meat in a six-quart, 15-pound pressure cooker. Add all the other ingredients and as much water as is necessary to bring the level to the maximum of the pan. Cover, bring up the pressure, and cook 30 minutes.

Strain the broth through cheesecloth and a fine strainer. Cool to coagulate any fat, and skim it off. Makes approximately 10 cups.

Chicken Broth

brodo di pollo

1 to 1⅓ kilograms (2 to 3 pounds) chicken, cut up (including necks, backs, carcass)

1 small beef or veal marrow bone (optional)

1 carrot, scrubbed and cut in half

1 celery stalk with leaves, washed and halved

3 ripe or canned peeled plum tomatoes (optional; do not use when a very clear broth is desired)

2½ teaspoons salt

4 peppercorns

1 bay leaf

9 to 10 cups cold water (approximate)

Place everything in a pressure cooker (six-quart, 15-pound size). Add water to cover or to the maximum fill mark. Close the pressure cooker, bring up to pressure, and cook 30 minutes. You may let the pressure fall of its own accord, or you may bring it down immediately. Open the pan, pour the broth through a cheesecloth-lined sieve into a clean receptacle. Cool to firm any fat, and skim it off. Makes about 10 cups.

To clarify meat or chicken broth: bring broth to a boil, add two egg whites slightly beaten, and, as the broth continues to boil for 2 minutes, beat the whites into the broth. Tiny particles left by the beef, bone, or chicken, even flavorings, will cling to the frothing egg whites.

Strain the hot broth through a cheesecloth-lined sieve into a clean receptacle.

Chicken-Beef Broth for Aspic and Soups

brodo di pollo e manzo per gelatina e zuppe

1½ large (1 kilo 300 grams or 46 ounce) cans chicken broth, well chilled
2 small (400 grams or 14 ounce) cans beef broth
1 onion, peeled
2 carrots, scrubbed
2 celery stalks
1 bay leaf
1 teaspoon dried tarragon
2 sprigs Italian parsley
2 egg whites, lightly beaten
½ cup medium dry sherry (optional), or to taste

The following recipe has been worked out for those occasions when you are using commercial broths and you wish to perk them up for use in aspic or other soups.

On opening the chicken broth, scoop out and discard the fat congealed on the top of the broth. Put the chicken broth in a soup or pasta pot with a colander for easy removal of the seasonings later.

Add the beef broth, vegetables, and herbs. Cover the pot, bring to a boil, lower the heat to simmer, and cook for ½ hour.

Lift out the colander, and discard the vegetables.

Bring the broth to a boil, add the egg whites, and stir vigorously for about 2 minutes. Let stand 5 minutes.

Pour the broth through a cheesecloth-lined sieve into a clean receptacle.

You may use the broth as is for soup or aspic or for freezing.

If you wish to add sherry, add it either before serving (for soup), after the gelatine has been dissolved in the broth (for aspic), or after thawing and bringing it to a boil (if the broth has been frozen).

You may add a bit more sherry than the recipe calls for, but remember that too much sherry overshadows the broth in a soup plate and turns aspic into wine jelly. Makes approximately 12 cups.

Aspic

3 packets (3 tablespoons) unflavored gelatine
3 cups chicken-beef broth

Soften the gelatine in one cup of the broth. Add the remaining 2 cups, and heat until the gelatine has completely dissolved.

Chill the aspic in the refrigerator, stirring

from time to time — or place the pan or bowl of aspic over ice cubes and stir — until it has reached the syrupy stage, just beginning to thicken. It is now ready to coat a pâté dish, pâté, a salad, or *antipasto.*

Extra aspic may be poured onto a sided cookie sheet, jelly-roll pan, or shallow roasting pan and placed in the refrigerator until firm. When it is time to serve salad or pâté, cut the extra aspic in tiny cubes and place them around the serving dish for decoration.

If your dish is to be served on a very hot day, add an extra half packet of gelatine to the broth to produce a more firm aspic.

Vegetable Broth

brodo di verdure

1 ½ quarts of water
1 tablespoon unsalted butter
2 potatoes, peeled, whole
1 small onion, peeled, whole
2 carrots, scrubbed and cut in half
2 celery stalks, washed and cut in half
3 plum tomatoes, peeled, canned, or very ripe and fresh
3 fresh basil leaves, or ½ teaspoon dried
3 sprigs Italian parsley
1 small bay leaf
1 ½ to 2 teaspoons salt, or to taste
3 peppercorns

Put the water and butter in the (six-quart, 15-pound) pressure cooker, uncovered, and bring to a boil.

Add the potatoes as soon as they are peeled, and let them start cooking as you prepare the rest. Add all the other ingredients, close the cooker, bring up to pressure, and cook 15 minutes.

Allow the pressure to fall of its own accord. Strain the broth through a sieve into a clean container.

Taste for salt, and adjust to please. Makes about 1½ quarts of delicate broth for soups, pasta, or rice. This broth also may be used by itself, dressed with a bit of chopped parsley and grated Parmesan cheese.

For a thick vegetable soup, pass the vegetables through a food mill or give them a spin in the food processor and return them to the broth.

Vegetable broth may be frozen in any size container suitable for your needs.

Fish Broth

brodo di pesce

1¼ kilograms (2½ pounds) fish (cheeks, heads and tails, meaty fish)

2 garlic cloves, peeled

4 tablespoons olive oil

4 anchovy filets

3 tablespoons chopped Italian parsley

1½ cups peeled plum tomatoes, canned or fresh

1 small onion, peeled

1 small carrot, scrubbed

1 small celery stalk with leaves, washed

2½ teaspoons salt, or to taste

1 bay leaf

1½ quarts warm water

If using whole fish, clean them, but reserve the heads and tails, which belong in the broth.

Sauté the garlic in the olive oil in a large (six-quart, 15-pound) pressure cooker until golden. Then discard.

Chop the anchovies with the parsley and add them to the flavored olive oil.

Cut the tomatoes in chunks, add to the pan, and cook, uncovered, for about 10 minutes. Add the fish and all the remaining ingredients.

Cover the pot, bring up the pressure, and cook 15 minutes. Let the pressure fall, taste for salt, and add as you please. Put the broth through a fine sieve, and use as desired. Fish broth may be frozen as soon as it is cool. Makes about 9 cups.

Appetizers

Antipasti

A discussion of *antipasti* — appetizers, hors d'oeuvres — is practically an impossibility: there are thousands of them, some simple, some complicated, many duplicated and multiplied, and all as bright and beautiful as autumn leaves. Like leaves, some are more antique than others, some still green and almost young. All of them serve the ancient purpose for which they were devised: to provide something to nibble on before a meal.

Antipasto is an Italian word derived from the Latin *ante* (as in *ante bellum*), meaning "before," and *prandium,* meaning "meal." *Antipasto* should be just that, a taste before a meal, not something to work against the meal, as in *anti*social. That heaping platter of all the glories an Italian grocery has to offer is quite misdirected.

Not every Italian meal, of course, is preceded by an *antipasto.* Appetizers generally are saved for special meals or are used to precede a normal but very light meal or to while away the time it takes for that "cook-and-serve" dish.

And, *antipasti* are becoming popular in another role today: often three or four or more, different in taste and texture, can make up a buffet dinner.

Antipasto is a game anyone can play. You can choose from the traditional, borrow from the classic, or invent your own. Some Italian *antipasti* end up as side dishes and, naturally, vice versa.

Furthermore, international influences are showing up more than ever on today's Italian table in the form of crackers, cheeses, hearts of palm, avocados, canned pâté and many others too numerous to list.

We have selected here a few newcomers to our scene, which blend or contrast happily with the older, more traditional *antipasti* we have written about before. Some call for classic preparation, some are tailored to modern methods, tools, and ingredients. All were chosen for taste and for the way they fit the American table today. Many either can be prepared ahead of time or require little preparation — and that ease and simplicity is very much part of today's Italian cooking.

Avocado with Anchovy Sauce

avocado in salsa d'acciuga

Sauce

3 flat anchovy filets, preserved in oil, or 2 salted anchovy filets
3 cocktail onions
1 teaspoon Dijon mustard
3 tablespoons olive oil
2 tablespoons wine vinegar
salt (optional)
white pepper to taste

2 avocados

If using anchovies in oil, drain them well. If using anchovies preserved in salt, rinse them thoroughly under cold running water and remove the spines. Pat dry with paper towels.

Mash the anchovies in a mortar with a pestle or in a blender or food processor. Cut the onions in half, and mash them into the anchovy paste. Stir in the mustard, oil, and vinegar, and work with the pestle (or blender or processor) until smooth and homogeneous.

Taste for salt (the anchovies should have added enough), and add as needed. Add a dash of pepper to taste.

Cut the avocados in half, remove the pits, and peel off the skins. Cut each half in four slices and place them on individual plates. Dress with sauce, and serve. For 4.

Artichokes, Jewish Style
(as done in the old Roman ghetto)

carciofi alla Giudia

1 globe artichoke per person for *antipasto* (or 2 per person if used as a side dish)
1 lemon
vegetable oil for deep frying
salt to taste

Clean and trim the artichokes (see pages 4 to 5), but leave the stems attached and do not remove the chokes. Soak in cold water with the juice of the lemon for about ½ hour to make the leaves less resistant to opening up.

Drain the artichokes thoroughly. A partial opening of the leaves is needed at this stage. You may do this by prying with your fingers or by using a lemon. Hold one artichoke in your left hand and a lemon in your right hand. Place the more pointed end of the lemon down into the center of the artichoke leaves. Push down, and twist the lemon back and forth, thus loosening the leaves and opening them slightly. The heat of the cooking oil will soften the leaves further to create a final wide-open, flowerlike effect.

Pour vegetable oil to the depth of approximately 5 inches in a deep frying pot. Heat to 149° to 163°C (300° to 325°F).

Using a pair of long-handled kitchen tongs, clasp the stem of an artichoke and immerse it in the hot oil. This will provoke quite a commotion in the oil, and its temperature will rise. Both will subside when the natural moisture of the artichoke has boiled away. After about 2 minutes, clasp the stem of the artichoke again with the tongs and press the head of the artichoke down on the bottom of the pot to encourage the leaves to open up like a flower's petals. Let the artichoke fry, turning it from time to time, until the stem and all the leaves are a golden brown.

Now, to add to the crispness of the artichoke, you may choose one of three methods for the final cooking:

1. Wet the tips of your fingers, and sprinkle some drops of water in the oil. This will not only provoke the temperature to rise but cause quite a lot of spattering, so take necessary precautions. Once the splashing subsides, return from the safe distance to which you had retreated and lift the artichoke from the oil. *Or:*

2. Have on another burner another pot with oil at about 204°C (400°F). Lift the artichoke from the first pot and immerse it in the second pot for a few seconds, then, with a slotted spoon, remove and drain it on paper toweling. *Or:*

3. Since this frying in a home situation should not be attempted with more than one or two artichokes at a time, when the first artichoke in the pot is golden brown, add a second, uncooked artichoke. This will make the oil temperature rise (it sounds like a contradiction, but it does work that way), so leave the already

golden artichoke to fry a few more seconds, then drain it, and continue to cook the second artichoke. Proceed to the third and fourth as your needs require.

Serve the artichokes well drained and warm, not hot. Salt to taste.

The whole procedure of *carciofi alla Giudia* seems more fussy than it actually is. No matter what, once you serve and taste them, it is all worthwhile.

Artichokes with Anchovy Dressing

carciofi con salsa d'acciuga

2 large artichokes, trimmed, boiled, drained, and cut in half

3 flat anchovy filets, drained of oil

3 small cocktail onions, chopped

1 teaspoon Dijon mustard

3 tablespoons olive oil

2 tablespoons wine vinegar

salt (optional)

white pepper to taste

In a mortar, mash the anchovies and onions to a paste.

Stir in the mustard, oil, and vinegar, and work with the pestle until the sauce is smooth and homogeneous.

Taste for salt (the anchovies should have added just the right amount), and add if needed. Add a sprinkling of white pepper to taste, and mix again.

Place cooked and cooled artichoke halves on a plate. Pour the sauce over them, and serve. Makes an antipasto for 2.

Crab Meat, Venetian Style

granzeola alla veneziana

450 grams (1 pound) cooked crab meat

2 to 3 tablespoons minced Italian parsley

juice of 1 large lemon

3 tablespoons olive oil

salt to taste

white pepper

Shred the crab meat into a small bowl. Mix in the parsley.

Add the lemon juice and olive oil, and mix well. Add salt to taste, but go gently, since the crab meat is usually salted in cooking.

Add a sprinkling of white pepper. Chill thoroughly, and serve on chilled plates. For 6.

Batter-Fried Mozzarella

mozzarella fritta

½ recipe Batter II (page 27)
115 grams (¼ pound) whole milk *mozzarella*
½ cup (approximate) unseasoned bread crumbs
vegetable oil for frying

Make the batter as previously directed, and let it stand for an hour before using.

Cut the cheese into small pieces about ½ inch square. Fresh *mozzarella* is best, but you can use the readily available processed *mozzarella* and still be pleased.

Dip the cheese in the batter, then in the bread crumbs, pressing lightly to get as many as possible to adhere.

Bring a small pan of vegetable oil (about 2 inches deep) to 170° C (340° F).

Fry a few pieces of *mozzarella* at a time until golden brown. Serve warm. For 2 (double the ingredients for 4 to 6 servings).

Mussels in Piquant Sauce

cozze in salsa piccante

1 kilogram (2 pounds) fresh mussels
2 tablespoons unsalted butter
2 tablespoons flour
¾ cup reserved mussel broth
1 tablespoon wine vinegar
2 tablespoons Dijon mustard
1 egg yolk
2 generous dashes Tabasco
freshly ground pepper to taste
1 tablespoon minced Italian parsley
salt (optional)

Scrub the mussels clean, remove the beards, and wash them thoroughly. Put them in a pot with ¼ cup water, cover, and steam a few minutes until the mussels open.

When the mussels are cool enough to handle, separate the two halves of the shells, loosen each mussel from the half shell to which it clings, and let it rest on a half shell on a warm plate in a warm place.

Filter the liquid from the pot through a cheesecloth-lined sieve and reserve.

Melt the butter in a saucepan, add the flour, and beat with a whisk. Cook over low flame for three minutes, then slowly add ¾ cup reserved mussel broth, stirring constantly. Bring to a low boil, stir in the vinegar and mustard, and cook for 2 minutes or until a creamy, saucelike consistency is reached. Let cool slightly, and beat in the egg yolk. Finally add the Tabasco, a bit of freshly ground pepper, and the parsley. Taste for salt, and correct if necessary. Spoon a bit of sauce over each mussel and serve. For 4.

Marinated Mushrooms

funghetti marinati

340 grams (¾ pound) small fresh mushrooms

1 garlic clove, peeled and cut in half

3 tablespoons olive oil

1 large sprig Italian parsley

freshly ground pepper

½ cup dry white wine

juice of ½ lemon .

1 tablespoon wine vinegar

1 bay leaf

2 whole cloves

1 teaspoon salt

Clean the mushrooms. Leave the smaller ones intact. Cut any larger ones in half.

Sauté the garlic in olive oil in a skillet large enough to hold the mushrooms in one layer. Discard the garlic when golden, and add the mushrooms, parsley, and a generous sprinkling of pepper. Sauté for 1 minute, stirring, until the mushrooms barely darken. Add the remaining ingredients, stir, lower the heat to a simmer, and cook, covered, for 5 minutes. Let cool, and then put the mushrooms and their liquid in a deep bowl or jar. Cover, and refrigerate for at least several hours. For 4.

Marinated mushrooms keep, and taste better, for several days when refrigerated.

Grilled Stuffed Mushrooms

funghi ripieni alla griglia

12 large fresh mushrooms

1 garlic clove, cut in half

285 grams (10 ounces) cooked ham, cubed

285 grams (10 ounces) Swiss cheese, cubed

3 sprigs Italian parsley

1 heaping tablespoon capers, rinsed and drained

2 tablespoons unseasoned bread crumbs

⅛ teaspoon dried oregano

freshly ground pepper

salt

2 to 3 tablespoons olive oil

Clean the mushrooms, and cut off the stems; reserve the stems for another use.

Rub a small chopping board or the food processor bowl with the garlic, then discard the garlic.

Place the ham and cheese in the bowl or on the board. Add the parsley leaves and bits of stems. Squeeze the capers dry in absorbent toweling, and add them. Chop or process the mixture until coarsely minced. Mix in the bread crumbs, oregano, and a generous amount of pepper. Taste for salt, and add some if the capers have not added enough. Dribble with oil to make a thick paste.

Fill the mushroom caps with the mince, and place them on a flameproof dish. Dribble with a little more oil.

Broil in a preheated broiler 5 to 6 minutes or until lightly browned. Serve warm. For 4.

These grilled mushrooms can be prepared ahead of time and reheated.

Roasted Sweet Peppers with Anchovies

peperoni all'acciughe

4 sweet peppers (red,
  green, or yellow)
1 50-gram (1¾-ounce) can
  flat anchovy filets,
  drained
4 tablespoons olive oil
1 large garlic clove, peeled
  and sliced thin
juice of ½ lemon

If using a gas stove, turn the grates of two burners upside down and place the peppers directly on them over a high flame. As the skins blacken, turn the peppers and continue roasting them until they are burnt and blistered.

If using an electric stove, place the peppers in the broiler and broil them, turning them 3 or 4 times to roast the skins thoroughly.

Slip the skins off under cold running water, cut the peppers in half, core them, and let them drain on absorbent toweling.

Cut the peppers in strips about 1 inch in width. Mince two of the anchovies and set them aside. Cut the remaining anchovies in halves or thirds, and place a piece of anchovy in the center of each strip of pepper. Roll up, and skewer with toothpicks.

Place the oil in a small saucepan, add the garlic, and sauté until golden, then discard the garlic. Let the pan cool a moment. Add the minced anchovies. Cook and stir over medium heat until the mince has disintegrated. Add the lemon juice, mix, and dress the peppers with this sauce. For 4.

Note: Plain roasted peppers are a traditional antipasto favorite served with olive oil and lemon juice.

Pepper-Celery-Olive Antipasto

peperoni, sedani, ed olive

2 stalks celery without
  leaves
2 sweet peppers (red,
  green, or yellow)
12 Spanish olives
4 tablespoons olive oil
juice of ½ lemon
1 tablespoon coarsely
  chopped Italian parsley

Clean the celery, and dice into ¼-inch pieces. Blanch in boiling salted water about 5 minutes or until tender yet still crisp. Drain immediately.

Roast the peppers (page 58) and then peel, core, and cut them into ½-inch cubes.

Cut six of the Spanish olives in half, and leave the rest whole. Place the celery, peppers, and olives in a small serving dish. Dress with the olive oil and lemon juice, and toss. Sprinkle with parsley, and serve. For 4.

This antipasto may be refrigerated for 24 hours. If so, bring to room temperature, and add the parsley just before serving.

Broiled Stuffed Tomatoes with Ham and Cheese

pomodori ripieni con prosciutto cotto e formaggio

4 medium-sized tomatoes
½ teaspoon salt
1 heaping tablespoon
  chopped Italian parsley
1 slice (28 grams or 1
  ounce) cooked ham
60 grams (2 ounces) Swiss
  cheese, cut in ¼-inch
  cubes
2 tablespoons unseasoned
  bread crumbs
1 tablespoon olive oil (approximate)

Cut off and discard the tops of the tomatoes, and empty the seeds and pulp into a sieve over a small bowl. Sprinkle the tomatoes with salt and turn them upside down to drain.

Place the ham on the chopped parsley, and chop coarsely.

Mix the ham and parsley with the cheese and bread crumbs, and fill the tomatoes with this mixture.

Work the tomato pulp and seeds with a spoon to release their juice, and put approximately 1 teaspoon juice in each tomato. Sprinkle each tomato with ½ to 1 teaspoon olive oil (depending on size).

Broil in a preheated broiler for 7 minutes or until toasted on top. For 2 to 4.

Broiled Stuffed Tomatoes

pomodori ripieni alla griglia

4 medium-sized tomatoes

½ teaspoon salt (approximate)

115 grams (4 ounces) whole milk *mozzarella*

¼ cup unseasoned bread crumbs

½ teaspoon dried oregano (approximate)

freshly ground pepper

1 tablespoon olive oil

Cut off and discard the tops of the tomatoes. Scoop out the seeds and inner pulp, and place in a sieve over a small bowl. Press the pulp against the sieve to collect whatever juice there is. Lightly salt the tomatoes, and turn them upside down to drain for 15 minutes.

Cut the *mozzarella* in small (⅛- to ¼-inch) cubes.

Turn the tomatoes right side up, and sprinkle about a teaspoon of bread crumbs into each. Sprinkle the bread crumbs with half the oregano. Fill the tomatoes with cheese, pressing it in gently. Sprinkle the cheese with the remaining bread crumbs to fill the cracks and to cover the tops. Add the remaining oregano and the pepper. Moisten each tomato with some of the reserved tomato juice and, finally, with about ½ teaspoon olive oil.

Preheat the broiler, and broil the filled tomatoes 7 to 10 minutes or until the bread crumbs and top cheese are toasted. For 4.

Note: This is a nice way to disguise out-of-season, store-bought tomatoes.

Seafood Cocktail

antipasto di mare

225 grams (½ pound) small squid, cleaned (page 251)

1½ liters (1½ quarts) fish broth (page 47)

225 grams (½ pound) baby cherrystone clams

225 grams (½ pound) mussels, scrubbed and with beards removed

225 grams (½ pound) shrimp, shelled

1 tablespoon capers, rinsed and drained

1 tablespoon chopped Italian parsley

juice of 1 lemon

4 tablespoons olive oil

salt and freshly ground pepper to taste

Cut the squid bodies in small strips or rings; but leave the tentacles whole unless too wide for a mouthful, in which case cut them in half lengthwise. Prepare the rest of the fish.

Put the squid in a soup pot. Add the fish broth. Bring to a boil, reduce the heat, cover, and simmer for 15 minutes.

Add the clams and mussels, and cook for 5 minutes.

Add the shrimp, and cook another 5 minutes.

Strain, reserving the liquid.

Remove the mollusks from their shells and place them in a serving bowl. Add the shrimp and squid. Chop the capers and add them and the parsley to the fish. Dress with lemon juice and olive oil.

Marinate in the refrigerator for at least ½ hour before serving. Toss well, add salt and pepper to please.

Seafood cocktail can be kept covered in the refrigerator 24 hours, after which and just before serving, add the parsley. For 4.

Salty Pastry for Tartlets

pasta salata per tartellette

1 ½ cups all-purpose un-
bleached flour

7 tablespoons unsalted
butter, very chilled

1 tablespoon vegetable
shortening, chilled

¾ teaspoon salt

¼ cup ice water

1 egg white beaten with ½
teaspoon water

Put the flour in the bowl of a food processor, steel or dough blade in place.

Cut the butter in ¼-inch cubes, and add to the flour. Add the shortening and salt. Process on/off for about 10 seconds until the mixture has the consistency of coarse meal.

Turn the machine on, and pour the water through the tube in a slow, steady stream. Process about 30 seconds or until the dough has formed a ball at one end of the blade. Remove the ball of dough, wrap it tightly in plastic wrap, and refrigerate for 2 hours.

When chilled, roll the dough on a floured surface to ¹/₁₆-inch thickness and cut in shapes (you can make rounds, ovals, or 2 crusts 8 inches in diameter).

Preheat oven to 230 ° C (450 ° F).

Spray pans with vegetable spray. Place the dough in pans. If using small pans, press one on top of a filled one to firm the dough into the curves and down the sides and bottom. Place aluminum pie weights, or beans, on the bottom dough. Place the pans on a cookie sheet, chill for 15 minutes, and then bake in a hot (230 ° C, 450 ° F) oven for 10 minutes.

Remove weights, and return to bake 5 more minutes or until golden and baked through.

Brush with the egg white-water mixture. Return pans to the oven for 3 more minutes with the heat off in order both to dry the egg white and to ensure a shine and sealed crust for the tartlets.

Makes approximately 18 small tartlets or 2 large crusts.

Once cooked, this pastry freezes well; just be sure your freezer container is sturdy enough to prevent any crushing when placed in storage.

Fill with your favorite filling for *antipasto*, such as crab meat and mayonnaise or *insalata russa* (page 64).

Crab Meat Filling for Tartlets

barchette di granchio

115 grams (4 ounces) cooked crab meat, shredded

1 tablespoon Marsala

1 teaspoon lemon juice

1 dash Tabasco sauce

85 grams (3 ounces) fresh mushrooms (approximate)

1½ tablespoons unsalted butter

sprinkle of salt

sprinkle of white pepper

1 teaspoon flour

¼ cup milk

1 egg yolk

unseasoned bread crumbs

6 to 12 pastry shells (pages 62 to 63)

Marinate the crab meat in the Marsala, lemon juice, and Tabasco for 10 minutes. Meanwhile, clean and thinly slice the mushrooms.

Melt a tablespoon of the butter in a small saucepan, and sauté the mushrooms in it. Add the salt and pepper, and continue cooking until the mushrooms release their natural juices (about 4 minutes). Scoop the mushrooms out of the pan, and add to the crab meat.

Melt the remaining ½ teaspoon butter in the pan juices over low heat. Whisk in the flour, and cook one minute. Add the milk, and cook and stir until thickened and smooth (about 4 minutes). Let cool slightly, and then whisk in the egg yolk. Mix well.

Add the egg sauce to the crab meat and mushrooms, and mix again. Fill 6 to 12 tartlet shells (pages 62 to 63) with the mixture. Sprinkle with bread crumbs, and place in a preheated broiler for 5 minutes. For 6.

Russian Salad

insalata russa

1 285-gram (10-ounce)
  package frozen peas and
  carrots
1 large all-purpose potato,
  boiled and skinned
5 tablespoons mayonnaise
  (pages 30 to 32)
3 tablespoons lemon juice
  (or more, to please)
2 rounded teaspoons
  capers, rinsed and
  drained
pinch of salt
white pepper to taste
6 to 10 pastry shells (optional)

Cook the peas and carrots in boiling salted water until tender but still a bit crisp, about 6 minutes. Drain well, and let cool in a colander or on absorbent toweling.

Mash ⅓ of the potato with the mayonnaise and work it with a fork until a soft, smooth consistency is reached.

Cut the remaining potato in cubes the size of the carrots.

Mix the potato, carrots, peas, and mayonnaise well. Add lemon juice and capers, salt, and a dash of pepper. Taste, and correct the seasonings as you wish. Use to fill tartlets or make a mold: line a suitable bowl with plastic wrap and fill it with the salad, pressing down lightly on the mixture. Refrigerate in the coldest part of the refrigerator for at least half an hour. Unmold, and serve as *antipasto* or as an accompaniment to fish or cold beef. For 4.

Savory Squid

calamari all'appetitosa

675 grams (1½ pounds)
  squid, fresh or frozen

6 tablespoons olive oil

1 red pepper pod or 2 generous dashes Tabasco
  sauce

2 garlic cloves, peeled and
  split in half

3 tablespoons unsalted
  butter

2 tablespoons minced fresh
  parsley

2½ tablespoons unsea-
  soned bread crumbs

juice of 1 lemon

salt to taste

Clean the squid (pages 251 to 252), cut the bodies in ½-inch rings and the larger tentacles in half lengthwise. Let the squid dry on absorbent toweling.

Put the oil in a sauté pan. Seed the red-pepper pod. Sauté the pepper and garlic in the oil until the garlic is golden, the pepper dark. Remove the flavorings, and add the squid to the oil. Sauté over high heat for 3 minutes, lower the heat, and simmer, uncovered, for 15 minutes or until tender. Squid releases its natural moisture during cooking, which makes for a fairly liquid sauce. If this should evaporate too much before the squid is cooked, add a little warm water.

When the squid is tender, add the butter. When the butter is melted, add the parsley and bread crumbs, stir well, and add the lemon juice. Stir again to obtain a homogeneous sauce. Taste for salt, and adjust.

Serve hot as a main dish for 2. Serve cold or warm as an *antipasto* for more.

Little Pizzas

Pizzette

There is really no perfect substitute for home-made *pizza* or *pizzette,* individual *pizzas;* and, with a bit of time and a food processor, the dough is simple to make, since it basically consists of flour, yeast, water, and salt. But, with the improved mass-produced frozen bread dough, there is a shortcut well worth trying.

Most supermarkets carry two or three brands of frozen bread dough, in packages that make three to five loaves of bread (depending on the brand). Because some of these doughs are a little sweeter than others, we urge you to experiment and use the least-sweet dough. A one-pound loaf, defrosted in the refrigerator either overnight or during the day (depending on when you want to serve the *pizza* or *pizzette*), makes 20 to 24 crisp, light, small *pizzas* for *antipasti,* snacks, or part of an informal meal. The *pizzette* cook in 15 to 20 minutes and can be reheated in a microwave oven or a toaster oven (or in a regular toaster, says one of our sons who puts the toaster on its side for reheating *pizzette* without losing any of the topping).

Handmade *Pizzette* Dough

2½ cups all-purpose un-
  bleached flour
1 packet active dry yeast
1 cup warm (50° C,
  120° F) water
½ teaspoon salt
olive oil

Place the flour in a mound on the counter or pastry board. Make a well in the center, and pour in the yeast. Add just a bit of warm water to the yeast, and begin to stir with a fork. As a paste starts to form, add more water. Keep on stirring and adding water until all the water has been absorbed. Start kneading with your hands. As you knead, the dough will continue to pick up any remaining flour. Use a dough scraper or metal spatula to collect any bits that have stuck to the counter. Add the salt, and continue to knead for about 15 minutes or until the dough is soft, smooth, and elastic. (To freeze *pizza* dough, see below.)

Roll into a sausage shape. Cut into 20 to 24 slices. Put dabs of oil (as many as there are slices of dough) on cookie sheets. Cover each dab of oil with a slice of dough, turning it around a bit to ensure that the bottom is oily. Brush the tops of the *pizzette* with oil. Cover with plastic wrap, and let rise in a warm place until doubled in size. A cold kitchen can take 2 hours; an oven with a pilot on takes half that time.

Preheat the oven to 230° C (450° F).

Once the *pizzette* have risen, flatten them down again, shaping them in rounds with their rims slightly thicker than their centers. Now you are ready for any topping you wish (see page 69).

To freeze the dough: after the kneading, roll into a sausage shape, lightly oil the whole surface, place on a cookie sheet, cover lightly with plastic wrap, and let rise in a warm place until double in size. Punch the dough down to sausage shape again, wrap tightly in the plastic wrap, and place in a plastic bag. Seal the bag, and store the dough in the freezer.

Food-Processor
Pizzette Dough

2½ cups all-purpose un-
  bleached flour
1 packet active dry yeast
½ teaspoon salt
⅔ to ¾ cup warm (48° C,
  115° F) water
olive oil

Preheat the oven to 93° C (200° F), turn off, and let cool to 27° C (80° F).

Place the dry ingredients in the bowl of the food processor, steel blade in place. Turn on the processor and slowly pour ½ cup water through the tube. The mixture at this time is a very fine grain, just beginning to stick together. Add the rest of the water very slowly, stopping the machine when a ball of dough has formed and begun to beat around the bowl. You many not need more than ⅔ of a cup of water, depending on the atmosphere of the kitchen. Lift the ball of dough out of the bowl, roll it in flour, and knead for a minute or two. Place about 1 tablespoon of oil in the bottom of a warm bowl, and twirl the ball of dough around in the oil until bowl and dough glisten. Cover with plastic wrap, place in a warm place, and let the dough rise until doubled in size. Proceed as with handmade *pizza* dough.

Commercially Frozen
Bread Dough

1 450-gram (1-pound) loaf
  frozen bread dough
olive oil

Lightly oil a 9″ × 5″ bread pan, place the frozen loaf in the pan, brush the top of the bread with oil, and cover with plastic wrap. Defrost in the refrigerator overnight (or during the day, depending on baking time).

When the loaf is soft but not yet risen, place it on a pastry board or counter and roll it into a long sausage shape. Cut into 20 to 24 thin slices.

Take the slices one at a time and shape them into round discs with your fingers. Place ten or twelve drops of oil, evenly spaced, on each of two cookie sheets. Set the slices of dough on the oil; swirl gently so the entire bottom of each slice is covered with oil. Brush the tops with a bit more oil. Cover the cookie sheets with plastic wrap, and let the dough rise until doubled in size.

Flatten the *pizzette* down again, pressing down on the centers to create thick rims. Brush once more with olive oil, and you are ready for your topping (see below).

Pizzette with Tomatoes and *Mozzarella*

pizzette con pomodori e mozzarella

1 recipe *pizzette* dough
(pages 67 to 68)

olive oil

2 cups (approximate)
canned peeled plum to-
matoes, drained and
slightly mashed

225 grams (8 ounces) fresh
mozzarella

½ teaspoon dried oregano

salt

freshly ground pepper

Preheat oven to 233 ° C (450 ° F).

When the *pizzette* have risen, press them down and shape them. Brush tops with olive oil.

Almost cover each piece of dough with mashed tomatoes. Shred, grate, or chop the *mozzarella* into very small pieces. Sprinkle the cheese over the *pizzette*. Add a light sprinkling of salt and pepper to your taste. Sprinkle the oregano over them all and dribble a drop or two of oil on each disc.

Bake the *pizzette* 15 to 20 minutes in a hot (230 ° C, 450 ° F) oven or until the cheese has melted and the rims of the dough have become crisp. Serve immediately.

Pizzette with Mushrooms and *Mozzarella*

pizzette con funghi e mozzarella

This is a variation of the preceding recipe: omit the oregano and add 225 grams (8 ounces) thinly sliced fresh mushrooms over the cheese. Sprinkle with oil, and bake as above.

Cheese-and-Spinach Turnovers

sfogliatine di spinaci e formaggio

1 285-gram (10-ounce) package of frozen chopped spinach

½ cup fresh *ricotta*

2 tablespoons grated Parmesan cheese

½ teaspoon freshly grated nutmeg

dash of freshly ground pepper

1 large egg, slightly beaten

450 grams (1 pound) chilled fresh puff pastry or 4 sheets frozen (pages 320 to 323)

60 grams (2 ounces) Muenster cheese cut into 20 cubes

Cook the spinach in boiling, salted water; drain well, cool, and squeeze out all remaining water.

Place the spinach in a bowl with the *ricotta*, Parmesan, nutmeg, and pepper. Mix well, and add 3 tablespoons beaten egg.

If using fresh puff pastry, roll it out to approximately ⅛-inch thickness. If using frozen puff pastry sheets, allow them 10 minutes to thaw, but do not let them reach room temperature.

Preheat oven to 190° C (400° F).

Cut the pastry in 20 4-inch discs, rerolling, as necessary, leftover scraps. Brush half the rim of each disc with beaten egg. Place a rounded teaspoon of spinach-*ricotta* mixture just off center of each disc, toward the egg-brushed side. Put a piece of Muenster on the mixture. Fold each disc in half, pressing the top rim firmly against the egged rim to seal in the filling. Go around the edge with the tines of a fork.

Place the filled pastries on ungreased cookie sheets and chill them in the refrigerator 15 minutes.

Brush the tops of pastries with the remaining egg. Bake 25 to 30 minutes in a hot 190° C (400° F) oven. Let cool a few moments before serving as *antipasto* or main dish for lunch. Serves as many as you decide.

Puff Pastries with Tomato and *Moz-zarella*

sfogliatine

225 grams (½ pound) fresh puff pastry, or 2 sheets frozen (pages 320 to 323)

115 grams (¼ pound) *mozzarella*, diced

3 tablespoons basic tomato sauce (page 40)

8 ripe black olives, cut in half

¼ teaspoon dried oregano (approximate)

1 large egg, beaten

pinch of salt

Preheat oven to 190° C (400° F).

If using fresh pastry, roll it out to ⅛-inch thickness. If using frozen puff pastry, thaw for about 10 minutes, but do not allow it to reach room temperature, cut each sheet in half, and roll out each half 1 inch wider and longer than originally. Cut out 14 to 16 4-inch discs.

Place 6 to 8 pieces of cheese just off center on one of the discs. Add about ½ teaspoon tomato sauce and half an olive to the cheese. Sprinkle with a bit of oregano and salt. Brush half the rim of pastry (the half on the side of the filling) with beaten egg. Fold the empty half of the disc over the cheese-tomato mixture, and press the edges firmly to seal. After you have done one, you will know the exact amount of cheese to add to the others as well as the exact positioning. Continue to place filling on half of each remaining disc, brush the rim, and press the edges together to seal. Go around the edge with the tines of a fork.

Brush the tops of the sealed pastries with the remaining egg, and place them all on an ungreased cookie sheet.

Bake in a hot (190° C, 400° F) oven 15 to 18 minutes or until well puffed and toasted. Let cool a moment or two before serving as *antipasto* or snack. Depending on appetite and occasion, serves 4 to 6.

Puff Pastries with Ham and *Ricotta*

sfogliatine con pro-
sciutto e ricotta

2 eggs, beaten

½ cup fresh *ricotta*

⅓ cup Parmesan, grated

115 grams (¼ pound) fresh *mozzarella*, grated

115 grams (¼ pound) cooked ham, diced

340 grams (¾ pound) fresh puff pastry or 3 sheets frozen (pages 320 to 323)

Place all but about 2 tablespoons egg in a one-quart bowl. Add all the cheeses and the ham. Mix well.

Preheat oven to 230° C (450° F).

Roll out the puff pastry to about ¹⁄₁₆-inch thickness, and cut into 3-inch squares. Frozen sheets rolled out make about 12 squares per sheet. You may make rounds, of course, in which case a circle 4 inches in diameter is a good size to work with. Reroll the leftover scraps for more rounds.

Brush two sides of the squares, or half the rims, with beaten egg. Place a teaspoon of filling just off the center of the square or circle, toward the egg-brushed side. Fold over, and seal firmly with your fingers and then around the edge with the tines of a fork.

Place on ungreased cookie sheets and put in the oven. Immediately reduce the heat to 200° C (400° F) and bake for 25 minutes or until puffed and toasted. Makes 36 squares or rounds.

Note: This particular filling lends itself deliciously to *risotto* (pages 134 to 137) and to *frittate* (pages 214 to 216).

Tuna Mousse

spuma di tonno

3 200-gram (7-ounce) cans
Italian-style tuna, or light
tuna packed in oil

2 packets (2 tablespoons)
gelatine

⅓ cup cold water

2½ tablespoons unsalted
butter

3 tablespoons all-purpose
unbleached flour

1 cup milk, hot

1 chicken bouillon cube

½ teaspoon dried basil, or
3 leaves fresh, chopped

¼ teaspoon salt

freshly ground pepper to
please

1 lemon

1 small cucumber, skin on,
sliced very thin

½ sweet red pepper or pi-
miento

Drain the tuna thoroughly, and put it in the bowl of a food processor with the steel blade in place. Process on/off until well broken up, and then process until smooth.

Soften the gelatine in the cold water, then heat over low flame until completely dissolved. Pour into the tuna, and process until absorbed.

Make a *besciamella:* melt the butter over low heat, then stir in the flour, and, finally, add the milk in a steady, slow steam. Break the bouillon cube in bits, and add to the pan. Add the basil, salt, and pepper. Cook, stirring constantly, over low heat for 4 minutes. Taste for seasonings, and correct if necessary.

Add the *besciamella* to the tuna mixture, and process briefly until incorporated.

Grate the lemon, and add the grated peel to the tuna; then squeeze and pour the juice through a sieve into the tuna mixture. Process on/off (or blend).

Pour the mixture into a fish mold (about 1½ liters or 1½ quarts) and place it in the refrigerator for at least 2 hours or until very firm. It can stay in the refrigerator up to 24 hours.

To unmold the mousse, place the form in warm water for about 5 minutes and then turn it out on a serving platter.

Make fish "scales" with the thinly sliced cucumber. Form tail, mouth, and eyes with bits of red sweet pepper or pimiento. Serve with Melba toast, toasted rounds of Italian bread, or crackers of your choice. For 10.

Venetian Pâté

pâté alla veneziana

3 tablespoons olive oil

3 tablespoons unsalted butter

3 rounded tablespoons minced Italian parsley

½ celery stalk, minced

2 medium onions, peeled and thinly sliced

5 fresh sage leaves, or about 1 teaspoon dried

1 teaspoon salt

½ teaspoon freshly ground pepper

1 cup chicken broth (page 44)

450 grams (1 pound) boneless chicken breast, cubed

1 kilogram (2 pounds) calves' liver, cubed

675 grams (1½ pounds) unsalted butter (450 grams or 1 pound whipped, 225 grams or ½ pound solid)

2½ teaspoons Dijon mustard

3 rounded teaspoons freshly grated nutmeg

6 tablespoons Italian brandy

grated rind of ½ large orange

1 cup medium cream

8 mammoth black ripe olives, pitted, chopped, or 1 black truffle, chopped

Sauté in butter and oil the parsley, celery, onions, and sage until limp. Add salt, pepper, and broth, and cook over low heat for 15 to 20 minutes or until most of the liquid has been cooked away. Add the chicken and liver, raise the heat, and cook for 6 to 10 minutes or until the meats are cooked and tender. Let cool.

Process the cooked, cooled meats in a food processor using the steel cutting blade or send them through a meat grinder twice.

The pâté is now ready for its final seasonings and butter. Because of the size of the recipe, you will find it easier to flavor the pâté in three installments, placing each installment in the bowl of a food processor or that of an electric mixer. Thus, to ⅓ of the processed (or ground) meats, add ⅓ of the butter; ⅓ each of the mustard, nutmeg, brandy, and orange rind; and ⅓ of the cream. Process or beat until smooth, creamy, and perfectly blended. Fold in the olives or truffle.

When all the pâté has been seasoned, mix the three batches together and chill in a 1¾-liter (two-quart) mold or in 4 half-liter (pint) molds, lined with plastic wrap or aspic (see pages 45 to 46; 75).

Venetian pâté can be frozen (without aspic) for up to 3 months, but on thawing you will find its texture changed. To correct this, just put it back in the food processor, steel blade in place, and process on/off briefly. Chill again, and then apply aspic, if desired.

Serve with thinly sliced toasted Italian or French bread or white Melba toast. Makes approximately 2,050 grams (4½ pounds). This is enough for 50 to 100 guests, depending, of course, on their appetites. The pâté recipe may be doubled, but in that event use only 1 kilogram (2 pounds) of butter.

Chicken Liver Mousse in Aspic

spuma di fegatini in gelatina

Aspic
2 packets (2 tablespoons) gelatine
2 cups chicken broth (page 44)
1 cup beef broth (page 43)

Besciamella
1 tablespoon unsalted butter
2 tablespoons all-purpose unbleached flour
¼ teaspoon freshly grated nutmeg
⅔ cup chicken broth, hot (page 44)

Mousse
400 grams (14 ounces, approximately 1½ cups) chicken livers, trimmed and chopped coarsely
4 tablespoons unsalted butter
4 fresh sage leaves, or ½ teaspoon dried sage
¾ teaspoon salt
freshly ground pepper to taste
½ cup heavy cream, whipped and chilled

Partially fill a large bowl with ice cubes, place a second bowl on the ice, and place them both in the freezer. Also, chill a 9″ × 5″ bread pan, preferably glass, in the freezer.

To make aspic: soften the gelatine in ½ cup of mixed broths. Add remaining broth, and heat until all the gelatine has dissolved. Set the aspic in the refrigerator to cool to the syrupy stage, just beginning to thicken.

To make a white sauce: melt the tablespoon of butter over medium heat. Stir in the flour and nutmeg. Continue stirring, and slowly add the ⅔ cup of hot chicken broth. Cook and stir 4 minutes. Remove from heat. Lay plastic wrap on the surface of the sauce (to prevent a skin from forming), and chill in the freezer while assembling the mousse.

To make mousse: sauté the chicken livers for 6 minutes in butter with the sage. Add salt and pepper to taste. Do not overcook. Process the livers with the pan juices in a food processor or put them through a food mill, using the finest disc, to reduce the livers to a paste. Place the processed liver in the chilled bowl over ice. Fold in the now chilled white sauce, mixing well. Fold in the chilled whipped cream. Fold in 1 cup of the chilled aspic mixture, and put the mousse in the freezer for 15 to 20 minutes.

Brush the inside of the chilled bread pan with

three or four coats of aspic, chilling the pan in the freezer after each coat.

Decoration

12 to 3 large black ripe olives

extra sage leaves or Italian parsley

piece of sweet red pepper or pimiento

6 sprigs Italian parsley

1 lemon

To decorate the mousse: cut the olives into petal-like slivers and the sweet pepper or pimiento into tiny rounds. Place the olive sections, black side down, in a treelike pattern on the stiffened aspic in the bottom of the bread pan. Put the extra sage leaves between the olive slivers. Place the pepper rounds here and there like a Christmas decoration. Then, add two more layers of aspic, chilling after each addition.

When the mousse is reasonably stiff from its stay in the freezer, spoon it down the center of the bread pan. Level it gently with a spatula, and spread it so it almost reaches the sides of the pan. Chill another 15 minutes. Pour the remaining aspic along the sides and over the top of the mousse. Cover with plastic wrap, and chill in the refrigerator 4 to 24 hours.

To serve: Dip the pan in warm water for 3 minutes and turn the mousse out on a serving platter. Decorate with sprigs of parsley and rounds of lemon. Serve with thin slices of toasted Italian or French bread. For 20 servings.

First Courses

Primi piatti

With or without an *antipasto,* the first course of an Italian meal consists of soup, pasta, or rice (never all three at once); and rarely are the rice or pasta dishes offered with second courses. First courses set the pace, reflect the mood, day, season, and market. More and more the first courses reflect the life-style of the group involved — who is working, where and when.

A short time ago, the first course of an Italian lunch was exquisitely timed for the arrival of the major wage earner of the family; but lately lunch is getting short shrift with the change to what are called American hours. Just as dinners have taken over the prime-meal-of-the-day slot, lunches in Italy are becoming more and more like the lunches in America, England, and many Western European countries.

Time once spent over the lunch, or *pranzo,* is converted now to a space in the evening for a leisurely dinner. But time spent preparing that meal now has been narrowed down. Hence, newer Italian recipes are shorter in preparation and cooking time than ever. Servings of various dishes are just a bit smaller and reflect not so much parsimony as a new concern for nutritional value, covering the proper balance of a meal without overwhelming the participant with calories. Whether one chooses soup or pasta or rice, we continue to believe that Italian first courses are the nicest way to begin any meal.

Soups

Minestre

Italian soups are just as famous as the country's pasta dishes, and we hope you will agree that there are days when nothing can soothe the palate and provide a proper beginning for a meal like a bowl of soup.

Some of the recipes are long cooking, others ready in a matter of minutes, especially if broth is kept on hand. In the past, of course, all of the soups were made from scratch and many were planned for a large family and simmered slowly on an ever-burning stove. But things have changed. Of course we like the image of the simmering pot, the idea of the aroma filling the kitchen with the promise of good soup. But above all, it is the soup we want, not the pot. And then, fewer and fewer people are at home to potwatch nowadays, in Italy or elsewhere.

So we have collected in this chapter some of Italy's new treats, or new versions of old favorites, which work well in the modern kitchen.

For general reference, the classic broths used in many of the following recipes are in the chapter on Batters, Butters, Basic Sauces, and Broths. Canned substitutes or bouillon cubes can always be used, but for the real thing you will want to make your own. Beef Broth is on page 43; Chicken Broth on page 44; Vegetable Broth on page 46; and Fish Broth on pages 47.

Artichoke Soup

minestra di carciofi

3 artichokes
1 lemon
1 leek
1 medium Idaho potato
1 celery stalk, cut in half
¼ cup olive oil
1½ teaspoons salt, or to taste
freshly ground pepper
1 beef bouillon cube
1 egg yolk
4 cups hot water (approximate)
2 tablespoons lemon juice

Clean and trim the artichokes (pages 4 to 5), and put them to soak in cold water with the juice of the lemon. (Save the lemon peel.)

Clean the leek, discard the dark green tops, and cut the white portion in ¼-inch rounds.

Peel the potato, cube ¾ of it, and mince the remainder.

Drain the artichoke pieces, and put all the vegetables in a soup pot. Add the oil, salt, and a generous sprinkling of pepper. Cook and stir over high heat for 2 minutes.

Dissolve the bouillon cube in the water, and add to the soup pot. (There should be just enough liquid to cover the vegetables by a fraction of an inch.)

Take half of the skin of the lemon used in the preparation of the artichokes, rinse it, and add it to the pot.

Bring the pot to a boil, stir, cover, and reduce the heat to simmer. Cook 20 minutes, stirring occasionally.

Uncover the pot, taste for seasonings, and adjust as you please. Cook another 10 minutes. Allow to cool for a few minutes. Remove the lemon rind.

Mix the egg yolk with the additional lemon juice, and gently stir into the soup. Serve with slices of hot Italian bread. For 4.

Lentil and Sausage Soup

zuppa di lenticchie e salsiccie

1 teaspoon coriander seeds
1 carrot, peeled
1 celery stalk with leaves, washed
1 onion, peeled and quartered
2 sprigs Italian parsley
2 Italian sweet sausages, skinned
3 tablespoons olive oil
2 cups dry white wine
2 cups chicken broth, hot
1 cup dried lentils, sorted and washed

Process, in a food processor with the steel cutting blade, the coriander, carrot, celery, onion, parsley, and sausages. (Or mince together by hand.)

Put the oil in a soup pot or pressure cooker (six-quart, 15-pound). Add the minced vegetables and sausages, and sauté over high heat, stirring constantly, until sizzling.

Add the wine, and cook until evaporated. Add the broth, and cover the pot. If using a conventional pot, bring to a boil, lower the heat, and cook slowly until the lentils are cooked (about ½ hour). If using a pressure cooker, bring up to 15 pounds pressure, and cook 20 minutes. Reduce the pressure immediately.

This is a very thick soup and is frequently garnished with additional sweet sausages baked to a crisp beforehand in a hot oven. For 4.

Lobster Soup

zuppa di aragosta

4 tablespoons olive oil

1 garlic clove, peeled

½ hot red pepper pod, seeded, or 2 dashes Tabasco sauce

4 anchovy filets, minced

4 tablespoons minced Italian parsley

4 peeled plum tomatoes, fresh or canned

1½ to 2 liters (quarts) fish broth (page 47), hot

4 slices Italian bread, crustless, cut in cubes

4 tablespoons unsalted butter

225 grams (½ pound) boiled shrimp, peeled and deveined

340 to 450 grams (¾ to 1 pound) boiled lobster meat (crab meat may be substituted)

1 tablespoon chilled, dry white wine per soup plate (optional)

Put the olive oil in a soup pot. Add the garlic and the pepper pod, and sauté over medium heat until golden. Discard the garlic and pepper. (If using Tabasco instead of red pepper, add it later, along with the tomatoes.)

Add the anchovies and the parsley to the oil. Cook over low heat until the anchovies practically dissolve.

Pass the tomatoes through a food mill or sieve into the olive oil and cook for 5 minutes.

Add the fish broth, bring to a boil, lower the heat, and let simmer for 15 minutes. Meanwhile, fry the bread cubes in the butter until golden brown.

Cut the shrimp in half lengthwise. Cut or break the lobster into pieces about the size of the shrimp. Add both shrimp and lobster to the broth, turn up the heat, and as soon as the soup comes to a boil, take it off the heat.

To serve, put the bread cubes in soup plates and ladle the soup over them. Add the wine and serve. For 6.

Minestrone, Genoa Style

minestrone genovese

1 celery stalk with leaves, minced

1 onion, minced

1 carrot, minced

2 slices *pancetta* or lean salt pork, cut in tiny cubes

1 sage leaf or 4 fresh basil leaves, minced

4 tablespoons olive oil

2 potatoes, peeled and cut in small pieces

2 carrots, peeled and cut in small rounds

2 leeks, cleaned, tops removed, sliced in thin rounds

2 tomatoes, peeled and quartered

1 onion, peeled, sliced in slivers

2 zucchini, cubed

1 handful escarole, washed, cut in bite-size pieces

3½ teaspoons salt

2 cups small macaroni (*tubetti*, shells, etc.)

2 to 3 tablespoons *pesto* (pages 36 to 39)

1 cup cooked shell beans, fresh or canned

2 tablespoons grated Parmesan cheese (approximate)

2 tablespoons grated *pecorino* cheese (approximate)

Place the first five ingredients in the olive oil in a six-quart pressure cooker or soup pot. Sauté until the bits of salt pork are translucent, the seasonings limp.

Add the next seven ingredients, water to cover (or up to the full line on the pressure cooker), salt, and stir.

If using the six-quart, 15-pound pressure cooker, seal the pot, bring the pressure to 15 pounds and cook for 30 minutes. Let the pressure fall of its own accord.

If using a soup pot, bring it to a boil, cover, lower the heat, and cook for about 2 hours.

When the soup is cooked, bring it to a boil, add the pasta, bring it back to a boil, and cook 15 minutes or until the pasta is cooked.

Add the *pesto* and beans. Stir well. Serve with the two grated cheeses. For 8.

Pasta and Bean Soup

pasta e fagioli

This is today's lighter version of a traditionally hearty soup of which Italy has many regional recipes.

You may make it with dried shell or kidney beans; these take quite a while to cook and, when using them, we turn to the pressure cooker (six-quart, 15-pound).

If they are in season, you should not pass up the chance to make *pasta e fagioli* with fresh shell beans. They are superior, and cook up in about 25 minutes in a conventional soup pot.

Or at any time of the year you may use canned shell or kidney beans, those that have been put up with only salt and water.

No matter what type of bean or pot you use, the soup will be thick. The pasta does not have to be *al dente* — some in fact prefer it slightly overcooked, as it will be when and if reheated.

Pasta e fagioli is a year-round soup, served at room temperature in the summer and hot, with a sprinkle of Parmesan cheese, the rest of the year.

Pasta and Bean Soup

pasta e fagioli
(continued)

2 cups soaked beans (1 cup dried to begin with), or 2 cups fresh shelled or 2 cups canned beans

2 slices lean and fat *prosciutto* (60 grams, 2 ounces), cubed

1 large garlic clove, peeled and halved

1 medium onion, peeled and halved

½ cup packed celery leaves

2 tablespoons olive oil

3 peeled plum tomatoes, canned or fresh, mashed

6 drops Tabasco sauce

1½ liters (6 cups) hot water (approximate)

3 to 4 teaspoons salt

1½ cups small macaroni (*tubetti*, shells, elbows)

2 white inner celery stalks, cut in ⅛-inch pieces

2 small tender carrots, cut like the celery

grated Parmesan cheese (optional)

If you are using dried beans and a pressure cooker: soak 1 cup of dried kidney or shell beans in abundant water with ⅛ cup of vegetable oil overnight or for 8 hours. Drain and rinse well.

Make a fine *battuto* by mincing or processing the *prosciutto,* garlic, onion, and celery leaves.

Put the olive oil in a six-quart pressure cooker.

Add the minced flavorings, and sauté until limp over medium-high heat. Add the tomatoes and Tabasco, and cook and stir over medium heat until the entire mixture has blended completely and looks like a sauce (about 4 minutes).

Add the soaked beans to the tomato mixture in the pressure cooker.

Add the water (enough to fill no more than half the pressure cooker) and 3 teaspoons of the salt. Cover the pressure cooker, bring the pressure up to 15 pounds, and cook 5 minutes. Reduce the pressure immediately.

Uncover the pressure cooker and stir in the pasta, chopped celery stalks, and carrots. Stir and cook on a low heat for about 12 minutes or until the pasta and beans are tender. Taste for salt (the *prosciutto* should have added enough), and add more if you need.

If you are using fresh beans and a conventional soup pot: sauté your minced flavorings in oil until limp. Add the tomatoes and Tabasco, and cook until the mixture has blended completely and looks like a sauce.

Add the fresh beans, along with the water, and 3 teaspoons of the salt. Bring the soup to a boil, cover, lower the heat, and simmer for about 15 minutes.

Uncover the pan and stir in the pasta, celery

stalks, and carrots. Bring to a boil, lower the heat, and cook about 12 minutes or until both pasta and beans are tender. Taste for salt, and add remaining salt as you please.

If you are using canned beans and a soup pot: proceed as above until the *battuto* and tomatoes have blended well.

Add the hot water and bring to a boil; add 3 teaspoons of the salt and the pasta, celery stalks, and carrots; and cook about 9 minutes.

Add the canned beans and their canning liquid to the soup pot.

Continue cooking another 3 to 4 minutes or until the pasta is tender.

Taste for salt, and add the last teaspoonful if you please. Serve at room temperature or hot, with grated Parmesan cheese for each to add as he or she wishes. For 4.

Turkey Broth for the Pressure Cooker

brodo di tacchino per la pentola a pressione

1 ½ kilos (about 3 pounds) fresh turkey meat and bone (wings, neck, back, uncooked carcass, a leg)

5 sprigs Italian parsley

1 medium onion, peeled and quartered

1 carrot, scrubbed

1 celery stalk with leaves, washed

1 bay leaf

4 teaspoons salt, or to taste

½ teaspoon dried tarragon

2 liters (2 quarts) cold water (approximate)

¼ cup cocktail sherry (optional), or to taste

Cut off and discard as much of the turkey skin and fat as possible. If you're using a carcass, cut it with a meat cleaver to fit into your pressure cooker.

Put all the ingredients, except the water, in a six-quart pressure cooker; then add as much water as necessary to fill to the maximum fill line.

Cover the pan, bring the pressure to 15 pounds, and cook 15 minutes. Allow the pressure to fall of its own accord. Strain the broth through a cheesecloth-lined sieve into a clean pot, and chill thoroughly.

Once the broth is chilled, scoop off any remaining fat or froth. Bring to a boil, and clarify with egg white (page 44).

Add sherry to taste.

Turkey broth may be used in your favorite egg-lemon soup, in *stracciatella,* with *pastina, cappelletti,* or *capellini,* or simply with grated Parmesan cheese. This broth may be frozen, or kept in the refrigerator 2 to 3 days. Makes 9 to 10 cups.

Vegetable Soup

zuppa di verdure

3 tablespoons olive oil

4 cups chicken broth, or 4 chicken bouillon cubes dissolved in 1 liter (1 quart) water

5 celery stalks with leaves, washed and chopped

1 heart of celery, chopped

2 leeks, cleaned and sliced thinly

1 large Idaho potato, peeled and thinly sliced

1 carrot, peeled and thinly sliced

⅓ cup tomato juice

1½ liters (about 6 cups) cold water, or to cover

1 zucchini, sliced paper thin

4 to 6 tablespoons grated Parmesan cheese

Put everything but the zucchini and cheese in a large saucepan. Bring to a boil, cover, lower the heat, and simmer for 25 minutes.

Uncover the pan, add the zucchini slices, and cook 1 minute. Serve, with Parmesan cheese for each to add as he or she pleases. For 6.

Pasta

Treatises exist on the historical, social, and economic impact of pasta, its geographical and cultural origins, and its nutritive power (or lack of it). The temptation to accept or dismiss the various theories is great, but we shall resist it.

Pasta, by now, is universal, and we assume that the difference between the commercially dried pasta and the homemade kind is well known. As for the many shapes, thanks to modern packaging, anybody who has entered a supermarket is familiar with at least some of them. The list of shapes is enormous and seemingly endless, compounded by the fact that in many cases the same kind of pasta has different names in different Italian regions; and the various names have been adopted variously by different manufacturers here. We will, when necessary, translate the Italian name for a shape of pasta into the name most currently used. Cases in point: *bucatini* are better known as *perciatelli* or "thin macaroni" (even if in Italy there is a tiny difference between them) and *farfalle* are better known as "bow macaroni."

As for the quality of commercial pasta, there are so many brands (imported and domestic) that it would be unfair for us to select one over another.

However, since all commercially made pasta basically consists of flour and water and, since the best flour for pasta is made with a high percentage of durum wheat (*farina di semola* in Italy, semolina here), a check on the list of ingredients on the package is a start toward a good choice. Cooked pasta reveals even more about its quality: poor pasta becomes mushy throughout or mushy outside and uncooked inside, a sorry state of affairs.

Pasta made with durum wheat flour resists the rigors of boiling better than others and cooks to, and retains better, that ephemeral state, *al dente,* which means cooked but still slightly firm to the bite. This is the most commonly used and pedestrian way of describing *al dente.* Actually, we cannot think of any way really to describe it. Good and well-cooked pasta speaks for itself. We have seen many people, accustomed to mushy, overcooked pasta, light up at the recognition of an excellent *al dente* dish and exclaim: "It's different! And it's better!"

The best recommendation we can make is that you try a few of the pasta brands available in your shopping area and settle on the one you like best. If this seems like easy advice, do remember that the same brand of pasta can cook differently in different locations, depending on humidity, altitude, or even the quality of the local water. A brand good in Miami could turn out quite badly in Denver and vice versa.

Homemade Pasta

pasta fatta in casa

The best pasta for pasta lovers is homemade. We suggest that the beginner make one or two batches completely by hand. It will give not only a creative experience but also a firsthand knowledge of how pasta dough should feel and an understanding of the whole process. And yet, while we sympathize with pasta purists and while we will always consider making pasta by hand a rewarding, satisfying experience, when pressed for time and especially when making pasta in large batches, we consider the pasta machine a necessity. It is a modest investment for a lifetime of rewards. And, when combined with the food processor, it becomes a miracle: home production of pasta is a cinch.

Also available on the market today, besides the hand-cranked pasta machine, are electric machines that speed pasta-making even more; and, naturally, we welcome them too.

Remember the old saying, "even a child can do it"? One of the more memorable experiences of life in our kitchen was having a six-year-old (who had never cracked an egg in his life) produce a batch of *fettuccine* all by himself. His joy at the accomplishment (and in eating it later) was the best compensation for the free pasta-making lesson.

For handmade pasta all you need is a solid, smooth, flat surface and a rolling pin. Their dimensions, naturally, will be dictated by the size of the batch that is to be prepared. On the average, a surface of about 20 × 24 inches should do. A formica counter top will do or, in a pinch, a large pastry board. If you use a board, put a slightly damp towel under it to keep it from shifting as you knead and roll.

An Italian rolling pin is advisable. Compared

to the common pastry rolling pin, the Italian is thinner and longer (about 2 inches in diameter and about 24 inches long, with no ball bearings in the handles), which makes rolling dough into large sheets much easier.

The ingredients for the pasta are eggs, all-purpose unbleached flour, and salt. Traditionally, most pasta *all'uovo* is made without salt, but the cooking water is well salted. We prefer to salt the pasta and cut down on the salt in the water.

As a rule of thumb, allow 1 egg and ¾ cup of flour for approximately one portion. The approximation is due to the fact that eggs are never alike, nor are flours, and the two tend to combine in different proportions under different conditions of humidity and temperature. The one-egg-per-portion rule, too, is only indicative: experience will let the maker decide on the number of eggs needed for the number of portions to be served. It depends on appetites and on the planned use of the dish — whether as a first course *all'italiana* or as a one-dish meal. We seem to strike a happy balance by following the 1-egg rule for up to three servings but then not increasing the number of eggs exactly with the number of portions above three. In other words, a 5-egg batch of pasta is sufficient for six or seven portions, a 6-egg batch for eight servings, and a 9-egg batch for twelve, as a first course.

Following is the description of the method that has worked well for us. It is a 3-egg rule because it suits the congenial gathering of four around a table; it also makes enough pasta for *cappelletti* for six (pages 120 to 124) and for a normal sized *lasagna* (pages 130 to 131).

Handmade Pasta

2¼ cups all-purpose un-
bleached flour

½ teaspoon salt

3 large eggs at room tem-
perature

Put the flour and salt in a mound on a pastry board or clean counter. Make a well in the center of the mound, and crack the eggs into it. With one hand cradling the outside of the mound, use the other hand to stir the eggs with a fork, breaking them up and stirring around and around, picking up flour. When the developing dough becomes too stiff to stir with the fork, put the fork aside, flour your hands, and begin kneading.

Work in as much of the remaining flour as the dough will take. Scrape the counter clean, flour it lightly, and knead for 6 to 12 minutes or so (depending on energy and expertise) until you have a smooth and elastic ball of dough. By now the counter should be virtually clean, and you can start to roll out the dough.

If you are rolling by hand: at this point, every motion should be directed toward accomplishing the job in the shortest possible time; otherwise the dough will tend to dry out, making rolling and final cutting difficult. Place the dough in the center of the rolling surface and flatten it as much as you can with your hands. Place the pin on the center of the dough and roll it out and away from you, then from the center toward you. Give it a 90-degree turn and roll it again, first from the center away, then from the center toward you. If in the process the dough should stick to the board or pin, sprinkle it very lightly with flour. Keep turning and rolling the pasta until you get a uniform thickness, about one millimeter ($^{1}/_{32}$-inch) or, better yet, the thickness of a dime.

Once you have mastered this way of rolling,

you can reach faster results by the "wrap around" method. Start rolling as for the previous method, but when you have reached a 3- to 4-millimeter (⅛-inch) thickness, flour the pasta lightly and place the pin on the edge closest to you. Roll the pin away, letting the pasta wrap around it in a roll. Bring the whole thing toward you, place the palms of your hands on the center of the roll, then push it away and let your hands slide, applying a gentle pressure, out toward the ends of the pin. Repeat a couple of times, then unroll the pasta, turn it 90 degrees, and repeat the procedure until you have reached the desired thickness.

If you are rolling with a pasta machine: open the rollers of the pasta machine to their widest gap, and send the flattened piece of dough through. Flour the piece, fold it in half, and send it through again fold first. Repeat 2 or 3 times until the dough loses its wrinkles and is very smooth.

Narrow the opening between the rollers one notch, and send the dough through once. Continue narrowing the opening, notch by notch, and roll the dough until it is the correct thickness. Usually this stage is reached on the next to last notch of the pasta machine when you are making *fettuccine, lasagne,* and *cannelloni. Tonnarelli* are just a bit thicker than *fettuccine.* The other pastas, *cappelletti* and *ravioli,* should have the dough rolled even thinner to facilitate filling and sealing.

2½ cups all-purpose un-
bleached flour
½ teaspoon salt
3 large eggs at room tem-
perature
1½ tablespoons water (ap-
proximate)

Food-Processor Pasta

This rule was worked out for the average-size processor. Naturally, if you have a larger processor, it should accommodate all the ingredients in one operation, and you should not have to do two batches.

Place the steel blade or dough blade, depending on the make, in the food processor.

Put 1½ cups of flour and half the salt in the processor bowl.

Lightly beat two of the eggs in a small bowl. Turn on the machine and slowly pour the beaten eggs through the tube. Process on/off until the mixture is like coarse meal. With the machine on, add 1 tablespoon water and continue processing until the dough forms a ball. Remove the dough, wrap it in plastic wrap, and set it aside.

Process the remaining ¾ cup of flour with the rest of the salt. Slightly beat the egg, and add it slowly to the flour as in the first batch. Finally, add the ½ tablespoon of water. Process until the dough has formed. Remove the dough from the processor. Flour the dough, flatten it a bit to an oval shape, and it is ready to roll by hand or machine (see preceding recipe).

CUTTING PASTA BY HAND

Fettuccine: Let your rolled dough rest on a clean kitchen towel for 10 to 15 minutes. The timing depends on the climate of the kitchen but should never be so long that the edges become brittle. Fold the semidried pasta up in a flat roll about 4 inches wide. With a very sharp knife, cut the roll in ribbons about ¼ inch wide.

After every few slices, stop cutting, pick up the *fettuccine,* and shake them out. Flour the toweling or counter slightly, and spread the cut pasta out to dry further. *Fettuccine* may be used at once or may continue to dry. The drier the *fettuccine,* the more fragile they are and the longer they take to cook.

Tonnarelli: Proceed as for *fettuccine,* but cut the pasta in ribbons as wide as the pasta is thick, the end result being perfectly square spaghetti. Spread the cut pasta as you would for *fettuccine,* but do not let them dry completely or they will break when they go into the pot.

Cappelletti: After rolling the dough almost paper thin, cut in 2-inch squares. If you are not filling the squares right away, cover them with a dampened and thoroughly wrung-out kitchen towel or plastic wrap to keep them from drying further. (See pages 120 to 124 for filling and folding.)

Ravioli or Agnolotti: After rolling the pasta as thin as for *cappelletti,* cover with a barely damp cloth or a piece of plastic wrap until it is time to add the filling and seal the pasta.

Lasagne: Roll out as for *fettuccine,* then cut in rectangles about the size of a postal card (4″ × 6″). (See page 130 for cooking.)

Cannelloni: Roll out the pasta as you would for *lasagne* and cut in 4″ × 5″ rectangles. (See page 127 for cooking.)

CONSERVING PASTA

Fettuccine can be dried completely and stored in airtight containers almost indefinitely. Very dry pasta takes about 5 to 6 minutes to cook, while very fresh pasta can cook up in 2 minutes or so, depending on that ever-present climatic element.

Tonnarelli are best used fresh, for the thin strands are very brittle when thoroughly dried.

Cappelletti, ravioli, agnolotti, and *cannelloni* can be filled and frozen immediately for long preservation. The first three can be cooked without thawing. So can the *cannelloni,* but dot with butter and cheese or cover with a sauce before putting them in the oven.

Green Pasta
pasta verde

Pasta verde is a variation on the pasta theme, in which a small amount of cooked spinach takes the place of one or more of the eggs in the dough, turning it green, pleasant to the eye and the taste. *Pasta verde,* when rolled with a pasta machine (which finishes the kneading), looks a bit raggedy on the first two or three passes through because of the water content in the spinach itself. Pay no attention; just keep on rolling. Hand kneading of *pasta verde* takes a bit longer, for the same reason, but the rewards are worth the small effort.

Pasta verde may be used by itself, combined with yellow handmade pasta, or used in making the various filled and layered pasta.

140 grams (5 ounces) fresh or frozen spinach (which, cooked and drained, becomes approximately 60 grams or 2 ounces)

pinch of salt

2 cups all-purpose unbleached flour

½ teaspooon salt

2 large eggs at room temperature

1 tablespoon water (optional)

If you are using fresh spinach: remove the stems, and wash thoroughly. Cook the leaves, with a pinch of salt, in the water that clings to them. Drain in a sieve, pressing the spinach against the side to remove as much water as possible, let cool, then squeeze dry with your hands.

If you are using frozen spinach: cook in a small amount of boiling salted water, drain, let cool, and squeeze dry as above.

Mince the spinach thoroughly, almost to a paste, either by hand or in a food processor with the steel blade.

If you are making the pasta by hand: treat the minced spinach as one of the eggs and proceed accordingly. If using the food processor, process and mix the minced and cooled spinach into the flour first. Then add the eggs, following the recipe on page 97. Do not add the water unless the dough refuses to come to a ball on the end of the blade.

Roll and use as you would yellow pasta.

COOKING PASTA

Whether it be commercial or homemade pasta, the rules for cooking it are simple. You should have a big pot, large enough to hold at least 3 liters (quarts) of water for 1 to 3 portions — and after that 1 liter of additional water per additional serving, a long wooden fork or spoon to stir the pasta, and a capacious colander for draining. (See pages 22 to 24 for more information on equipment.)

Water for pasta should be boiling and should be salted with 1 teaspoon of salt per quart or liter of water just before you put in the pasta. Once the pasta is in the pot, give it a gentle stir and cover the pot for a moment until it comes back to a boil. Then uncover and let boil.

Cooking times (after coming back to a boil) range from 1 to 2 minutes for fresh, homemade pasta to 7 to 8 minutes for thin commercial *spaghetti* to 12 to 15 minutes for sturdier pasta, such as *rigatoni*. Generally, we find that pasta cooks more quickly than manufacturers of commercial pasta advise. Thus, scoop out a strand from time to time, test it, and let your taste be your guide. Remove the pasta from heat and drain the minute it has reached the famous *al dente* stage.

Once your pasta is drained, mix it with the sauce immediately and serve and begin. Pasta is the one dish that must be eaten the minute it is served, with no standing on protocol, since that would offend the cook as well as the true pasta lover.

The following sauces, which fall into loosely constructed categories dependent on a principal ingredient, are some new favorites we feel are splendid additions to the traditional and meatless sauces of our other two books.

Pasta with Fish Sauces

Pasta with Salmon and Peas

pasta al salmone e piselli

340 grams (¾ pound) fresh salmon (approximate)

1 small garlic clove, peeled and halved

6 tablespoons unsalted butter

salt to taste

1 285-gram (10-ounce) package frozen tiny peas

2 tablespoons chopped Italian parsley

1 3-egg recipe homemade egg pasta

freshly ground pepper to taste

juice of 1 lemon

Skin and bone the fish. Cut in 1-inch cubes.

In a large (10-inch) frying pan, sauté the garlic in butter for 1 minute. Add the salmon, stir gently, and cook a minute or two, but not enough to cause loss of color. Salt lightly.

Boil the peas in salted water until just tender. Drain the peas thoroughly and add them to the salmon. Add parsley, and cook and stir for 1 minute. Remove the garlic.

Cook the pasta in boiling salted water until *al dente*. Drain immediately, dress with the salmon and peas. Add a good sprinkling of freshly ground pepper and the lemon juice, toss lightly, and serve. For 4.

Note: This sauce is also good with medium-sized macaroni — spirals, shells, *ziti, penne.*

Pasta with Tuna and Clam Sauce

pasta con tonno e vongole

4 tablespoons olive oil

1 garlic clove, peeled

1 hot red pepper pod, seeded, or 3 dashes Tabasco sauce

450 grams (1 pound) peeled ripe plum tomatoes, or canned variety

2 140-gram (5-ounce) cans baby clams

1 100-gram (3½-ounce) can Italian style or chunk light tuna in oil

3 tablespoons chopped Italian parsley

800 grams (1¾ pounds) spaghetti

8 teaspoons salt

Put olive oil in a large sauté pan to cover the bottom. Fry the garlic clove and pepper pod in the oil until the garlic is golden. Discard these two flavorings, let the pan cool a minute, then add the plum tomatoes. (Add Tabasco if using it in place of the pepper pod.) Raise the heat, bring back to a boil. Drain the clams, reserving the liquid. Drain the tuna and break up the chunks. Add clams and tuna to the tomatoes and, when once again the sauce boils, lower the heat and let simmer about 20 minutes. Add the parsley, and cook another 2 minutes. Taste, and adjust seasonings as desired, including adding a bit of the reserved clam juice.

Bring 8 liters (8 quarts) of water to a boil, add the salt and spaghetti, and cook until *al dente*. Drain thoroughly. Dress with sauce, and serve. (No cheese, please.) For 8.

Note: This dish readily divides or multiplies for smaller or larger gatherings.

Spaghetti with Cherrystone Clam Sauce

spaghetti mare d'estate

1½ to 2 kilograms (3 to 4 pounds) small cherry-stone clams

2 cloves garlic, peeled

5 tablespoons olive oil

1 small onion, peeled

450 grams (1 pound) ripe fresh plum tomatoes

8 fresh basil leaves

1 teaspoon salt

freshly ground pepper to taste

400 grams (14 ounces) thin spaghetti

3 tablespoons chopped Italian parsley

This is for, and only for, those lucky enough to have access to small cherrystone clams, ripe plum tomatoes, and garden fresh herbs. Only then can one know what is the taste of "a summer sea."

Soak the clams a few hours or overnight in salt water to let them excrete sand. Wash the clams carefully in cold water.

In a pan large enough to contain the clams, sauté in 2 tablespoons of the olive oil 1 garlic clove until golden.

Add the clams, raise the heat, cover the pan, and cook about 3 minutes or until the clam shells are open, stirring a couple of times. Remove the pan from the heat, and let cool.

Mince together the onion, basil, and remaining garlic clove, and place in the remaining olive oil in a sauté pan over medium heat. Sauté until barely golden and limp.

Wash the tomatoes, and pass them through a food mill directly into the sauté pan with the onion, basil, and garlic. Add salt and a generous sprinkling of pepper. Stir, bring to a boil, then simmer for 10 to 15 minutes, stirring occasionally.

Remove the clams from their shells, directly over the pan they were cooked in, to conserve all the natural juices. Set aside the clams, and strain the juices with the first garlic clove into a cup. Add ½ cup of the clam juice to the tomato sauce. Add the clams, and cook another 5 minutes.

Cook the spaghetti in at least 5 liters (5 quarts) boiling water salted with 5 teaspoons salt. When the pasta is *al dente,* drain thoroughly and place in a serving dish. Dress with the sauce, and sprinkle with the minced parsley. Toss, and serve. For 4.

Baby Clam Sauce, Sicilian Style

salsa con vongole alla siciliana

3 tablespoons unsalted
  butter
1 tablespoon olive oil
4 anchovy filets, minced
200 grams (7 ounces)
  canned baby clams
2 tablespoons clam juice
1 garlic clove, peeled
6 tablespoons (approxi-
  mate) unseasoned bread
  crumbs browned in 1
  teaspoon olive oil
2 tablespoons chopped
  Italian parsley

This recipe was developed for use with Japanese canned baby clams because so many of us have no source of fresh baby clams and because the Japanese canned varieties are far superior for sauces to the tough, canned, minced clams used in some American fish chowders.

Melt the butter in a small saucepan. Add the olive oil and minced anchovies, and cook for 2 minutes. Drain the clams, preserving 2 tablespoons of the juice, and add both clams and juice to the saucepan. Add the garlic clove (skewered with a wooden pick for easy removal at the end of cooking), and simmer the sauce for 5 minutes. Remove and discard garlic.

Toast the bread crumbs until nicely browned in a skillet. (You need not add oil, if using one of the new nonstick surfaces; otherwise, add about a teaspoon of olive oil.)

Serve the sauce with 300 to 400 grams (about ¾ to ⅘ pound) homemade *pasta verde* cut in thin *fettuccine* (for 3 to 4 people) and sprinkle with the bread crumbs and the minced parsley.

Thin Spaghetti with Crab Meat Sauce

spaghettini al granchio

400 grams (14 ounces)
  spaghettini
6 tablespoons olive oil
1 garlic clove, peeled and
  halved
6 anchovy filets
140 grams (5 ounces)
  cooked crab meat
2 tablespoons chopped
  Italian parsley
3 tablespoons unseasoned
  bread crumbs browned in
  1 teaspoon olive oil

Like the sauce made with baby clams, this is one of those extra-quick dishes that dispel forever the notion that gourmet food is achieved only with elaborate techniques and intimidating lists of ingredients.

Frozen, cooked crab meat works perfectly well for this dish; but if you have access to fresh crabs, all the better. And do reserve some extra claws for decoration and enjoyment.

Bring at least 4 liters (approximately 4 quarts) water to a boil, salt it with 1 teaspoon salt per liter of water, and cook the *spaghettini*.

In the meantime, put 6 tablespoons of oil in a skillet, and sauté the garlic in it. When golden, remove the garlic, and add the anchovies to the oil. Over low heat, chop and stir the anchovies until they are almost dissolved in the oil. Add the crab meat and the parsley, stir, and remove from heat.

In another small skillet or frying pan put the teaspoon of oil and brown the bread crumbs over moderate heat until toasted.

When the *spaghettini* are cooked *al dente* drain them well, dress with the crab-meat sauce, sprinkle with bread crumbs, toss, and serve. For 4.

Spaghetti with Shrimp and Fresh Tomatoes

spaghetti agli scampi e pomodori

1 clove garlic, peeled

3 tablespoons olive oil

450 grams (1 pound) fresh shrimp, deveined

1 cup dry white wine

450 grams (1 pound) fresh plum tomatoes, peeled and quartered (seeded if you wish)

salt to taste

1 tablespoon chopped Italian parsley

400 grams (14 ounces) spaghetti

Crush the garlic and sauté it in the olive oil in a medium-sized sauté pan until golden. Discard the garlic, add the shrimp, and cook for 3 minutes or until bright coral in color.

Add the wine and let it sizzle and evaporate about 2 minutes.

Add the tomatoes, and bring to a boil. Lower the heat and simmer, stirring from time to time, about 10 minutes. Very ripe tomatoes should have disintegrated rapidly and the liquids of the sauce reduced. Add salt, stir, and taste. Add the parsley.

Cook the spaghetti in at least 4 liters (4 quarts) boiling salted water until *al dente*. Drain well, and mix with the sauce in the sauté pan. Serve immediately. For 4.

Pasta *alla Sarah Caldwell*

2 cups peeled plum tomatoes

1 dried hot red pepper pod, seeded, or several drops of Tabasco sauce to taste

4 tablespoons olive oil

5 fresh basil leaves, chopped

1 teaspoon salt

freshly ground pepper

½ cup chopped Italian parsley

2 tablespoons unsalted butter

340 grams (12 ounces) cooked fresh lobster or shrimp

¼ cup brandy, warmed

1 4-egg recipe homemade pasta (pages 93 to 96)

There are all kinds of reasons behind the name of a dish. This particular pasta sauce was named for Sarah Caldwell the day we answered her invitation to cook pasta on stage for a special performance of Offenbach's *Orpheus in the Underworld* by the Opera Company of Boston. Our cast-size caldron steamed with fresh egg pasta, and the sauce was ladled out to music. We have cut the proportions to suit a table for six: it makes a memorable dinner, with or without music.

Put the tomatoes through a food mill, using the finest disc. Cook the pepper pod in the olive oil over medium heat until dark and then discard. Cool the olive oil a moment, and then add tomatoes, basil, salt, and a good sprinkling of pepper. (If using Tabasco, add it with the tomatoes.) Bring the pan to a boil, lower the heat, and simmer for about 15 minutes or until the sauce has thickened.

Stir in the parsley, and remove from heat.

Melt the butter in a medium-sized saucepan, add the lobster or shrimp. Stir, and cook for two minutes. Add the brandy, and flame it. Stir and mix everything into the tomato sauce.

Cook the pasta 2 to 3 minutes (or until *al dente*) in at least 4 liters (4 quarts) boiling, salted water. Drain thoroughly, and dress with the sauce. For 6.

Pasta with Cheese Sauce

"Tossed" *Fettuccine*

fettuccine sciué-sciué

When we asked the cook of a Gaeta eatery (restaurant would be too imposing a name for such a few tables under a pergola near a beach) why he called his *fettuccine sciué-sciué*, he did not answer, he demonstrated. Holding a large, long-handled skillet piled with hot *fettuccine*, he sprinkled the pasta with shredded *mozzarella* and then with expert motions he flipped the pasta several times in the air as if it were an omelet. Each time he tossed the pasta he chanted a loud "Shoooo-ay!" "It means nothing . . . it is to give me courage," he explained. He also explained that, when mixed his way, none of the melting *mozzarella* is lost on the spoon and fork needed for conventional tossing. We prefer the conventional way (for big batches), losing a few grams of *mozzarella* but avoiding the risk of redoing the kitchen. Do as you prefer; it is delicious any way you toss it.

8 to 10 ripe plum tomatoes, peeled, or 2 cups canned

6 tablespoons unsalted butter

6 fresh basil leaves

1 teaspoon salt

freshly ground pepper to taste

1 3-egg recipe *fettuccine* (pages 95 to 99)

3 tablespoons minced Italian parsley

225 grams (½ pound) fresh *mozzarella* cheese, shredded

Pass the tomatoes through a food mill or, if using canned tomatoes, cut them in chunks or mash them with a fork.

Melt the butter in a large skillet or sauté pan. Add the tomatoes, basil, salt, and pepper. Stir, bring to a boil, then simmer for 15 minutes. Taste, and adjust for salt.

Cook the *fettuccine al dente* in at least 4 liters (4 quarts) of boiling salted water, and drain them well. Put the *fettuccine* in the skillet with the sauce, add the parsley, raise the heat, and toss well.

Remove from heat, sprinkle with *mozzarella,*

toss *sciué-sciué* or mix well, and serve immediately.

There is a third way of doing all this: put about half the drained *fettuccine* in a warm serving bowl, add some sauce and parsley and some of the *mozzarella*. Mix gently. Then add the last of the *fettuccine* and the rest of the sauce, parsley and cheese, and mix again. But do it quickly. *Sciué-sciué* should be eaten while the *mozzarella* is still melted and creamy. For 4.

Pasta with Meat Sauces

Spaghetti, Charcoal Makers' Style

spaghetti alla carbonara

3 slices *pancetta* or lean salt pork cut as thick as bacon

2½ tablespoons olive oil

generous amount of freshly ground pepper

3 medium eggs

grated Parmesan cheese to please

450 grams (1 pound) spaghetti

If using salt pork, it is advisable to blanch it first in boiling water for 2 to 3 minutes to remove excess salt.

Cut the salt pork or *pancetta* in tiny pieces and sauté them in the oil until the fat is translucent.

Add freshly grated pepper to the salt pork or *pancetta.*

Break the eggs into an unheated serving platter or bowl. Beat the eggs until whites and yolks are blended. Add more pepper to the eggs.

Cook the pasta in abundant boiling salted water until *al dente.* Drain well, reserving a tablespoon or two of the pasta water.

Place drained spaghetti on beaten eggs, and mix immediately and thoroughly so that the heat of the pasta cooks the eggs.

Add the salt pork and its oil to the pasta, and toss again. If by any chance the pasta seems a little dry, add the reserved pasta water and toss again. Serve with more pepper and Parmesan cheese on the side for those who wish it; it is up to your table mates to choose. For 4.

Spaghetti *alla Paolo*

This sauce has a recent but glorious history: we began it as an attempt at a welcoming dish of *spaghetti alla carbonara* for our returning son Paolo, only to find the larder short on salt pork but with two extra and unsuspected Italian sausages, a bit of *mozzarella* (it had not all gone into a previous dish), and some egg yolks (their whites departed in meringues). Such are the coincidences of history and cuisine. Now we go out of our way to make this fortuitous aggregation of ingredients happen again and again.

85 grams (3 ounces) lean salt pork

2 Italian sweet sausages (no fennel seeds)

4 tablespoons olive oil

400 grams (14 ounces) spaghetti

4 egg yolks

2 tablespoons milk

freshly ground pepper

115 grams (4 ounces) *mozzarella* cheese, shredded

While the pasta water (at least 4 liters or 4 quarts) comes to a boil, cube the salt pork. Blanch in boiling water for 2 minutes (if necessary) to remove excess salt.

Skin the sausages and crumble them.

Put the olive oil in a small saucepan, add the salt pork and sausages, and cook over medium heat until cooked but not crisp.

When the pasta water boils, salt it and put in the spaghetti.

Put the egg yolks, milk, and a generous amount of pepper in a serving bowl. Beat with a fork until homogeneous.

Drain the pasta, and pour it immediately over the egg mixture. Toss well and, when the heat of the pasta has cooked the eggs, add the salt pork and sausages with their warm oil.

Toss, and add the *mozzarella.* Toss again, and serve. For 4 — and the honored guest is allowed to eat his portion out of the serving bowl.

Rigatoni with Sausages and Mushrooms

rigatoni, salsiccie, e funghi

170 grams (6 ounces) *rigatoni*

115 grams (4 ounces) fresh mushrooms

1 garlic clove, peeled

3 tablespoons olive oil

2 Italian sweet sausages

1 tablespoon chopped Italian parsley

salt to taste

freshly ground pepper

2 tablespoons unsalted butter

grated Parmesan cheese to taste

Put the pasta in at least 4 liters (4 quarts) boiling salted water.

While the pasta cooks, clean and chop coarsely most of the mushrooms; slice the remaining few.

In a skillet, large enough to contain the pasta once cooked, sauté the garlic in the oil. Once the garlic is golden, press it with a fork to release its flavor and then discard. Add the mushrooms to the pan, and stir. Skin the sausages and shred them directly into the skillet. Add salt to taste and a generous amount of freshly ground pepper. Cook and stir over medium heat until mushrooms and sausages are cooked, 5 to 10 minutes.

Once the pasta is cooked, drain well and add it to the skillet. Toss everything thoroughly, dot with butter, and cook over low heat for 2 minutes. Serve with grated Parmesan cheese. For 2.

Pasta with Chicken Livers

tagliatelle coi fegatini

1 small onion, peeled

4 tablespoons unsalted butter

2 tablespoons olive oil

2 cups ripe plum tomatoes, peeled, or 2 cups canned plum tomatoes

2 cups chicken livers

1 bay leaf

½ teaspoon salt, or to taste

freshly ground pepper

4 tablespoons grated Parmesan cheese (approximate)

400 grams (14 ounces) tagliatelle

Mince the onion and sauté it in 2 tablespoons of the butter and the olive oil until golden.

Put the tomatoes through a food mill or coarse sieve.

Clean and chop the livers.

Once the onion is golden, scoop half of it into another saucepan along with the remaining butter. Add the chicken livers, and sauté over high heat 4 to 5 minutes.

Add the tomatoes and bay leaf to the onion in the first saucepan, bring to a boil, then lower the heat, and simmer for 10 minutes.

Stir the chicken livers into the simmered tomato sauce. Taste for salt, adjust as you wish. Add pepper to taste, simmer 5 more minutes.

Cook the *tagliatelle* in at least 4 liters (4 quarts) boiling salted water until *al dente*. Drain thoroughly. Dress with sauce. Serve with Parmesan cheese. For 4.

Pasta with Vegetable Sauces

Vermicelli with Super-Quick Tomato Sauce
vermicelli al pomodoro rapidissimi

200 grams (7 ounces) *vermicelli* or *spaghettini*

1 small onion, peeled

2 tablespoons unsalted butter

3 or 4 fresh basil leaves

1 cup pure tomato juice

freshly ground pepper to taste

grated Parmesan cheese to taste

Grandmother, or even Aunt Teresa, would have disowned us for even thinking of such a sauce. But then neither would have believed that any of their Italian descendants would one day purchase and drink *puro succo di pomodoro* — plain tomato juice.

Put the pasta water (at least 3 liters or 3 quarts) to boil. When it does, salt it and start cooking the *vermicelli*. While they cook:

Mince the onion and sauté it in the butter until golden in a skillet large enough to hold the pasta once it is cooked. Chop the basil coarsely, add to the onion, and stir. Add the tomato juice. Bring to a boil, add the pepper, and simmer for 4 minutes or until the *vermicelli* in their pot of water are barely *al dente*. Thoroughly drain the pasta, put it with the sauce, raise the heat, and stir and toss for a minute or two or until the pasta's starch has thickened the sauce to coat the pasta. Sprinkle with grated Parmesan cheese to taste. Serve at once. For 2. Double for 4.

Pasta with Mushroom Sauce

tonnarelli ai funghi

4 tablespoons unsalted butter

1 medium onion, peeled and minced

340 grams (12 ounces) fresh mushrooms

½ teaspoon salt, or to taste

3 tablespoons dry Marsala wine

½ cup medium cream

freshly ground pepper

400 grams (14 ounces) tonnarelli or fettuccine

2 tablespoons minced Italian parsley

4 tablespoons grated Parmesan cheese

Melt the butter in a saucepan over low heat. Add the minced onion, and cook until limp.

Clean and slice thinly the mushrooms and add them to the onion. Cook 4 to 5 minutes or until the mushrooms begin to release their moisture. Add salt.

Stir in the Marsala, raise the heat, and cook until the wine has evaporated.

Lower the heat, stir in the cream. Taste for salt. Add a generous sprinkling of pepper.

Cook the pasta in at least 4 liters (4 quarts) of boiling salted water, drain thoroughly, and place in a warm serving bowl. Dress with the sauce, add the parsley and Parmesan cheese. Toss well, and serve. For 4.

Macaroni with Summer Sauce

maccheróni al sugo d'estate

1 small eggplant (225 grams, ½ pound, approximate)

salt

1 medium onion, peeled

2 to 3 slices bacon

1 garlic clove, peeled

3 tablespoons olive oil (approximate)

1 tablespoon unsalted butter

2 sweet green peppers

1 sweet red and 1 yellow pepper

1 chicken bouillon cube

freshly ground pepper

flour

oil for frying

450 grams (1 pound) small shaped macaroni, preferably shells

4 tablespoons (approximate) grated Parmesan or sweet *Provolone* cheese

1 tablespoon finely chopped Italian parsley

If you are not familiar with the taste of eggplant and peppers with pasta, this is just the introduction you may need. This is a sauce that really calls for six appetites in order to use the vegetables without wasting any or creating a leftover that with reheating will lose its texture.

Peel the eggplant and cut it in julienne strips. Spread the strips out in the bottom of a large colander, sprinkle them liberally with salt, and let them sit until they have given up their bitter juices (about 20 minutes).

Slice the onion paper thin; cut the bacon crosswise into narrow strips; mince the garlic.

Sauté the onion, bacon, and garlic in a large sauté pan with the olive oil and butter until limp and translucent.

Wash and core the peppers and cut them in strips as you did the eggplant. Add the peppers to the sauté pan.

Add the bouillon cube and a good sprinkling of pepper. Stir, lower the heat, cover the pan, and let simmer for 20 minutes or until the peppers are well cooked. Stir occasionally. If the sauce dries out before the peppers are cooked to your taste, add a tablespoon or so of hot water.

While the sauce cooks, rinse the eggplant briefly and pat dry on absorbent toweling. Shake the strips in a plastic bag with flour.

Bring the frying oil to a high heat (180°C, 375°F) and fry a handful of eggplant strips at a time. Remove from the oil when golden and let them dry on absorbent toweling.

Cook the pasta in at least 6 liters (6 quarts) boiling salted water until *al dente*. Drain thoroughly, and stir into the pepper sauce. Toss well, and place in a serving dish. Sprinkle with the fried eggplant and parsley. Serve, with the grated cheese and extra olive oil to be added as each pleases. For 6.

Ziti with Fresh Tomatoes

ziti con pomodori freschi

675 grams (1½ pounds) very ripe tomatoes (plum or salad)
1½ garlic cloves, peeled
15 to 20 fresh basil leaves
1 tablespoon chopped Italian parsley
¼ teaspoon dried oregano
1½ teaspoons salt
freshly ground pepper
4 tablespoons olive oil
170 grams (6 ounces) fresh whole milk *mozzarella,* chopped coarsely
400 grams (14 ounces) macaroni, preferably *ziti*

Peel and seed the tomatoes, saving as much juice as possible. Cut the tomatoes in bite-size chunks and place them in your pasta serving bowl along with their juice.

Mince the garlic, basil, and parsley; add them, together with the oregano, to the tomatoes.

Season with salt and pepper (ten or so twists of the mill should give the proper amount). Add the olive oil and *mozzarella*. Mix well, and let rest 1 hour at room temperature.

Cook the pasta in at least 4 liters (4 quarts) boiling salted water until *al dente*. Drain thoroughly, and add to the tomato-and-cheese mixture. Toss well, and serve immediately on warm plates. For 4.

Spaghetti with Lemon Sauce

spaghetti al limone

400 grams (14 ounces) spaghetti or *spaghettini*
grated zest of 1 lemon
1 cup medium cream
¼ cup vodka or *grappa*
juice of ½ lemon
⅛ teaspoon freshly grated nutmeg

The name may evoke a pungent taste, but the dish is a most delicate one with only the fragrance of lemon. The original recipe uses a shot of *grappa,* the fiery drink of the Alps. We have substituted vodka because of its availability on the market and also because it adds an even more delicate flavor. If you can find a good *grappa* in your area, be daring and use it.

Put the pasta to cook in at least 4 liters (4 quarts) boiling salted water.

Grate the zest of the lemon, but be careful not to grate any of the white part of the peel.

In a large skillet over very low heat put the cream and the zest and let them steep for 5 minutes. Add the vodka, and stir in the lemon juice and the nutmeg.

Drain the pasta when it is barely *al dente,* add to the sauce in the skillet. Raise the heat to medium, and stir and toss the spaghetti until the pasta has absorbed most of the liquid and the sauce is thick and creamy. Serve hot. For 4.

Fettuccine with Mushrooms and Ham

fettuccine ai funghi e prosciutto

225 grams (½ pound) mushrooms

115 grams (¼ pound) cooked ham (delicatessen slices are fine)

5 tablespoons unsalted butter

½ teaspoon salt

1 tablespoon coarsely chopped Italian parsley

¾ cup medium (all-purpose) cream

5 tablespoons grated Parmesan cheese

1 3-egg batch homemade *fettuccine* (pages 95 to 99)

Wash the mushrooms quickly and gently in lukewarm water, and dry with paper towels (or brush them clean with a mushroom brush). Slice thinly. Cut the ham in 1-inch julienne strips.

Melt 3 tablespoons of the butter in a large sauté pan, and cook the mushrooms about 2 minutes or until they are just beginning to lose their crispness and give up their natural juices. Add the salt. Stir in the ham bits and the parsley, and remove from heat.

Put the remaining butter in the pasta serving bowl and set it over the pasta pot as its water comes to a boil. Add the cream and Parmesan cheese and leave the bowl over the hot water until the ingredients have blended to a cream sauce.

Cook the pasta in 4 to 6 liters (quarts) salted water, drain thoroughly, and place in serving bowl. Mix well, add the mushrooms and ham, and serve. Additional Parmesan may be added as desired. For 4.

Spaghetti with Sweet-Pepper Sauce

spaghetti ai peperoni

1 medium sweet onion

2 sweet peppers, green, red, or yellow

4 tablespoons olive oil

1 tablespoon wine vinegar

1½ to 2 cups peeled plum tomatoes (fresh or canned), cut in chunks

½ teaspoon salt, or to taste

freshly grated pepper

400 grams (14 ounces) spaghetti

2 tablespoons chopped Italian parsley

Cut the onion in thin slices.

Clean and seed the peppers and cut them in very thin strips, more or less the thickness of the spaghetti.

Sauté the onion and peppers in the oil and, when almost limp, add the vinegar. When the vinegar has evaporated, add the tomatoes. Bring to a boil, add salt and pepper to taste, lower the heat, and simmer 15 minutes, stirring occasionally.

In the meantime, cook the spaghetti in at least 4 liters (4 quarts) boiling salted water until *al dente*. Drain well, and place in a serving bowl. Dress with the sauce and chopped parsley. Toss well, and serve. For 4.

Pasta with Artichokes

pasta ai carciofi

2 large artichokes, cleaned
and trimmed (pages 4 to
5)

juice of 1 lemon

10 to 12 full sprigs Italian
parsley

1 garlic clove, peeled

1 medium onion, peeled

5 tablespoons olive oil

¼ teaspoon dried marjoram

1 beef bouillon cube,
crushed

¾ teaspoon salt

freshly ground pepper

1 teaspoon quick-mixing
flour

⅔ cup light cream

1 3-egg recipe homemade
pasta (pages 93 to 97),
or 340 grams (¾ pound)
spaghetti

grated Parmesan cheese

Cut off the artichoke stems and slice in rounds.
Cut the artichokes in thin wedges. Put all in a
bowl of cold water with the lemon juice.

Mince the parsley, garlic, and onion.

Heat the oil over moderate heat in a large
saucepan. Add the mince, and cook until limp.
Drain and add the artichoke pieces. Stir gently,
and add the marjoram, bouillon cube, salt, and
pepper. Cook for 4 minutes or until the artichoke wedges are tender but still have a little bit
of crispness. Sprinkle in the flour. Stir, add ½
cup of the cream, and cook on very low heat
another 3 minutes.

Taste for salt, and adjust to please. Add remaining cream if the sauce is too thick.

Bring 4 liters (4 quarts) water to a boil, salt it
with 1 teaspoon salt per liter, add the pasta, and
cook until *al dente*.

Drain the pasta and put it in a serving dish.
Dress with the artichoke sauce, and serve with
Parmesan cheese on the side. For 4.

Filled, Layered, Rolled Pasta Dishes

Cappelletti

115 grams (4 ounces) lean pork

85 grams (3 ounces) white meat of turkey

1 tablespoon unsalted butter

115 grams (4 ounces) cooked ham

2 eggs

¼ teaspoon salt

¼ teaspoon white pepper

½ teaspoon freshly ground coriander

¼ teaspoon freshly grated nutmeg

1 heaping tablespoon grated Parmesan cheese

1 3-egg recipe *pasta all'uovo* (page 95)

Chop the pork and turkey coarsely, and sauté in butter until tender and cooked, about 6 minutes.

Coarsely chop the ham. Grind all three meats to a paste either by sending them through a meat grinder twice or by processing them with the steel blade in a food processor.

Stir in the eggs one at a time, then add salt, pepper, coriander, nutmeg, and Parmesan. Mix well.

Sauté a teaspoon or so of the filling for a minute or two in the butter remaining in the pan, taste for flavoring, and adjust seasoning for the entire recipe if needed.

Make your pasta recipe (pages 93 to 97) and cut into 2-inch squares. Since the pasta must be moist to seal in the filling, cover most of the squares with plastic wrap or a dampened, thoroughly wrung out, clean dish towel while filling the first few squares.

With a demitasse spoon or a pastry bag, place a small dab of filling in the center of each square. Fold the square in half on the diagonal and seal the filling in by pressing the edges firmly with your fingers. (If the dough has dried, moisten the edges slightly with a bit of water on a fingertip.)

You now have a stuffed triangle. Take the two corners of the base and wrap them around the tip of your finger. Press the corners together so that they stick. Fold the third corner back on itself. There is your first *cappelletto*, or "little hat." Keep filling, pressing, and turning until all the dough and stuffing is used.

Makes approximately 150 *cappelletti,* or enough for 6 servings with *ragù* (pages 35 to 36) or with a sauce of unsalted butter, cream, and Parmesan cheese, or 8 to 10 servings with broth from *bollito misto.*

Cappelletti may be made ahead of cooking time and allowed to dry on a floured dish towel or cookie sheet. They may be frozen once they have dried an hour; put the cookie tin in the freezer until the *cappelletti* are frozen, then pack them in freezer containers and seal well.

Frozen *cappelletti* take a bit more time to cook than those freshly made, but the flavor remains the same.

Pork-Veal-Ham Filling for *Cappelletti* or *Cannelloni*

ripieno per cappelletti o cannelloni

Filling

60 grams (2 ounces) cooked ham, about 2 or 3 delicatessen slices

115 grams (4 ounces) lean pork

140 grams (5 ounces) veal (may be boneless stew meat, cuttings from veal breast, etc.)

60 grams (2 ounces) *mortadella*, about 2 or 3 slices

1 tablespoon unsalted butter

¼ teaspoon freshly ground pepper

½ teaspoon salt, or to taste

12 coriander seeds, freshly ground

¼ teaspoon freshly grated nutmeg

1 tablespoon minced Italian parsley

1 or 2 dashes Worcestershire sauce (optional)

3 tablespoons grated Parmesan cheese

1 egg

It is no secret that the making of *cappelletti* or *cannelloni* is time-consuming, but the delightful end result is nothing short of utterly rewarding. In the interest of cutting time, the following recipe has been worked out to make enough filling for about 150 *cappelletti*, or for 48 *cappelletti* and 8 *cannelloni*, either for freezing (in 1 or 2 containers depending on your use), or for using half immediately and freezing the other half. *Cappelletti* should be allowed to dry about an hour before freezing to prevent their sticking together. *Cannelloni* may be placed in a buttered freezer-to-oven dish and frozen as soon as they are filled.

Cube or very coarsely chop the four meats.

Melt the butter in a sauté pan, add the meats, pepper, and salt and cook, stirring, until the pink color has gone.

Place the cooked meats in the food processor bowl. Add the coriander, nutmeg, parsley, Worcestershire sauce (if desired), and cheese. Process on/off until the meats are very finely minced. (Or mince the meats well by hand, or send them twice through a meat grinder; then add seasonings and cheese, and blend well.) Add the egg, and process (or blend) to mix in well. Taste for seasonings, and adjust to please.

Makes approximately 1¾ cups filling.

Pasta

¾ cup all-purpose un-
  bleached flour
1 egg
¼ teaspoon salt

Follow the instructions for pasta on pages 93-98. This amount will make approximately 48 *cappelletti* or 8 *cannelloni,* using about ½ the filling recipe.

To fill, shape, and cook *cappelletti* see pages 120 to 121. These *cappelletti* may be served with just butter and grated Parmesan cheese or with cream sauce (page 124). *Cappelletti* may also be cooked and served in broth (pages 43 to 47) and served with grated Parmesan cheese to please. Forty-eight *cappelletti* with butter and cream sauce serve approximately 2 people. When this amount is cooked in and served with broth, it can almost appease the appetites of 6.

To fill cannelloni: cut the pasta in eight 4″ × 5″ rectangles. Bring 2 to 3 liters (quarts) of water to a boil, add 2 to 3 teaspoons salt, add the pasta, and let it cook 2 minutes after it rises to the top of the water. Remove with a slotted spoon into a pan of cold water and then on to clean dish towels.

Divide and spread the filling down the center of each pasta rectangle. Roll up and place seam side down in a buttered baking dish.

Sauce

½ recipe *besciamella*
  (pages 41 to 42)
1 tablespoon unsalted butter
2 tablespoons grated Par-
  mesan cheese (approxi-
  mate)

To complete cannelloni: cover the *cannelloni* with the *besciamella,* dot with butter, sprinkle with the cheese. Bake in a 177° C (350° F) oven until toasted (about 15 minutes). Serves 4.

Cappelletti in Cream Sauce

cappelletti alla panna

1½ cups medium (all-purpose) cream

3 tablespoons unsalted butter

¼ teaspoon freshly grated nutmeg, or to taste

6 tablespoons grated Parmesan cheese

1 recipe *cappelletti* (pages 120 to 121)

Bring 8 liters (8 quarts) of water to a boil, and add 8 teaspoons salt.

Place your serving dish on top of the water and in it put the cream, butter, nutmeg, and cheese. Stir briefly, and let the heat from the pot below warm the cream and melt the cheese and butter.

When the water boils, put the serving dish in a warm oven.

Add the *cappelletti* to the boiling water, and cook until the pasta is completely cooked. Drain carefully, and put in the serving dish with the cream and cheese. Toss gently, and serve. For 6.

Ravioli with Filberts
ravioli alle nocciole

The addition of filberts (hazelnuts) to the traditional ingredients for *ricotta ravioli* gives a new dimension to an old favorite. When made with the (optional) almond paste, these *ravioli* even have a hint of Middle Eastern flavor. At one time Italian cooking was definitely influenced by the mid-east trade, and thus the flavor of *ravioli alle nocciole* is not really new. Just delicious.

The ingredients are enough to fill approximately 36 *ravioli* or 4 servings (no seconds, please), but are easily multiplied for more or, if you wish, for freezing.

Pasta
¾ cup all-purpose un-
bleached flour
1 egg
1 tablespoon oil (vegetable
or olive)
¼ teaspoon salt

Mix and knead as described on pages 93 to 96. Divide the dough into two equal pieces, roll out, and leave protected by plastic wrap or clean kitchen towels while you make the filling and the sauce.

Filling
60 grams (2 ounces)
shelled filberts
30 grams (1 ounce) almond
paste (optional)
60 grams (2 ounces) *ricotta*
cheese
40 grams (1¾ ounces)
grated Parmesan cheese
1 egg yolk
⅛ teaspoon freshly grated
nutmeg
⅛ teaspoon salt
1 tablespoon milk

Roast the filberts in a skillet over medium heat for a few minutes, shaking frequently, until the brown skins begin to crackle and peel off. Remove from heat, wrap the filberts in a clean cloth, and rub and shake to remove all the brown skins.

Put the peeled nuts in a mortar and turn them into a floury paste. Or do the same with a rolling pin over a hard, smooth surface. Add the almond paste (if using it), and mix well.

Put the nut mixture in a bowl, add the *ricotta* and Parmesan, and mix well. Add the egg yolk, nutmeg, and salt, and mix again. Stir in the milk, but only enough to obtain a smooth paste. Cover, and let rest.

If using a food processor, roughly chop the cleaned filberts and put them in the bowl with the steel blade in place. Process until the nuts have turned to a floury paste. Add the almond paste (optional), and process briefly. Add the remaining ingredients, and process until a smooth compound is obtained. Let rest.

To assemble ravioli: position little dabs of filling in even rows on one of the sheets of pasta so that each dab will be in the center of a 2-inch square. Cover with the other sheet of pasta and with your fingers press down around each bit of filling. Cut between the rows of filling with a pastry cutter, and place the filled squares on a flour-dusted cloth or cookie sheet.

Sauce

4 tablespoons unsalted butter
4 tablespoons light cream
grated Parmesan cheese

Put the butter in a saucepan over very low heat and cook, stirring, until it is light brown. Do not burn. Warm the cream in a second pan. Do this while the *ravioli* are cooking.

To cook ravioli: put at least 6 liters (6 quarts) of water to boil. Salt with 6 teaspoons of salt.

Lower the *ravioli* into the boiling water with a slotted spoon, bring the water back to a boil, and then sustain the heat at a slow boil. Cook the *ravioli* for 4 minutes after they float to the surface. Scoop them out with a slotted spoon, draining them well. Place *ravioli* in a warm serving bowl, cover with the brown butter and the cream, toss gently, and serve with grated Parmesan cheese aside. For 4.

Saint's Day *Cannelloni*

cannelloni del curato

Pasta

¾ cup all-purpose un-
 bleached flour
1 egg
¼ teaspoon salt

Filling

1 small carrot, scrubbed
 and peeled
½ stalk celery, washed
1 small garlic clove, peeled
1 small onion, peeled
1 tablespoon olive oil
4 tablespoons unsalted
 butter
140 grams (5 ounces)
 white meat of chicken
 (about half a chicken
 breast)
115 grams (4 ounces)
 cooked ham
freshly ground pepper
1 bay leaf
½ cup dry white wine
3 tablespoons all-purpose
 unbleached flour
1 cup milk, hot
¼ teaspoon salt
1 egg, lightly beaten
4 tablespoons grated Par-
 mesan cheese (approxi-
 mate)
1 tablespoon unseasoned
 bread crumbs
1 tablespoon unsalted butter

Once, on the patron saint's day of every Italian village, farmers would bring tokens of their best produce to the curate. The tradition still goes on in some villages, and this recipe is an homage to it. It uses the traditional flavorings and the best of the chicken and pork: chicken breast and cooked ham.

Prepare the pasta as on pages 93 to 96 and cut in 4″ × 5″ rectangles. Cook in at least 3 liters (3 quarts) of boiling salted water to which you have added a tablespoon oil. When the *cannelloni* are *al dente,* remove them to drain on clean kitchen toweling.

Mince the vegetables together, and sauté the mince until golden in the oil and 2 tablespoons of the butter. Cut the chicken meat in small pieces and add it to the sauté pan. Cook 4 minutes. Cube the ham, and add it to the pan along with pepper and bay leaf. Cook another 5 minutes, stirring occasionally. Taste for salt, and add as desired. Add the wine, and cook until the wine is evaporated. Let cool.

To make a thick besciamella: melt the remaining 2 tablespoons of butter over low heat; add the flour, and stir with a whisk until it is absorbed by the butter. Pour in the milk slowly and steadily, stirring all the time. Raise the heat to moderate, and cook at least 4 minutes or until a reasonably thick sauce has been achieved. Let cool.

Remove the bay leaf from the cooked meats and, with a food processor or a meat grinder, reduce them and their juice to a coarse paste. Mix the meats with the cooled *besciamella,* and add the egg and 2 tablespoons Parmesan cheese. Stir well. Let rest.

Sauce

2 tablespoons unsalted
butter

2 tablespoons all-purpose
unbleached flour

1 cup milk

¼ teaspoon nutmeg

¼ teaspoon salt

To assemble: butter a baking dish or four individual au gratin dishes, and preheat the oven to 200° C (400° F). Prepare a light *besciamella*:

Proceed as you did earlier with the thick *besciamella*.

Distribute the filling on the *cannelloni* pieces. Roll up the *cannelloni* and place them, fold side down, in the baking dish(es). Cover the *cannelloni* with the *besciamella* and sprinkle them with the last of the Parmesan cheese and the bread crumbs. Dot with the last tablespoon of butter, and bake 15 minutes or until the top is golden and the *cannelloni* are heated through. For 4.

Squash *Ravioli*

ravioli alla zucca

Filling
60 grams (2 ounces)
    cooked pureed winter
    squash (fresh or frozen)
4 tablespoons grated Par-
    mesan cheese (approxi-
    mate)
1 egg
¼ teaspoon freshly grated
    nutmeg
1 tablespoon milk (optional)

Pasta
1 recipe *filbert ravioli*
    (pages 125 to 126)

Sauce
4 tablespoons unsalted
    butter
4 tablespoons light cream
grated Parmesan cheese

Mix together all the ingredients for the filling, stirring until you have a thick but spreadable paste. Depending on the moisture of the squash, you may want to add a little more Parmesan to thicken the paste or a bit of milk to thin it. Let rest for 15 minutes.

Make a recipe as for filbert-*ravioli* dough, fill with the squash filling, and cut the *ravioli*.

Put at least 6 liters (6 quarts) of water to boil. While the water heats, make the sauce: put the cream and butter in the serving bowl and set it on top of the pasta pot as the water comes to a boil, thus melting the butter into the cream. Put the serving bowl in a warm oven until the *ravioli* are done.

Salt the *ravioli* water with 6 teaspoons salt. Lower the *ravioli* into the boiling water with a slotted spoon, and reduce the heat to a low boil. Cook the *ravioli* 4 minutes after they float to the surface.

Using a slotted spoon, scoop out the *ravioli* when cooked, and put them in the warm serving bowl. Dress with sauce, toss gently, and serve with Parmesan cheese on the side. For 4.

Lasagne with Mushroom Sauce

lasagne al sugo di funghi

Pasta
1 4-egg recipe *pasta all'uovo* (page 95)
1 recipe *besciamella* (page 41 to 42)

Mushroom Sauce
15 parsley sprigs
1 garlic clove, peeled
1 fresh rosemary sprig or 1 teaspoon dried
6 tablespoons unsalted butter
3 tablespoons olive oil
3 cups peeled plum tomatoes, preferably fresh
½ cup tomato puree
½ cup water
675 grams (1½ pounds) fresh mushrooms
2 to 3 dried Italian mushrooms, soaked in warm water about 30 minutes
1½ teaspoons salt
¾ cup grated Parmesan cheese
½ cup unseasoned bread crumbs

Make the egg pasta, cut it into *lasagne* (4″ × 5″), and dry briefly on clean dish towels or floured cookie sheets.

Make the *besciamella* and let it cool.

Process or mince by hand the parsley, garlic, and rosemary, and sauté them in butter and olive oil until limp, about 5 minutes.

Pass the tomatoes through a food mill, and add to the flavored olive oil. Add the tomato puree and water, bring to a boil, then lower the heat, and simmer about 20 minutes.

Clean and slice the mushrooms in thick slices. Add to the simmering sauce. Squeeze dry the soaked mushrooms and slice them in thin strips. Add them to the sauce. Sprinkle with salt, stir, cover, and continue cooking until the full 20 minutes is up and the sauce has darkened in color and has condensed to the point that it can coat a spoon.

Bring a pot of water to a boil, add salt, and cook the *lasagne,* a few at a time. With a slotted spoon, remove the *lasagne* when they float to the top and are *al dente,* and drop them into a pot of cold water to stop the cooking process. Remove from cold water and spread them on kitchen toweling.

Preheat oven to 177° C (350° F).

Make a thin layer of mushroom sauce in the bottom of a *lasagne* baking dish (14″ × 10″ × 3″). Arrange the first layer of *lasagne* so that the pasta comes up the sides and ends. Cover with another thin layer of sauce. Follow that with a layer of *besciamella,* dropping it in tablespoonsful about 2 inches apart. Sprinkle with Parmesan cheese. Add another layer of pasta, pressing down to spread the *besciamella.* Add a layer of sauce, one of *besciamella,* some Parmesan cheese, and then repeat with the pasta, sauces, and cheese until you have used all the ingredients, aiming to finish with a layer of Parmesan. Sprinkle with bread crumbs. Tuck any overhanging bits of pasta down into the sides of the dish.

Bake in a moderate 177 ° C (350 ° F) oven 30 minutes. Cool for at least 15 minutes before cutting. Baked *lasagne* keeps at least 3 days in the refrigerator, is easy to freeze if wrapped well, and can easily go from freezer to oven. For 8 to 10.

Lasagne with Bolognese Meat Sauce

lasagne al ragù

Pasta

1 4-egg recipe *pasta all'uovo* (page 95) or *pasta verde* (pages 99 to 101) or half and half

Fillings

1 recipe *Bolognese ragù,* (pages 35 to 36)

1 recipe *besciamella* (pages 41 to 42)

1 kilo (2 pounds) shredded fresh *mozzarella*

Parmesan cheese to please

Make the pasta, *ragù,* and *besciamella.* The layering of this *lasagne* is just like the one with mushroom sauce (pages 130 to 131), except that the Parmesan is added only as a topping.

Cook the pasta. Spread in a *lasagne*-baking dish a layer of sauce, a layer of pasta, one of *besciamella,* one of *mozzarella,* and repeat, starting with the pasta. If you wish, you may alternate layers of green pasta with layers of the white.

When your dish is complete, bake it ½ hour in a moderate 177 ° C (350 ° F) oven. Let cool at least 15 minutes before serving. Baked *lasagne* freezes well if wrapped properly; it can also go from freezer to oven and bake in about 45 minutes. It is delicious reheated after a day or two in the refrigerator. For 8 to 10.

Crêpes with Mushrooms, Ham, Cheese

crespelle ai funghi, prosciutto, formaggio

Crespelle

4 tablespoons all-purpose unbleached flour
1 tablespoon grated Parmesan cheese
½ cup milk
¼ teaspoon salt
2 eggs
vegetable oil for frying

Filling

140 grams (5 ounces) fresh mushrooms
2 tablespoons unsalted butter
salt to taste
pepper to taste
85 grams (3 ounces) cooked ham
85 grams (3 ounces) shredded *Fontina* or Muenster cheese
1 egg yolk
3 sprigs Italian parsley

2 tablespoons unsalted butter
5 tablespoons unseasoned bread crumbs
2 tablespoons grated Parmesan cheese

Mix the flour and cheese together in a small bowl. Stir in part of the milk to make a paste, add a little more milk, and make a cream. Stir in the salt and then the eggs one at a time. Add any remaining milk, and beat well. Let rest 10 to 15 minutes.

Heat a small frying or omelet pan, brush with oil, and pour in enough of the *crespelle* batter to cover the bottom of the pan. Cook one side, then the other, until light golden. Remove to a plate. Repeat with the remaining batter. Makes eight 6- to 7-inch *crespelle*.

Clean and slice the mushrooms, and sauté them briefly in butter. Add salt and pepper to taste, and let cool.

Cut the ham in thin julienne strips. Mix the ham with the shredded cheese. Stir in the mushrooms, the egg yolk, and the parsley.

For the assembly, have all of the above prepared, plus:

Butter 4 individual oven-proof dishes or 1 larger dish. Sprinkle with a tablespoon or so of the bread crumbs. Mix remaining crumbs with the cheese. Cut the remaining butter in tiny pieces.

Put 2 heaping tablespoons filling in the center of a *crespella*. Fold two opposite sides of the *crespella* over the center so they barely meet. Fold the other two sides to close the package. Place, fold side down, in the oven dish. Repeat with the rest of the filling and *crespelle*. Dot with butter. Sprinkle with cheese–bread crumb mixture.

Bake in a moderate (177 ° C, 350 ° F) oven for 15 minutes or until golden on top. Serves 4.

Crespelle may also be served with ½ recipe light *besciamella* (pages 41 to 42), in place of the dotted butter, for a creamier dish.

Rice

Riso

Rice, or *risotto,* when cooked at the same time and in the same pot as the sauce which glorifies it, is served, like pasta, as a first course. In northern Italy, where most of the rice is grown, the making of *risotti* is a long-honored tradition. A mince of flavorings and herbs is sautéed in butter or olive oil until wilted. Then the rice is added and sautéed until it crackles. From a simmering pot of homemade stock a ladle of broth (chicken, beef, fish, or vegetable) is poured into the rice. A wooden spoon is used to stir the grains as the cooking continues over a steady heat, neither too high (which would result in rice cooked outside but hard inside) nor too low (which would give you a soupy rice). More broth is added as the rice absorbs both broth and flavorings. The end result is a creamy dish of plumped-up, tender rice, each grain separate, delicately flavored yet firm, *al dente* like good pasta. Sprinkled with Parmesan cheese and served immediately, *risotti* are as famous as pasta dishes on the Italian table and a pleasure to the palate.

The above traditional technique still stands and works wonderfully with imported Italian rice as well as with many American rices. It will not work with instant rice, which cannot take the long cooking time (about 40 minutes) and thus cannot absorb the flavorings and accents so necessary to *risotto*. If we have the time, we prefer the traditional, grand method. If we do not have the time, there are still ways to make *risotto* in the modern kitchen. Here are two ways to go, depending on the cookware as well as the rice in the market.

For pans, use a medium to heavy conventional saucepan with a good cover that really seals in the vapors. A three-liter (three-quart) size is good for 4 people.

Or, you can use a pressure cooker, preferably one of the new electric models with a fail-safe lock and a thermostat control. Like an electric frying pan, it can cook wherever you wish it to stand. Replacing the cook's hand to stir and eye to watch sounds like heresy, and perhaps it is (or may be so considered), but the experiments we have carried out with pressure cookers in our own and other kitchens tasted just like the slow-cooking version; the texture of the rice was perfect, and it took ⅓ of the time required by the traditional method. Hence, we recommend a pressure cooker. We think they are foolproof for most *risotti*; and the only time we use a normal saucepan is when certain ingredients, such as fish, would be ruined by the time the rice is cooked.

As for the rice, there are many, many brands you may use. Imported Italian rice can be found in specialty shops, which carry other Italian delicacies. It comes under the names Arborio and

Vialone, and it is the best available here for *risotti*. It is a short-grain rice with amazing capabilities of absorbing sauces and becoming round and fat, yet staying in separate grains when cooked. But be careful. Sometimes imported rices have been sitting on a shelf or have been in transit so long that they have spoiled.

We have tried as many of the United States brands as possible and have found that the "extra-fancy long-grain" produced and marketed as suitable for Armenian and Greek dishes works well in *risotto,* although it does not swell as much as we would like. The Carolina long-grain is also good. From Arkansas comes an "extra-long-grain rice," which seems to work the best of all. Under the Riceland name come four different types. The "extra-long-grain" cooks in 14 minutes in a closed saucepan or in 5 minutes in a pressure cooker. The "extra-long-grain enriched" rice (called Chefway) is perhaps even better, having been treated to retain all the natural nutrients. It cooks in 25 minutes in the saucepan, in 8 minutes in the pressure cooker. There is also the "converted natural long-grain rice," which is just a little less plump after cooking than "extra-long-grain enriched rice"; it takes 20 minutes in a conventional pan, 7 minutes in a pressure cooker. In the end, as with so many products, your choice of rice depends on your market and your kitchen. We have only one word of warning: in using a pressure cooker, be sure to bring the pressure down and stir the rice well the minute the cooking time is up.

As we have said previously, *risotti* are nearly always first courses. One of the few exceptions is *risotto alla milanese,* made with saffron and marrow bone. For tradition's sake this *risotto* is paired with *osso buco,* veal shanks in an herb sauce, as a second course.

While most *risotti* are cooked with their sauce-making ingredients, some are made with the simple addition of a pasta sauce, as in *risotto al ragù.* The rice is cooked with a bit of butter and the usual amount of broth for just a little less than the usual time. Then the sauce is added, and the cooking is completed, in 5 to 10 minutes, depending on the rice. Try it with your own favorite sauce. After all, like *antipasti, risotti* is a game any cook can play.

If you make a larger batch of *risotto* than you need, you have *avanzi,* which can serve a next-day use. Such could be called leftovers, but they really are a planned surplus. *Avanzi* lend themselves to another rice recipe, which is popular for snacks: *supplì.* (See *risotti* on pages 140 to 141, 143.)

Many *risotti* can be used for *supplì,* but the classic is *risotto al ragù, risotto* with Bolognese meat sauce (pages 35 to 36).

Rice is also a favorite in salads in the summer, in soups all year around, and in filling vegetables — tomatoes, peppers, and zucchini. (See pages 148, 272, 274.)

When it comes to the broth used in *risotto,* we nominate homemade broth — chicken, beef, vegetable, or fish, depending on the recipe (pages 43 to 47). In a pinch, we make broth from bouillon cubes. Among canned broths, there is a wide difference in available brands. We suggest tasting various types and using the lightest and most genuine in flavor. Many broths contain more fat than we like, so we always chill canned broth so that the fat can be scooped off and discarded before adding the broth to the rice.

Risotto with Artichokes

risotto ai carciofi

1 small onion, peeled
1 clove garlic, peeled
5 sprigs Italian parsley
4 tablespoons olive oil
2 medium artichokes, trimmed, dechoked, and cut in thin wedges
juice of ½ lemon
1 teaspoon salt
1½ cups extra-long-grain enriched rice
3 cups chicken broth, hot
4 tablespoons grated Parmesan cheese

Mince finely the onion, garlic, and parsley, and sauté in olive oil in a saucepan or pressure cooker until limp. (See the discussion of pans and rices, pages 134 to 136.)

Add the artichokes, and continue cooking about 4 minutes.

Add the lemon juice, the salt, and the rice. Cook and stir until the rice crackles. Add the hot broth, and cover the pan.

If using a saucepan, lower the heat and cook 25 minutes or until the rice is tender. If using a pressure cooker, bring the pressure to 15 pounds, cook 8 minutes, and lower the pressure immediately.

When the rice is cooked, stir it well, add the Parmesan cheese, taste for salt, and adjust as necessary. Transfer to a hot serving dish, and serve immediately. For 4.

Rice with Asparagus

riso con asparagi

1 medium onion, peeled and minced
4 tablespoons unsalted butter
1½ cups extra-long-grain enriched rice
3 cups vegetable or chicken broth, hot
450 grams (1 pound) fresh asparagus
60 grams (about 2 ounces) *mozzarella* cheese, shredded
3 to 4 tablespoons grated Parmesan cheese, or to taste

Sauté the onion until golden in the butter in a saucepan or pressure cooker. (See the discussion of pans and rices, pages 134 to 136.)

Add the rice, and stir and cook until the rice crackles. Add the broth, cover the pan. If using a saucepan, lower the heat and cook 20 minutes. If using a pressure cooker, bring the pressure to 15 pounds and cook 5 minutes. Lower the pressure immediately.

While the rice is cooking, break off and discard the ends of the asparagus. Wash and then cut the stalks in ½-inch pieces if thick, 1-inch pieces if thin.

When the rice has cooked, add the asparagus and continue to cook in the uncovered pan for 4 to 5 minutes.

Stir in the *mozzarella.* Transfer to a hot serving dish, sprinkle with Parmesan cheese, and serve immediately. For 4.

Risotto with Chestnuts and Almonds

risotto alle castagne e mandorle

200 grams (7 ounces, approximate) dried chestnuts

1 bay leaf

1 small onion, peeled and minced

4 tablespoons unsalted butter

1½ cups extra-long-grain enriched rice

3 cups beef broth, hot

½ cup light cream

⅓ cup sliced almonds

¼ cup vodka

3 tablespoons grated Parmesan cheese

Soak the chestnuts in lukewarm water for 1 hour. Cook them at a low boil in salted water with the bay leaf until tender (20 to 30 minutes). Let the chestnuts cool, then peel and clean them of any brown skin still clinging to the nut meat. Chop coarsely or crumble the nuts, and reserve.

Sauté the minced onion in 2 tablespoons of the butter until limp. Add the rice and half the chestnuts, and sauté for 2 minutes or until the rice crackles.

Add the broth, stir, and cover the pan. If using a saucepan, bring to a boil, lower the heat, and cook 25 minutes or until the rice is tender. If using a pressure cooker, bring the pressure to 15 pounds and cook 8 minutes. Lower pressure immediately. (See the discussion of pans and rices, pages 134 to 136.)

While the rice is cooking, put the cream, remaining chestnuts, almonds, and vodka in a saucepan and cook over very low heat for 5 minutes. Mash a few of the chestnuts against the side of the pan and stir them into the sauce.

When the rice is done, add the sauce to it along with the remaining 2 tablespoons butter and the cheese. Mix well, place on a hot serving dish, and serve immediately. For 4.

Risotto with Chicken Livers

risotto coi fegatini

1 small onion, peeled

4 or 5 fresh sage leaves, or 1 teaspoon dried, crushed sage leaves

¼ cup olive oil

225 grams (½ pound) chicken livers

⅓ cup dry white wine

½ teaspoon salt

1¼ cups extra-long-grain enriched rice

2½ cups chicken broth, hot

60 grams (2 ounces) *mozzarella* cheese, shredded or grated

5 sprigs Italian parsley, chopped with a bit of tender stem

Mince finely or process (with the steel blade) the onion and sage.

Sauté the mince in olive oil until limp.

Chop the chicken livers coarsely, and sauté 2 to 3 minutes in the onion-sage mixture. Add the wine, and cook over medium heat until the wine has evaporated.

Add the salt and the rice. Cook and stir until the rice crackles.

Add the broth, cover the pan. If using a pressure cooker, bring the pressure to 15 pounds and cook 8 minutes. Bring down the pressure immediately. If using a saucepan, bring to a boil, lower the heat, and cook 25 minutes. (See the discussion of pans and rices, pages 134 to 136.)

As soon as the rice is cooked, stir in the grated *mozzarella* and chopped parsley. Transfer to a hot serving dish, and serve at once. For 4.

Risotto with Eggs

risotto all'uovo

1½ cups extra-long-grain enriched rice

2 tablespoons unsalted butter

3 cups chicken broth, hot

2 egg yolks

½ cup whole milk

¾ cup freshly grated Parmesan cheese

½ teaspoon freshly grated nutmeg

pinch of salt

Sauté the rice with the butter in a saucepan or pressure cooker until it crackles. (See the discussion of pans and rices, pages 134 to 136.)

Add the hot broth, bring to a boil, and cover the pan. Cook 25 minutes or until tender in a saucepan, 8 minutes in a pressure cooker at a 15-pound pressure, and bring down the pressure immediately.

Meanwhile, beat the egg yolks well. Add the milk, cheese, nutmeg, and salt, and beat again until the mixture is smooth.

When the rice is cooked, add the egg mixture slowly, stirring constantly until the whole pan of rice is golden and creamy.

Place on a hot serving dish, and serve immediately. For 4.

Risotto with Ham and Three Cheeses

risotto al prosciutto e tre formaggi

1 small onion, peeled and minced

3 tablespoons unsalted butter

1½ cups extra-long-grain enriched rice

1 teaspoon salt

3¼ cups hot water

1 egg, beaten

60 grams (2 ounces) cooked ham, diced

¼ cup fresh *ricotta*

2 tablespoons grated Parmesan cheese

60 grams (2 ounces) fresh *mozzarella* cheese, grated

Sauté the onion in the butter in a saucepan or pressure cooker until limp. (See the discussion of pans and rices, pages 134 to 136.)

Add the rice and stir and cook until the grains begin to crackle.

Add the salt and water, stir, and cover the pan. If using a saucepan, bring up to a boil, lower the heat, and cook 20 minutes. If using a pressure cooker, bring up the pressure to 15 pounds and cook 7 minutes. Lower the pressure immediately.

When the rice has cooked as described, add the egg mixed with the ham and the cheeses to the pan. Stir, and continue to cook, uncovered, for 3 minutes or until the rice has been cooked completely. Transfer to a hot serving platter, and serve immediately. For 4.

This recipe also makes excellent *supplì* (page 152).

Risotto with Lemon

risotto al limone

2 rounded tablespoons minced onion (about ½ medium onion)

4 tablespoons unsalted butter

1½ cups extra-long-grain enriched rice

½ teaspoon salt

½ cup dry white wine

grated rind of 1 lemon

3 cups chicken broth, hot

juice of 1 lemon

2 to 3 tablespoons chopped Italian parsley

3 tablespoons light cream or milk

Sauté the onion in the butter in a saucepan or pressure cooker until limp. (See the discussion of pans and rices, pages 134 to 136.) Add the rice and salt, and cook until the rice crackles. Add the wine and the lemon rind, and cook until the wine has evaporated. Add the hot broth, and cover the pan. With a saucepan, bring to a boil, lower the heat, and cook 25 minutes or until the rice is tender. With a pressure cooker, bring the pressure to 15 pounds, and cook 8 minutes. Bring the pressure down immediately.

Uncover the rice, stir in the lemon juice and parsley. Cook about 30 seconds over medium heat. Stir in the cream. Transfer to a hot serving platter, and serve immediately. For 4.

Risotto with Lobster

risotto all'aragosta

1½- to ¾-kilo (1¼- to 1½-pound) lobster

4 tablespoons unsalted butter

1 celery stalk, minced

1 onion, peeled and minced

1 garlic clove, peeled and minced

1½ cups extra-long-grain enriched rice

1 packet Italian powdered saffron

½ teaspoon salt

5 tablespoons dry sherry

3 cups chicken broth, hot

2 to 3 tablespoons chopped Italian parsley

In boiling the lobster, be sure the water is abundant (at least 6 liters or 6 quarts) and as salty as sea water (1 tablespoon salt per liter). Do not overboil: 10 minutes after the pot comes back to a boil is enough for small lobsters.

Let the lobster cool enough to handle easily. Remove the meat from the shell. Slice the tail in neat rounds and reserve. Cut up the rest of the meat in ¼- to ½-inch pieces. Reserve the roe if you wish.

Melt the butter in a saucepan or pressure cooker. (See the discussion of pans and rices, pages 134 to 136.)

Add the minced flavorings, and sauté until limp.

Add the rice, saffron, and salt. Continue cooking until the rice crackles. Add the sherry, and cook until it has evaporated.

Add the hot broth and the cut-up lobster claws (and roe if you wish). Cover the pan. If using a conventional pan, bring to a boil, lower the heat, and cook for 25 minutes. If using a pressure cooker, cover, bring the pressure to 15 pounds, and cook 8 minutes.

When the rice is tender, stir it, put the mixture in a hot serving dish, and dress with the reserved lobster tail pieces and the chopped parsley. Serve immediately. For 4.

Risotto Milanese

risotto alla milanese

6 tablespoons unsalted butter

1 small onion, peeled and minced

1 tablespoon bone marrow

1¼ cup extra-long-grain enriched rice

1 packet Italian powdered saffron

3 cups broth, preferably homemade, half beef, half chicken (pages 45 to 46)

6 tablespoons freshly grated Parmesan cheese

Melt the butter in a pressure cooker or conventional saucepan (see discussion of pans and rices, pages 134 to 136). Add the onion, and sauté until golden.

Add the bone marrow, and cook 1 minute.

Add the rice and saffron, and cook and stir until the rice crackles.

Add 2½ cups of the broth, cover the pan, and bring to a boil; lower the heat, and cook about 25 minutes. If using a pressure cooker, bring to 15 pounds pressure and cook 8 minutes. Reduce the pressure immediately.

Uncover the rice, stir, and add the last of the broth. Cook 1 minute, stirring all the while. Add the Parmesan cheese. Stir again. Transfer to a hot platter and serve. For 4.

Risotto with Mushrooms

risotto ai funghi

1 large garlic clove, peeled and cut in half

¼ cup olive oil

225 grams (½ pound) mushrooms, cleaned and sliced

1 teaspoon salt, or to taste

juice of ½ lemon

1½ cups extra-long-grain enriched rice

1½ tablespoons unsalted butter

1 packet powdered saffron

3 cups broth, half beef, half chicken, hot

2 tablespoons chopped Italian parsley

freshly grated Parmesan cheese

Sauté the garlic in the olive oil until golden. Discard the garlic.

Add the mushrooms, and stir and cook over medium heat until they give up their natural moisture. Add salt and lemon juice, and remove from heat.

Put the rice and butter in a large saucepan or pressure-cooking pan. Cook until the rice begins to crackle. Stir in the saffron.

Add the broth, cover, bring to a boil. If using a saucepan, cook 20 minutes or until the rice is almost tender. If using a pressure cooker, bring the pressure to 15 pounds and cook 7 minutes. Reduce the pressure immediately. (See the discussion of pans and rices, pages 134 to 136.)

After the timed cooking, add the mushrooms, stir, and continue cooking about 4 minutes or until the rice is completely cooked but *al dente*.

Stir in the parsley.

Place the rice in a hot serving dish. Serve immediately with Parmesan cheese to taste. For 4.

Risotto with Mushrooms, Sausages, and Bacon

risotto ai funghi, salsiccie, e pancetta affumicata

3 tablespoons unsalted butter

2 Italian sweet sausages

2 thick slices bacon

5 small or 3 large fresh sage leaves, or 1 teaspoon dried whole sage leaf

4 sprigs Italian parsley, minced

115 grams (about 4 ounces) mushrooms, sliced

juice of 1 lemon

1 teaspoon salt, or to taste

1¼ cups extra-long-grain enriched rice

3 cups hot water

3 tablespoons grated Parmesan cheese

Put the butter in a saucepan or pressure cooker. (See the discussion of pans and rices, pages 134 to 136.)

Remove the casing from the sausages and break up the meat. Cut the bacon in ½-inch cubes. Put both meats with the sage and parsley in the pan and sauté briefly until the meats lose their color.

Add the mushrooms, and continue cooking another 2 to 3 minutes. Add half the lemon juice, stir, and add the salt and rice. Continue cooking until the rice crackles. Add the hot water, and cover.

If using a saucepan, bring to a boil, lower the heat, and simmer for 25 minutes. If using a pressure cooker, bring the pressure to 15 pounds and cook 8 minutes; then bring pressure down immediately.

When the rice is cooked, add another tablespoon lemon juice (or more as you please) and stir. Transfer to a hot serving dish, sprinkle with the Parmesan cheese, and serve immediately. For 4.

Risotto with Prosciutto

risotto al prosciutto

Rice

2 tablespoons unsalted butter

1 tablespoon olive oil

1 small onion, peeled and minced

2 fresh sage leaves, chopped, or ½ teaspoon dried sage leaves

1¼ cups extra-long-grain enriched rice

2½ cups chicken broth, hot

3 slices *prosciutto* or cooked ham, cut in thin strips

⅓ cup grated Parmesan cheese

Sauce

3 tablespoons unsalted butter

3 tablespoons all-purpose unbleached flour

1 cup hot milk

¼ teaspoon salt

white pepper

¼ teaspoon freshly grated nutmeg

3 tablespoons unseasoned bread crumbs

Preheat oven to 177°C (350°F).

Put the butter, olive oil, minced onion, and sage in a flameproof casserole over medium heat. Cook until the onion is limp and slightly golden.

Add the rice, and continue cooking until the rice crackles.

Add the hot chicken broth, stir, and, when the rice-broth mixture comes to a boil, cover the casserole and put it in the oven for 20 minutes.

While the rice is in the oven, prepare the sauce: place the butter and flour in a saucepan over medium heat and stir until the butter is melted. Slowly add the hot milk, stirring and cooking for 4 minutes. Season with salt, a generous sprinkling of pepper, and nutmeg, and set aside.

When the rice is cooked, stir in the ham strips, half the Parmesan cheese, and half the sauce. Put remaining sauce on top of the rice. Mix remaining cheese with the bread crumbs and sprinkle it over the sauce.

Return casserole to a very hot oven (260°C, 500°F) for 5 minutes or until the top is toasted and the cheese melted. For 4, generously.

Rice with Shrimp and Mushrooms

*riso con gamberetti
e funghi*

Rice

2 tablespoons unsalted
  butter
1½ cups extra-long-grain
  enriched rice
3 cups vegetable broth
  (page 46), hot

Shrimp

12 tablespoons unsalted
  butter
2 tablespoons olive oil
140 grams (5 ounces, or
  about 1½ dozen) fresh
  medium shrimp, shelled
  and deveined
1 large bay leaf
140 grams (5 ounces ap-
  proximately, or about 2
  cups) mushrooms,
  cleaned and sliced
½ teaspoon salt, or to taste
2 tablespoons brandy
½ cup medium cream

To prepare the rice, melt the butter in a sauce-pan or pressure-cooking pan, add the rice, and cook until the rice crackles, stirring occasionally. Add the broth. Bring to a boil, cover, and, if using a saucepan, lower the heat and cook 25 minutes or until the rice is tender. If using a pressure cooker, cover, bring the pressure to 15 pounds, and cook 8 minutes.

Meanwhile, in a sauté pan, melt the butter with the olive oil.

Add the shrimp and bay leaf. Stir and cook until the shrimp is coral in color. Add the mushrooms, cook 2 minutes. Add the salt and brandy, and cook until the brandy is partially evaporated, about a minute or two.

When the rice is cooked, add the cream, stir, and cook for another minute.

Place the rice in a hot serving dish, put the shrimp and mushroom mixture and its sauce on top. Serve immediately. For 4.

Risotto with Shrimp and Mussels

risotto ai gamberetti e cozze

2 dozen mussels

1 tablespoon olive oil

3 tablespoons unsalted butter

1 garlic clove

1 dried hot red pepper pod, seeded, or 2 dashes Tabasco sauce

225 grams (½ pound) shrimp, cleaned

3 tablespoons minced Italian parsley

½ cup dry white wine

2 tablespoons unsalted butter

1¼ cup extra-long-grain enriched rice

2½ cups fish broth (page 47), hot

Scrub the mussels well, and pull out their beards. Place mussels and the olive oil in a frying pan or saucepan, cover snugly, and cook over medium heat for 4 minutes or until the mussels have opened. When cool enough to handle, remove the meat from the shells and reserve in a bowl. Strain the pan juices onto the mussels.

Melt the butter in a sauté pan, add the garlic and red pepper, and cook until the garlic is golden and the pepper darkened. Remove both these flavorings, and add the shrimp and parsley. Stir and cook until the shrimp have turned coral pink. Add Tabasco (if using it). Add the wine, and cook a couple of minutes until it is partially evaporated. Add the mussels and their juice, remove from the heat, cover, and set aside.

Put the butter in a pressure cooker or saucepan over medium heat. (See the discussion of pans and rices, pages 134 to 136.) Add and cook the rice, stirring, until the rice crackles. Add the hot fish broth, cover, and bring to a boil or up to a 15-pound pressure. If using a conventional saucepan, cook, covered, for 25 minutes or until the rice is tender. If using a pressure cooker, cook 8 minutes, then bring the pressure down immediately.

When the rice has cooked, stir in the shrimp and mussels and their juice. Transfer to a hot serving dish, and serve immediately. For 4.

Risotto with Tomatoes and Basil

risotto al pomodoro fresco e basilico

100 grams (3½ ounces) onion, minced

4 tablespoons unsalted butter

450 grams (1 pound) fresh, very ripe, plum tomatoes, peeled

1 teaspoon salt, or to taste

freshly ground pepper to taste

10 fresh basil leaves, chopped coarsely

1¼ cups extra-long-grain enriched rice

2 cups chicken broth, hot

60 grams (2 ounces) *mozzarella* cheese, grated

4 to 5 sprigs Italian parsley, chopped with some stem

This *risotto* was made to capture the flavor of ripe summer tomatoes and fresh basil. Of course you can make it at other times of the year, substituting canned tomatoes for the sun-ripened ones and dried basil for the fresh, but it is worth a trip to a farmer's market in season to get the most out of the dish.

Sauté the minced onion in the butter in a saucepan or pressure-cooking pan until limp.

Cut the tomatoes in chunks, and push them through a sieve or a food mill or process them briefly with the steel blade. Add the tomatoes to the onion.

Add salt, pepper, and basil leaves.

Add the rice, stir, and cook 3 minutes.

Add the broth, cover the pan, and cook until tender, 25 minutes in a saucepan, 8 minutes in a pressure cooker after the pressure has reached 15 pounds. (See the discussion of pans and rices, pages 134 to 136.)

When the rice is cooked, stir in the *mozzarella* and sprinkle it with parsley. Transfer to a hot serving dish. Serve immediately. For 4.

Risotto with Tomatoes and Prosciutto

risotto al pomodoro e prosciutto

½ onion, peeled and finely diced

4 tablespoons unsalted butter

1 large ripe salad tomato, 2 or 3 plum tomatoes, peeled and seeded

85 grams (about 3 ounces) prosciutto, in ⅛-inch-thick slices

1¼ cups extra-long-grain enriched rice

1¾ cups chicken broth, hot

115 grams (4 ounces) large mushrooms, cleaned and sliced

60 grams (2 ounces) fresh mozzarella cheese, grated

grated Parmesan cheese to taste

Put the onion with 3 tablespoons of the butter in a saucepan or pressure-cooking pan. (See the discussion of pans and rices, pages 134 to 136.) Sauté over medium heat until limp.

Add the tomato (there should be about ⅔ cup tomato pulp) and stir well.

Cut the *prosciutto* in tiny cubes (⅛- to ¼-inch) and add them to the tomato-onion mixture.

Stir in the rice, and cook until it crackles.

Pour in the broth and cover the pot. If using a conventional pan, bring to a boil, lower the heat, and cook 25 minutes. If using a pressure cooker, bring it to a 15-pound pressure, cook 8 minutes, then reduce the pressure immediately.

While the rice cooks, sauté the mushrooms with the last of the butter for 1 minute, stirring constantly.

When the rice is cooked, stir in the mushrooms and the *mozzarella*. Place in a hot serving dish with Parmesan cheese to please. For 4.

Risotto with Turkey

risotto col tacchino

1 large celery stalk with leaves, washed

1 large white onion, peeled

5 tablespoons unsalted butter

225 grams (½ pound) white meat of turkey (breast or wings)

giblets of 2 chickens

1 teaspoon salt

1¼ cups extra-long-grain enriched rice

2½ cups chicken broth, hot

450 grams (1 pound) fresh peas (or one 280-gram, 10-ounce package frozen)

115 grams (4 ounces) fresh mushrooms, or 4 to 5 Italian dried mushrooms soaked ½ hour in warm water and drained

1 tablespoon olive oil

60 grams (2 ounces) *mozzarella* cheese, grated

2 to 3 tablespoons grated Parmesan cheese

This particular dish used to be made with veal and dried mushrooms and carried the distinguished name of *risotto alla padovana* (*risotto* in the style of Padua). Like all *risotti*, it called for homemade chicken broth, gentle cooking, and about 40 minutes of the dedicated cook's time.

With skyrocketing veal prices, an abundance of turkey in the average market, and the perfection of the pressure-cooker, the recipe has changed and the time been cut down; but the palatability remains. It is an all-time favorite with friends and family on both sides of the ocean.

Mince finely the celery and onion. Sauté the mince over medium heat in 4 tablespoons of the butter until limp. Use a large saucepan with a good cover or a pressure-cooker. (See the discussion of pans and rices, pages 134 to 136.)

Chop the turkey meat coarsely; trim off the fat and gristle, chop the chicken giblets, and add both meats to the pan. When the meats are well browned, add the salt and the rice. Stir and cook until the rice crackles and the liquid is mostly evaporated.

Add the hot broth. If using a saucepan, bring to a boil, cover, lower the heat, and cook 25 minutes. If using a pressure pan, cover, bring the pressure to 15 pounds, and cook 8 minutes. Lower the pressure immediately.

While the rice is cooking, cook the peas in boiling salted water until just tender. Drain immediately.

Slice and then sauté the mushrooms in the last of the butter and the olive oil until just tender.

The minute the rice is cooked, stir in the peas, mushrooms, and *mozzarella*. Mix well. Place in a hot serving dish, sprinkle with Parmesan cheese, and serve immediately. For 4.

Rice with Veal Kidneys and Mushrooms

*riso con rognoni
e funghi*

2 medium onions, peeled
 and minced
6 tablespoons unsalted
 butter
1 ¼ cups extra-long-grain
 enriched rice
2 ½ cups beef broth, hot
340 grams (¾ pound) veal
 kidneys (about 2 kid-
 neys)
2 to 3 tablespoons minced
 Italian parsley
200 grams (7 ounces) fresh
 mushrooms, cleaned and
 sliced
1 teaspoon salt, or to taste
1 packet Italian powdered
 saffron (optional)
2 tablespoons brandy
3 tablespoons grated Par-
 mesan cheese

Sauté half the onion in 2 tablespoons of the butter until golden. Add the rice, and cook and stir until it crackles. Add all but 2 tablespoons of the broth, cover, bring to a boil or up to 15 pounds pressure depending on the pan you are using, and cook accordingly: 25 minutes in a saucepan, 8 minutes in a pressure cooker. (See the discussion of pans and rices, pages 134 to 136.)

Clean the kidneys of membrane and fat and cut into thin slices.

Sauté the remaining onion and the parsley in 2 tablespoons of the remaining butter until lightly golden.

Add the kidneys, and sauté 2 minutes or until the kidneys lose their color. Add the mushrooms and salt and the saffron if desired. Cook, stirring, until the mushrooms begin to release their moisture. Add the brandy and let it partially evaporate. Add the reserved broth, and cook over very low heat for 2 to 3 minutes.

Stir the remaining butter and Parmesan cheese into the cooked rice and place on a hot serving plate. Make a well in the center of the rice and put the kidney-mushroom mixture in it. Dribble the kidney sauce over all. Serve immediately. For 4.

Rice Croquettes

suppli

1 recipe *risotto* (pages
    137, 140, 141, 143)
    room temperature
1 egg
¾ to 1 teaspoon freshly
    grated nutmeg
115 grams (¼ pound) soft
    cheese (fresh *mozzarella*,
    Muenster, Fontina), cut
    into ½-inch cubes
1 cup unseasoned bread
    crumbs, approximate
vegetable oil for frying

Place the *risotto* in a bowl. Break in the egg, sprinkle with nutmeg, and mix well with a fork.

With your fingers, scoop up about a tablespoon of the rice mixture. Place a cube or two of cheese in the center of that handheld mound of rice and put another tablespoon of rice on top. Shape the rice into a firm, rounded oval (like a big egg) and roll it in bread crumbs. Compact the *suppli* well with both hands.

Set it aside and continue scooping, shaping, and rolling until all the rice mixture has been turned into *suppli*.

Put about ½ inch vegetable oil in a large frying pan. Bring it to a high heat and, with the aid of a slotted spoon, lower the *suppli* one by one into the pan. Put in as many as will fit comfortably. Fry deep brown on one side; turn, and fry the other side. Remove to drain on absorbent paper toweling. Serve warm. Makes 8 to 12 *suppli*, enough for 4 to 6. *Suppli* heat up well in the oven if you have to make them ahead of time.

Second Courses

Secondi piatti

We have spoken so far of *antipasti* and first courses; and it follows that second courses are "main dishes" or what are often called "entrées." These run the gamut from meats and poultry and fish to eggs and vegetables; and they should be paired thoughtfully with whatever you choose to go before them.

By and large, beef and veal are such luxuries throughout the Italian peninsula that they are used more selectively by Italians than by Americans. Pork, easier to raise and market, appears more frequently and in more different forms (in *antipasti* as well as in first and second courses) than it does on the average American table. Poultry, once prized for the elegant flavor of homegrown birds, has developed into a major industry in recent years and is, therefore, highly available but, alas, has more fat and is less flavorful than before. Fresh fish from the sea or the lakes is priced high and consumed to the last of even little-known species, many of which are underused in this country. Eggs, often in *frittata* (omelet) form, complete the roster of second courses.

All Italian second courses tend to be a bit smaller than what many people consider main dishes. Spices and herbs are used carefully to perk up flavors, wine vinegar and lemon to override fat. Most meat and poultry is cut thinly for sautéed dishes, then pounded to make it even thinner so that it is more tender and yields more portions. Sauces, made from oil, butter, flavorings, and the natural juices of meat and fish, share honors with the main ingredient.

In this chapter, under the usual headings of beef, veal, lamb, and so forth, you will find many quick-cooking dishes as well as some of the longer and more traditional second courses. Yet even the preparation of these has been speeded up by new techniques.

We have tried to gear the recipes to the ingredients one finds in the average non-Italian market, but we have left the Italian touch of herbs and seasonings as we found it.

Beef and Veal

Manzo e vitello

Beef Rolls

involtini di manzo

Rolls

1 1-kilo (2-pound) piece of bottom round (semifrozen, at least 3 hours, for easy slicing)

225 grams (½ pound) cooked ham, sliced

½ celery stalk, washed

½ carrot, scrubbed

2 tablespoons unseasoned bread crumbs

flour

Cut the beef into the thinnest possible slices. Cut off and discard any fat. Place the slices between 2 pieces of wax paper or plastic wrap, and pound the meat with the side of a "meat-tenderizer" mallet to make it even thinner and more tender.

Cut the beef slices in rectangles approximately 3″ × 4″ and reserve any trimmings.

Cut the ham slices in half and place them on the beef.

Mince the beef trimmings in a food processor or by hand. Add the celery and carrot to the minced beef, and process or chop finely by hand.

Add the bread crumbs to the mince, and mix well.

Place a small amount of the minced beef–bread crumb mixture on each piece of ham-covered beef.

Sauce

60 grams (2 ounces) very lean salt pork (or *pancetta*), cut in ¼-inch cubes

1 stalk celery, washed

1 garlic clove, peeled

1 small onion, peeled

2 tablespoons olive oil

½ cup dry white wine

1¾ cups plain tomato juice

1 bay leaf

1 clove

1 teaspoon salt

freshly ground pepper to taste

2 tablespoons chopped Italian parsley

Roll up the beef slices and skewer them with wooden picks. Dredge the beef rolls in flour.

For the sauce, start with a *battuto:* mince or process together the salt pork, celery, garlic, and onion.

Put the olive oil in a (six-liter, or six-quart) pressure cooker or large conventional saucepan, and sauté the beef rolls until thoroughly browned.

Add the *battuto,* and cook until wilted. Add the wine, and cook and stir until the wine is nearly evaporated (about 2 minutes). Add the tomato juice, bay leaf, clove, salt, and pepper to please.

If using a pressure cooker, bring it to a 15-pound pressure and cook 7 minutes. Bring the pressure down at once. If cooking in a conventional saucepan, cover, lower the heat, and simmer until the beef rolls are tender and cooked (about half an hour). Stir from time to time, while the rolls cook, to make sure they do not stick to the bottom. If the sauce thickens too much, add a bit of hot water, stir, and bring to a boil again.

Remove the beef rolls to a deep-serving platter. Strain the sauce over the beef. Sprinkle with parsley and serve. For 4 to 6.

Beef and Pork Meat Loaf

polpettone di manzo e maiale

2 slices day-old Italian bread, crustless

⅓ cup milk (approximate)

450 grams (1 pound) ground lean beef

200 grams (7 ounces) Italian sweet sausages, skinned

2 eggs, raw

⅓ cup grated Parmesan cheese

leaves of 6 sprigs Italian parsley, chopped

½ teaspoon salt

freshly ground pepper to taste

¼ teaspoon freshly grated nutmeg

dash of Worcestershire sauce

100 grams (about 3 ounces) *prosciutto* or boiled ham, sliced thinly

2 hard-cooked eggs, shelled

Preheat oven to 177° C (350° F).

Place the bread in a small bowl and add only enough milk to soak it through. Let stand for a few minutes.

Place beef and sausages in the bowl of a food processor. Squeeze out the bread and add it to the meats. Process on/off to mix it well. (Or blend well by hand with a fork.)

Add the raw eggs, cheese, parsley, salt, pepper, nutmeg, and Worcestershire sauce to the meats. Process on/off briefly. (Or mix thoroughly by hand.)

Butter or oil a large (about 20-inches-long) piece of aluminum foil. Spread the mixture out into an 8″ × 10″ rectangle. Cover with ham slices. Place the 2 hard-cooked eggs end to end in the center of the rectangle. Bring up the sides of the aluminum foil to make a salami-shaped package. Seal the ends.

Place the meat loaf in a bread pan. Bake in a moderate (177° C, 350° F) oven about an hour. Let it cool before removing the foil and slicing. For 4.

Meat Croquettes

polpette di manzo

2 slices day-old Italian
  bread, crustless

½ cup milk

1 garlic clove, peeled

1 cup Italian parsley leaves

4 boiled potatoes, skinned

450 grams (1 pound)
  cooked beef (boiled or
  roasted) or roast pork

3 eggs

½ cup unseasoned bread
  crumbs

2 tablespoons grated Par-
  mesan cheese

1 teaspoon freshly grated
  nutmeg

1 teaspoon salt

freshly ground pepper to
  taste

olive oil

2 lemons, cut in wedges

Put the bread to soak in the milk.

Cut the garlic in half and place it in a food processor. Add the parsley leaves, and process on/off until finely minced. Add the potatoes. Scrape down the sides of the bowl. Process until the mixture forms a paste. Remove the contents to a bowl. (Or mince the garlic and parsley well by hand, cube and thoroughly wash the potatoes, and blend well.)

Process the meat on/off until minced. (Or mince by hand.) Add it to the potato mixture.

Squeeze the milk out of the bread and shred it into the bowl with the meat mixture. Add the eggs, bread crumbs, cheese, nutmeg, salt, and half the pepper, and mix well. The mixture should be moist enough to hold its shape when formed into balls about 1½ inches in diameter. If not, add a bit of the leftover milk. If too moist, add a bit more of the bread crumbs.

Form the mixture into 24 small *polpette*. Roll in the remaining bread crumbs. Heat olive oil, ½ inch deep, to frying temperature (190° C, 375° F approximately) in a frying or sauté pan. Fry croquettes quickly, 2 to 3 minutes a side. Drain on a paper towel. Serve with wedges of lemon. For 4.

Pot Roast for the Pressure Cooker

stufato di manzo per la pentola a pressione

675 grams (1½ pounds) beef (shell sirloin or top round)

½ slice (30 grams, 1 ounce) lean salt pork or *pancetta*

3 cloves

½ onion, peeled

½ carrot, scrubbed

1 small celery stalk, washed

2 cups dry red wine

piece of stick cinnamon (about 1 inch)

olive oil

flour

¾ teaspoon salt, or to taste

freshly ground pepper

1 tablespoon tomato paste dissolved in ½ cup water

This is a stew you can marinate early in the day and cook in approximately 10 minutes in a pressure cooker. The fragrance and flavor of the sauce is typical of northern Italian winter food at its best.

Cut small slits here and there in the beef, and fill the slits with small pieces of salt pork. Stick cloves in the meat at random.

Mince together the onion, carrot, and celery. Place beef, mince, wine, and cinnamon in a dish or sturdy plastic bag just large enough to hold all comfortably. Turn the meat (or bag) back and forth to distribute the mince. Marinate for 6 hours.

Place enough oil to cover the bottom of a six-quart pressure cooker. Flour the meat and brown it over medium heat. Add salt and pepper and the mince from the marinade. Continue cooking until the mince is limp.

Add the marinade and the diluted tomato paste. Add more water just to cover the meat. Seal the pressure cooker, bring the pressure to 15 pounds, and cook for 10 minutes. Let the pressure fall of its own accord (about 4 minutes). For 4.

Potatoes, cut in half, can be cooked at the same time as the stew. Place the pressure cooker's rack over the browned meat with its mince and put the potatoes on it. Proceed with the pressure cooking.

Roast Tenderloin of Beef

filetto di manzo arrosto

1½ kilos (3½ pounds) boneless tenderloin of beef (well-marbled bottom or top round may be substituted)

1 small carrot, scrubbed

½ medium onion, peeled

1 short celery stalk, washed

1 sprig fresh rosemary, or ½ teaspoon dried rosemary

4 fresh sage leaves, or ½ teaspoon dried sage leaves

2 bay leaves

⅛ teaspoon dried tarragon, or 3 to 4 fresh leaves

⅔ cup red wine vinegar

salt to taste

freshly ground pepper to taste

4 to 5 tablespoons olive oil

If using tenderloin or top round, tie the meat in the shape of a salami. Bottom round is usually uniform enough to cook without tying.

Cut the carrot, onion, and celery into pieces and place them in a food-processor bowl with a steel blade. Add rosemary, sage, bay leaf, and tarragon, and process on/off until finely minced. (Or mince vegetables and herbs well by hand.)

Put the meat in a sturdy plastic bag or in a bowl just large enough to hold it. Add the minced vegetables and herbs, pour on the vinegar, salt, and pepper. Close the bag or cover the bowl with plastic wrap. Marinate in the refrigerator at least 9 hours. Turn the meat or bag 4 times while marinating.

Preheat oven to 200° C (400° F).

Remove the meat from the marinade and scrape off any bits of mince; save the marinade. Brown the meat in the olive oil in a sauté pan on top of the stove. Remove meat to roasting pan.

Strain the marinade. Reserve the mince. Pour 3 tablespoons of the marinating liquid over the meat and place it in the hot oven.

Sauté the mince in the pan used for browning the meat, then strain the flavored oil into the marinade and baste the meat with this mixture 3 times during roasting.

Roast the meat 45 to 55 minutes or until the meat thermometer registers 60° C (140° F) or rare.

Place the meat on a platter, remove the string that ties it, and pour the pan juices over the roast. Slice thinly. For 6 to 8.

Tenderloin of Beef, Marco Polo

filetto alla Marco Polo

2 kilos (4½ pounds) bone-
  less beef tenderloin
4 slices fresh ginger
2 jiggers (3 ounces)
  cognac
1 small garlic clove, peeled
  and cut lengthwise in
  slivers
dash of soy sauce
dry red wine
olive oil

Cut off and discard all long tendons and fat around the outside of the tenderloin.

Place the meat in a dish just large enough to accommodate it. (If you do not have the right size, make one of heavy-duty aluminum foil or use a sturdy plastic bag and later seal it well.)

Add the ginger, cognac, garlic, and soy sauce to the bowl or bag. Pour on enough red wine to come about halfway up the side of the meat. Cover, and marinate for 2 to 3 hours, turning from time to time.

Preheat oven to 260° C (500° F).

Barely cover the bottom of a sauté pan with olive oil, and brown the meat in it over high heat, turning it until evenly and nicely browned on all sides.

Transfer the beef to a roasting pan and roast it in a hot (260° C, 500° F) oven 25 minutes. Turn off the heat and let the meat stay in the cooling oven until the meat thermometer registers 60° C (140° F). For 6 to 8.

Veal and *Prosciutto* Birds

*involtini di vitello
e prosciutto*

4 slices veal round

4 slices *prosciutto*

4 tablespoons grated *mozzarella* cheese

½ teaspoon crumbled dried sage, or 1 fresh sage leaf

1 tablespoon unsalted butter

1 ½ tablespoons olive oil

Cover the veal with plastic wrap or wax paper, and pound it with the flat side of a meat pounder or the flat side of a heavy knife to make it even and thin.

Place a slice of *prosciutto* to cover each slice of veal. Sprinkle with *mozzarella;* add a sprinkling of sage.

Roll up each piece of veal, being careful to keep the filling in place. Skewer shut with a wooden pick.

Heat the butter and oil in a small skillet, add the veal rolls, cook for about 5 minutes, turning the rolls as they brown.

Serve immediately. For 2. Halve for one, or multiply for many, but do not cut or multiply the amounts of butter and oil exactly; just use enough to coat the bottom of the pan.

Rolled Breast of Veal for the Pressure Cooker

rollato di vitello per la pentola a pressione

400 grams (14 ounces) boned breast of veal

3 thin slices cooked ham or prosciutto

3 tablespoons chopped Italian parsley

1 teaspoon capers, rinsed

4 fresh sage leaves or ½ teaspoon dried sage leaves

1 tablespoon snipped chives

60 grams (2 ounces) Gruyère, Muenster, or Jarlsberg cheese, sliced thinly

2 hard-cooked eggs, shelled

freshly ground pepper

4 tablespoons olive oil

1 tablespoon unsalted butter

1 cup dry white wine

1 cup hot water with ½ chicken bouillon cube dissolved in it or 1 cup chicken broth

4 to 6 potatoes, peeled (optional)

Place the veal breast between sheets of wax paper and pound it well with a meat pounder to make it even and thin. Remove the paper.

Place the *prosciutto* on the veal, leaving a small border all around.

Mince finely the parsley, capers, sage, and chives. Spread the herb mince over the ham. Place cheese slices over the herbs.

Place the eggs in the center of the narrower end of the veal. Roll the veal up; skewer the opening; tuck in and skewer both ends; tie the roll like a salami with butcher's string; then remove the skewers. Sprinkle generously with pepper.

Put the oil and butter in a six-quart pressure cooker and brown the veal roll thoroughly.

Add the wine, cook until it has evaporated, then add the water with the bouillon cube or broth.

Place the pan's rack over the veal, and place the potatoes (if desired) on the rack. Cover the pan, bring the pressure to 15 pounds, and cook for 12 minutes. Bring the pressure down immediately. Remove the rolled veal and let it cool at least 20 minutes before cutting.

Simmer the sauce to reduce it a bit and serve it with the rolled veal (and the potatoes if you have chosen to cook them). For 4.

Stuffed Veal Breast

petto di vitello ripieno

1 kilo (2 pounds) boned breast of veal (approximate)

salt to taste

freshly ground pepper to taste

3 slices lean salt pork, blanched or *pancetta*

2 small carrots, peeled

1 zucchini

1 sweet red pepper

green tops of 4 scallions, chopped

1 tablespoon olive oil

4 fresh sage leaves or ½ teaspoon dried sage

2 sprigs fresh rosemary or 1 teaspoon dried rosemary

1 garlic clove, peeled

Preheat oven to 200 ° C (400 ° F).

Pound the veal breast thin between two sheets of wax paper. Sprinkle very lightly with salt and pepper. Cut the *pancetta* or salt pork in small strips and sprinkle them over the veal.

Cut the carrots in half lengthwise. Cut the ends off the zucchini and cut it in half lengthwise. Take the top off the pepper, discard it along with the seeds and core, and cut the pepper in 8 strips lengthwise.

Place the carrots at the narrow end of the veal about an inch from the edge and parallel to it.

Lay the zucchini halves next to the carrots. Add the pepper strips next to the zucchini. Make a row of chopped scallions running the length of the pepper strips.

Beginning with the narrow end of the veal, roll up the meat. Skewer the roll shut along the lengthwise opening; tuck the ends in and skewer them too. Tie the roll as you would a salami and remove the skewers.

Put the olive oil in a plastic cooking bag and add to it the sage, rosemary, and garlic. Insert the veal roll, close the bag perfectly, place it in a baking dish, and make four small slits in the top of the bag. Bake the veal in the hot (200 ° C, 400 ° F) oven for 25 to 30 minutes.

Remove the roll from the oven and place it on a platter. Strain the juices into a small saucepan and heat; cook down a bit for a thicker sauce if desired. Pour sauce over the veal roll. For 4.

Veal on Skewers, Sicilian Style

spiedini alla siciliana

1 kilo (2 pounds) veal, preferably top round, semi-frozen for 3 to 4 hours for easy slicing

115 grams (¼ pound) Sicilian or dry salted *ricotta,* or *feta* cheese

115 grams (¼ pound) thinly sliced *prosciutto*

1 cup coarse unseasoned bread crumbs

½ cup olive oil, approximately

3 small onions, peeled

24 bay leaves

1½ teaspoons dried oregano

1½ teaspoons salt (approximate)

Slice the veal as thinly as possible — to make at least 8 slices. Place the slices between sheets of wax paper or plastic wrap and pound them with the flat side of a meat pounder to make the slices even thinner. Trim off and discard all fat. Cut each slice of veal in half.

Chop the cheese, mince the *prosciutto.* Mix these ingredients with the bread crumbs. Dampen with a bit of the olive oil, just enough to hold the mixture together.

Put a teaspoon of cheese-ham mixture in the center of each slice of meat. Fold the corners of the veal in and over the filling to enclose it.

Cut the onions in quarters lengthwise. Cut off the root end at the base of each quarter.

Slide a wedge of quartered onion onto a skewer. Follow with a bay leaf and a filled packet of veal, and continue with onion, bay leaf, and meat until each skewer holds 4 veal packets. Finish each skewer with a bay leaf and onion piece.

Slide a second skewer up through the various pieces to hold them firmly.

Mix the rest of the olive oil together with the salt and oregano.

Brush the filled skewers with the flavored oil and place them over hot coals on an outdoor grill or in a preheated broiler. Grill, turning as the meat browns, and brush several times with oil as the veal cooks. For 4.

Corned Beef and Cabbage, Italian Style

bollito irlandese all' italiana

1 piece lean corned beef brisket, weighing 1½ to 2 kilos (about 3 to 4 pounds)

1 cabbage, boiled and spread open as for stuffed cabbage (page 264)

1 recipe *sala d'acciuga* (page 53)

This recipe evolved after a long and noisy dinner with friends and relatives of a certain nationality. The Italians do not have corned beef, but the Italian treatment of this staple in the American diet has produced raves from the Irish sector and thus merits inclusion in this book.

Place the corned beef in a six-quart pressure cooker with 3 cups water (or the amount specified by the manufacturer). Cover the pressure cooker, bring to a 15-pound pressure, and cook 60 minutes. Let the pressure fall of its own accord. (Or boil the corned beef in water to cover until tender, about 2 hours per kilogram or 1 hour per pound.)

While the corned beef is cooking, trim the cabbage and boil as directed on page 264. Cool a bit and open up the leaves.

Make the *salsa d'acciuga* (page 53).

When the corned beef is cooked, slice it neatly. Take 1 or 2 slices and cut in small strips. Place the pieces of corned beef between the leaves of the cabbage. Pour half the *salsa d'acciuga* over the cabbage, and serve the rest on the side with the corned beef. A perfect accompaniment is red potatoes boiled with their skins on. For 8.

Chili con Carne, Roman Style

chili con carne alla romana

450 grams (1 pound) stew beef

225 grams (½ pound) pork shoulder

225 grams (½ pound) pork rind (usually found on the pork shoulder)

½ cup vinegar

3 teaspoons salt

2 or 3 sweet peppers

2 large yellow onions, peeled

1 450-gram (1-pound) can kidney or shell beans

2 cups peeled plum tomatoes, fresh or canned

3 tablespoons olive oil

freshly ground pepper to taste

¾ tablespoon Tabasco sauce

2 tablespoons Worcestershire sauce

½ teaspoon dried oregano

1 teaspoon paprika

½ cup dry red wine

In other, less permissive, times, this recipe would have strained international relations, and perhaps Teddy Roosevelt and his Rough Riders would have stormed up San Giovanni Hill in Rome. Yet we think it can compete with any chili we have tasted outside of San Antonio, Texas. A pressure cooker is a must, however.

Prepare all the meats: cut the beef and pork shoulder in ½-inch cubes and cut the pork rind in 3 or 4 pieces.

Place the rind in a six-quart pressure cooker. Add 4 cups water, the vinegar, and 2 teaspoons salt. Bring to a 15-pound pressure and cook for 8 minutes. Bring pressure down immediately and remove and cut the rind into ½-inch strips.

Roast the peppers (page 58), rinse off the skins, core, and cut into bite-size pieces.

Chop the onions coarsely.

Drain the beans, reserving ½ cup of the canning liquid.

Mash or process the tomatoes to a puree.

In the pressure cooker, brown the meats in the olive oil over high heat for 1 minute. Add the onion, and cook and stir until limp. Add 1 more teaspoon salt, a generous amount of freshly ground pepper, and the Tabasco sauce, Worcestershire sauce, oregano, and paprika. Stir, add the wine, and cook until it has evaporated.

Add the pork rind, about a quarter of the peppers, the tomatoes, and ½ cup of the beans' canning liquid.

Stir, and taste for salt and flavorings, adding more Tabasco if desired. Seal the pressure cooker, bring to a 15-pound pressure, and cook for 15 minutes. Bring down the pressure immediately.

Mash 3 to 4 tablespoons of the beans and add to the pot along with all the rest of the beans. Add remaining peppers. Bring the pot to a boil and cook, uncovered, for 5 minutes.

Serve with hot, crusty Italian bread. For the fullest of flavor, let rest 1 to 2 hours and warm before serving. For 6.

Pork

Maiale

Boneless Pork Loin with Orange Sauce

lombo di maiale all'arancia

1 kilo (2 pounds) fresh pork loin, boneless

6 tablespoons olive oil

1½ cups dry white wine

2 oranges

2 tablespoons wine vinegar

1 tablespoon fresh rosemary leaves or 2 teaspoons dried rosemary

1 tablespoon juniper berries (if available)

2 bay leaves

½ teaspoon salt

1 teaspoon freshly ground pepper

Tie the loin with butcher's string as you would a salami.

Make a marinade with 2 tablespoons of the oil, the wine, the juice of 1½ oranges, the vinegar, and the rosemary.

Put the pork loin in a container that fits it snugly. Add the marinade, and let stand for at least an hour, turning the loin occasionally.

Grind and mix together the juniper berries, bay leaves, salt, and pepper.

Lift the loin from the marinade, let it drain a bit, and then roll it in the juniper-berry mince.

In a pressure cooker or a flameproof casserole, with a close-fitting cover and large enough to hold the loin neatly, add the remaining 4 tablespoons of olive oil. Brown the loin thoroughly in the oil.

Peel a spiral of the zest from one of the squeezed oranges and add it to the pressure cooker or casserole. Add also the marinade and any of the juniper mince which did not cling to the pork.

If you are using a casserole, bring to a boil, cover, lower the heat, and let simmer for about 1¼ hours, turning the loin occasionally. If the liquids in the casserole should evaporate too fast, add some hot water. The loin is done when it is tender and no pink juice appears when you prick it with a fork.

Once done, lift the loin from the casserole and let it rest 10 minutes before removing the string and cutting it into slices. Pour pan juices over the sliced pork and decorate it with thin slices of the remaining half orange. In the event that the pan juices are too concentrated, add a little hot water, bring to a boil, then use. If the juices are too thin, boil them down a bit before serving over the pork.

If you are using a pressure cooker, seal the pan and, once the pressure reaches 15 pounds, cook for 25 minutes. Lower the pressure, remove the pork to a platter, and let rest 10 to 15 minutes. Remove the string and slice the meat.

Boil the pan juices down to a saucelike consistency and serve over the meat. For 6.

Tipsy Pork Roast

porchetta umbriaca

1 kilo (2 pounds) boned
  pork roast
leaves of 2 sprigs Italian
  parsley
6 juniper berries, crushed
1 garlic clove, peeled
freshly ground pepper
½ teaspoon salt, or to taste
⅓ to ½ cup gin

Preheat oven to 177° C (350° F).

Open up the boned roast. Mince together the parsley, juniper, and garlic. Spread the minced mixture down the center of the pork. Sprinkle generously with pepper and half the salt.

Tie the roast in the shape of a salami. Place it in a bowl or sturdy plastic bag. Add the gin and cover (or tie the bag) and let marinate 1 to 2 hours, turning occasionally.

Place the marinated pork in a small roasting pan. Sprinkle with the remaining salt. Add more pepper if you need.

Roast for 1½ to 2 hours or until the meat thermometer registers 77° C (170° F). Turn and baste occasionally with the marinade during roasting. For 4.

Herbed, Breaded Pork Cutlets

cotolette di maiale all'erbe

1 tablespoon fresh rose-
  mary leaves or 2 tea-
  spoons dried rosemary
½ bay leaf
6 juniper berries
5 sprigs Italian parsley
¾ cup unseasoned bread
  crumbs
2 eggs
½ teaspoon Dijon mustard
450 to 675 grams (1 to 1½
  pounds) lean pork cut in
  thin slices (may be from
  leg, boned loin, or thin
  chops without bone)
vegetable oil for frying
salt to taste
freshly ground pepper to
  taste
1 lemon, cut in wedges

Place the herbs, including the parsley leaves and tender stems, in the bowl of a food processor or on a chopping board and mince. (The juniper berries may be a bit recalcitrant, but if this is the case just crush them with a knife on the chopping board before adding to the other flavorings.) Add the bread crumbs, and mix well. Place the mixture in a soup bowl.

Beat the eggs in another bowl. Add mustard to the eggs, and mix.

Trim the pork slices of any extra fat. Dip them in the beaten egg, then in the herbed bread crumbs. Let rest a few minutes, and repeat dipping and breading.

Fry the cutlets in the smallest amount of vegetable oil necessary, about ¼ inch deep. When golden brown on both sides, remove to drain on paper toweling. Sprinkle with a little salt and pepper to please. Serve with the lemon wedges. For 4.

Marinated Pork Chops

cotolette di maiale marinate

1 garlic clove, peeled
2 1-inch-thick pork loin
   chops
¼ cup wine vinegar
⅓ cup olive oil
1 teaspoon salt
½ teaspoon freshly ground
   pepper
1 bay leaf, crumbled
leaves of 1 sprig rosemary
   or 1 teaspoon dried rosemary

Sliver the garlic clove and place 2 or 3 slivers in small slits in each of the pork chops. Add any remaining slivers to the vinegar, oil, salt, pepper, bay leaf, and rosemary. Mix well. Pour over the chops and let stand at least 1½ hours.

Preheat the broiler for 15 minutes, then broil the chops until thoroughly browned on both sides and well done in the center (about 14 minutes).

Baste with the marinade at least once during cooking. Serve immediately. For 2. Double for 4.

A typical accompaniment to this and other pork dishes is *mostarda di Cremona,* sweet-sour pickled fruits, for which, if we do not have any on hand, we substitute old-fashioned watermelon-rind pickles, which provide a similar contrast in flavor and texture.

Roast Pork with Mustard

maiale arrosto alla senape

1 2½-kilo (5½-pound) loin
   of pork
1 tablespoon fresh rose-
   mary leaves or 2 tea-
   spoons dried rosemary
10 juniper berries, crushed
1 clove garlic, peeled
4 teaspoons salt
10 peppercorns
4 tablespoons mustard

Preheat oven to 163° C (325° F).

Trim and discard excess fat from the loin, leaving only a moderate layer on the top.

Mince rosemary, juniper berries, garlic, salt, and pepper. Place a third of the mince here and there in the pork's natural cavities or between the bones.

Mix remaining two-thirds of the mince with the mustard, and spread it over the top of the loin.

Roast in moderate oven (163° C, 325° F) about 3 hours or until the meat thermometer registers 71° C (160° F), and the mustard-mince topping is crisp and browned. Let stand 10 to 15 minutes before carving.

This roast reheats well. It is also very good cold. For 8.

Pork and Turkey Croquettes

polpette di maiale e tacchino

450 grams (1 pound) lean pork, boneless

225 grams (½ pound) white meat of turkey (breast or meat of 1 or 2 wings, depending on size)

2 slices Italian bread, crustless

½ cup dry white wine

10 coriander seeds

½ teaspoon salt

freshly ground pepper to taste

1 285-gram (10-ounce) package frozen chopped spinach, cooked or 140 grams (5 ounces) fresh spinach, chopped, cooked, and squeezed dry

1 egg

2 tablespoons grated Parmesan cheese

¾ cup unseasoned bread crumbs (approximate)

vegetable oil for frying

1 lemon, cut in wedges

Cut the pork in chunks and process on/off, using the steel blade, until it is in small pieces; or chop coarsely by hand. Add the turkey meat, and process or chop until the meats are well mixed and almost minced.

Shred the bread and soak it briefly in the wine. Add the bread to the meats.

Grind the coriander seeds in a mill, and add them to the meats along with the salt and pepper to taste.

Add the cooked spinach and egg and cheese. Process on/off just enough to mix in the additions. (Or blend the mixture by hand in a bowl.)

Form into small *polpette* or croquettes about 2½ inches in diameter and 1 inch thick. Flatten slightly. Dip in the bread crumbs, and turn to coat all sides.

Fry in ½ inch of oil until golden brown on both sides. Serve with wedges of lemon. For 4.

Lamb

Agnello

Roast Baby (New Zealand) Lamb

agnello arrosto

1 2- to 2½-kilo (4½- to 5½-
  pound) New Zealand leg
  of lamb, frozen or the
  equivalent leg of lamb
10 sprigs Italian parsley
10 sprigs fresh rosemary or
  5 teaspoons dried rose-
  mary
3 teaspoons salt
freshly ground pepper to
  taste
5 tablespoons + 1 tea-
  spoon olive oil
1 cup dry white wine
8 medium potatoes

The closest thing to baby lamb in many markets is frozen New Zealand leg of lamb, and we
recommend it for its size and quality.

Twenty-four hours before roasting time, put the
lamb in the refrigerator to thaw.

Preheat oven to 200° C (400° F). Cut off and
discard any excess fat from the lamb, leaving
just a thin layer on the top side of the leg.

Mince together the parsley, half the rosemary, 1 teaspoon salt, and pepper to taste. Add
1 teaspoon olive oil. Mix so that the mince becomes a paste. Make deep slits in the outside of
the leg and fill them with the mince.

Pour 3 tablespoons of the oil in a deep roasting pan. Put in the lamb and brush it with the
oil. Sprinkle the lamb with 1 teaspoon salt and
as much pepper as you wish. Roast 1½ hours at
200° C (400° F).

Meanwhile, peel the potatoes and cut them in
1-inch cubes. Put remaining 2 tablespoons of oil
in a large sauté pan. Add remaining 5 sprigs

(or 2½ teaspoons) rosemary, the last teaspoon of salt, and pepper to please. Cook and stir over medium heat until the potatoes are warmed through and show signs of coloring.

Remove the roast from the oven, and drain off excess fat from the pan. Add the wine, stirring it into the pan juices. Add the sautéed potatoes and baste them with the pan juices.

Lower oven heat to 177 ° C (350 ° F) and continue cooking 35 to 40 minutes or until the meat thermometer registers 65 ° C (about 150 ° F).

Remove the lamb from the pan and let it rest about 15 minutes on a warm serving platter before cutting.

Test the potatoes after removing the lamb. If they are not quite done, stir, baste well, and continue to cook them at high oven heat for about 15 minutes. If they are done, keep them warm at low heat until serving time. For 8.

Lamb on Skewers

spiedini d'agnello

560 grams (1 ¼ pounds)
   lean lamb, boneless

4 tablespoons olive oil

3 sprigs fresh rosemary or
   2 teaspoons dried

1 teaspoon salt

freshly ground pepper to
   taste

dash of Tabasco sauce

juice of 1 lemon

5 small artichokes

3 leeks

2 red sweet peppers

115 grams (4 ounces)
   mushrooms

Cut the lamb in bite-size pieces. Place in a bowl and sprinkle with the oil, rosemary, salt, pepper, Tabasco, and 1 tablespoon of the lemon juice. Turn over and over to coat all the pieces with the seasonings. Cover and refrigerate for at least an hour.

Prepare the artichokes (pages 4 to 5), and cut them in half. Soak in water to which you have added the remaining lemon juice.

Cut off and discard the roots and green tops of the leeks. Blanch the whites of the leeks in salted boiling water for 3 minutes. Drain immediately.

Roast the peppers (pages 58), slip off their skins, core, and cut into bite-size pieces.

Clean the mushrooms as necesary and cut off the bases of their stems; cut in half if very large.

When the leeks have cooled, slice in ½-inch rounds.

The above is enough to fill about 1 dozen 10-inch skewers. Count your meat pieces so that you can allow about the same number for each skewer, with a piece of lamb at each end.

Skewer a piece of lamb, add a slice of leek, then follow with pepper, artichoke, lamb, mushroom, and so forth, finishing the skewer with another piece of lamb. The vegetable line-up is for you to decide, but do not brush off any pieces of rosemary clinging to the meat.

Skewers may be cooked on an oiled hot griddle, in an oiled broiler, in a large frying pan, or, even better, over the coals of an outdoor grill.

Brush the skewers with any remaining marinade during cooking. Add a sprinkle of salt and pepper after the meat has browned. Remove from heat when the meat is cooked and browned on all sides but still pink inside. For 4 to 6.

This recipe does not require a leg of lamb to complete. It lends itself nicely to what supermarkets label "lamb combination" or "lamb steaks."

Leg of Lamb with Gin

coscia d'agnello al gin

1 leg spring lamb (about 2 kilos, 4 pounds)

2 slices lean bacon or salt pork or *pancetta*

1 tablespoon fresh rosemary leaves or 2 teaspoons dried rosemary

1 small garlic clove, peeled

½ teaspoon salt (approximate)

freshly ground pepper to taste

2 tablespoons juniper berries

6 anchovy filets

1 tablespoon Dijon mustard

5 tablespoons olive oil

1 tablespoon fine unseasoned bread crumbs (approximate)

½ cup dry white wine

½ cup gin

Preheat oven to 220° C (425° F).

Trim the lamb of all excess fat, leaving just a thin layer on the top side of the roast.

Mince together bacon or salt pork or *pancetta,* rosemary, and garlic. Add salt and a generous amount of pepper to the mince. Mix well.

Make slits in and around the leg, and insert portions of the mince in each.

Crush the juniper berries with the anchovy filets. Add the mustard, a scant tablespoon of the olive oil, and just enough bread crumbs to make a paste.

Spread the paste over the top and sides of the lamb.

Put 3 tablespoons of the olive oil in the bottom of a roasting pan. Place the lamb in the pan and roast it for 15 minutes in a hot (220° C, 425° F) oven.

Pour the wine and one more tablespoon of olive oil over the lamb. Baste and bake another 15 minutes.

Pour gin over the leg and baste once. Then reduce the heat to 200° C (390° F) and continue roasting 1 hour. Baste occasionally.

Reduce heat to 190° C (375° F) and continue roasting for 30 to 40 minutes more or until the meat thermometer registers 71° C (160° F).

Place the lamb on a warm serving platter.

Sieve the pan juices into a saucepan, taste for seasoning, and adjust as necessary. Heat and serve with the lamb. For 6.

Lamb with Barolo

agnello al Barolo

800 to 900 grams (1 pound
12 ounces to 2 pounds)
lamb (neck or shoulder,
boned)

flour for dredging

1 onion, peeled

4 tablespoons olive oil

1 tablespoon fresh rose-
mary leaves or 2 tea-
spoons dried rosemary

1 small garlic clove, peeled

leaves of 3 sprigs Italian
parsley

2 cloves, crushed

2 teaspoons salt (approximate)

freshly ground pepper to
taste

2 cups Barolo or other robust red wine

1 beef bouillon cube dis-
solved in ½ cup hot
water or ½ cup beef
broth (page 43)

Cut the lamb in 1½- to 2-inch cubes, dredge in flour, and pat gently to remove excess flour.

Slice the onion paper thin and sauté in the olive oil until limp. Add the cubed lamb and brown it thoroughly.

Mince together the rosemary, garlic, parsley, and cloves. Add to the lamb. Add salt and pepper.

Add the wine and the bouillon cube and its water to the stew.

If you are using a conventional pot, cover, bring to a boil, lower the heat, and simmer 25 minutes, stirring occasionally. Then uncover and cook another 15 minutes or until the meat is tender, the sauce reduced a bit.

If you are using a six-quart pressure-cooker, seal the pan, bring the pressure to 15 pounds, and cook 8 minutes. Bring the pressure down immediately, remove the meat to a warm serving dish, and keep warm. Boil the sauce for 5 minutes or so until it has been reduced.

For 4 to 6. Serve with the meat sauce and mashed potatoes.

Braised Leg of Lamb

agnello brasato

1 leg spring lamb, the smallest possible (not over 1½ kilos, 3 pounds, 6 ounces)

4 tablespoons unsalted butter

4 tablespoons olive oil

1 onion, peeled

1 carrot, scrubbed

1 garlic clove, peeled

1 small celery stalk with leaves, washed

1 tablespoon fresh rosemary leaves or 2 teaspoons dried rosemary

½ cup wine vinegar

½ cup dry white wine

1 beef bouillon cube dissolved in ½ cup water or ½ cup beef broth (page 43)

salt to taste

freshly ground pepper to taste

Trim the lamb of any excess fat.

In a top-of-the-stove pan large enough to hold the lamb and with a good cover, melt the butter with the oil. Brown the lamb in the butter and oil, turning it frequently.

Mince together the onion, carrot, garlic, celery, and rosemary. Add to the pan, and stir and cook until the mince is limp.

Add the vinegar, the wine, and the bouillon cube and water.

Bring the liquids to a boil, cover the pan, and lower the heat.

Cook, turning the lamb occasionally and stirring the mince around, for at least 1 hour or until the meat is tender and has absorbed most of the liquid.

If, during cooking, the liquids evaporate too quickly, add more wine.

Remove the leg from the pan to a serving platter. Bring the liquid to a boil, strain, and serve with the lamb. For 4.

Lamb Roast, Umbrian Style

arrosto d'agnello

1½ kilos (3 pounds, 6 ounces) leg of lamb

1 very small garlic clove, peeled

6 sprigs fresh rosemary or 2 teaspoons dried rosemary

1 teaspoon salt, or to taste

freshly ground pepper to taste

2 to 3 cups red wine, preferably a good Chianti

Trim off excess fat from the lamb. Make 6 to 8 slits in the meat. Cut the garlic lengthwise in very thin slivers and put them in the slits. Place rosemary leaves in with the garlic.

Place the lamb in a pan, bowl, or extra-sturdy plastic bag. Add salt and pepper, wine, and any remaining rosemary. Marinate at least 2 hours. Place lamb on a rack and drain for half an hour, reserving the marinade.

Preheat oven to 200° C (400° F).

Place the lamb in a roasting pan in the hot oven for 15 minutes.

Baste with marinade, lower the heat to 177° C (350° F), and continue cooking for 1 hour. Baste occasionally.

Remove the lamb from the oven when the meat thermometer registers 66° C (150° F). Let the roast rest for 15 minutes before carving. For 4.

Golden-Fried Lamb Steaks

agnello fritto dorato

675 to 900 grams (1½ to 2
   pounds) lamb steaks,
   thinly sliced or lean
   shoulder chops, thinly
   sliced
4 juniper berries, crushed
2 cloves
1 sprig fresh rosemary or 1
   teaspoon dried rosemary
3 fresh sage leaves or ½
   teaspoon dried sage
1 small onion, peeled
1 small garlic clove, peeled
1 teaspoon salt, or to taste
freshly ground pepper
1 cup dry white wine
flour for dredging
1 tablespoon chopped Italian parsley
2 eggs, beaten
unseasoned bread crumbs
4 tablespoons unsalted
   butter
3 tablespoons olive oil
1 lemon, cut in wedges

Cut off and discard any excess fat from the lamb, and pound slices with the flat side of a meat mallet to make them flat and even.

Place the juniper berries and the cloves in a mortar and grind them well.

Mince rosemary, sage, onion, and garlic and add them to the mortar. Grind briefly to mix.

Place the lamb, flavorings, salt, pepper, and wine in a deep dish. Turn the meat over and over to coat it well. Marinate for at least 1 hour.

Drain the lamb and dredge it in flour. Add parsley to the beaten eggs and dip the lamb in the egg mixture, then in the bread crumbs. Let rest a few minutes.

Melt the butter in the olive oil in a sauté pan and, when hot, fry the lamb steaks until golden on both sides. Drain well and place on a warm serving platter.

Serve immediately, with lemon wedges. For 4.

Lamb Stew

spezzatino d'agnello

2 medium onions, peeled

1 celery stalk, washed

1 garlic clove, peeled

1 sprig fresh rosemary or 1
teaspoon dried rosemary

2 tablespoons olive oil

3 tablespoons unsalted
butter

675 to 900 grams (1½ to 2
pounds) lamb (neck or
shoulder) cubed

¾ cup dry white wine

350 grams (¾ pound) car-
rots, peeled

170 grams (about 6
ounces) small white
onions, peeled

1 beef bouillon cube, crumbled

freshly ground pepper

salt to taste

1 tablespoon chopped Italian parsley

Start with a *battuto:* mince the onion, celery, garlic, and rosemary, and sauté in oil and butter in a large skillet until limp.

Add the lamb and brown it lightly.

Add the wine and let it evaporate partially.

Slice the carrots in thin rounds and add them to the lamb. Add the onions, the crumbled bouillon cube, and a generous amount of pepper. Add barely enough water to cover.

Cover the skillet, and cook over low heat for about 15 minutes, stirring occasionally. Then taste for salt, add if necessary, and cook, uncovered, for another 10 to 15 minutes or until the lamb is tender.

Sprinkle with parsley, stir well, and serve. For 4.

Poultry

Pollame

Rock Cornish Hens
galletti

Rock Cornish Hen with Almond-Prune Stuffing
galletto ripieno alle mandorle e prugne

1 Rock Cornish hen
1 Italian sweet sausage, skinned
5 dried prunes, pitted
¼ cup blanched, slivered almonds
1 thick slice day-old Italian bread, crustless
½ cup milk
½ to ¾ teaspoon salt
2 slices lean bacon
freshly ground pepper
2 to 3 tablespoons olive oil
½ cup dry white wine or ¼ cup dry vermouth

Remove and discard the hen's neck; clean and reserve the giblets. Cut the sausage into small pieces. Cut the prunes into quarters. Chop the almonds coarsely. Break up and soak the bread in the milk.

Add the sausage, giblets, and prunes to the almonds, and chop or process until all the ingredients are well chopped and about the same size.

Squeeze the milk from the bread and add the bread to the stuffing. Mix well.

Salt the hen's cavity, then stuff both the cavity and the neck pouch with the almond-prune mixture. Skewer both openings closed.

Place the bacon on the bird's breast and tie the wings and legs close to the body. Sprinkle liberally with pepper.

In a skillet or pressure-cooking pan, brown hen in the oil.

If you are baking: preheat the oven to 200° C (400° F). Place the hen in a baking dish just large enough to hold it. Bake for 15 minutes. Add the wine and baste the hen.

Lower the heat to 190° C (375° F) and continue baking 30 to 40 minutes or until the meat is tender.

If you are using a six-quart pressure cooker: lift the hen out after it is browned, put in the pan's rack, place the bird on it, add the wine, cover, and bring the pressure to 15 pounds. Cook 12 minutes. Let the pressure drop of its own accord.

Once the hen is cooked, place it on a hot platter. Degrease the pan, if necessary, and serve the pan's juices with the hen. For 2.

Rock Cornish Hen Stuffed with Mushrooms and Sausage

galletto ripieno ai funghi e salsiccia

2 Rock Cornish hens
1 lemon, halved
4 tablespoons olive oil
2 sprigs fresh rosemary or 2 teaspoons dried rosemary
4 fresh sage leaves, chopped or ½ teaspoon dried sage leaves
1 large celery stalk, washed and cut in thin slices
1 dozen mushrooms, cleaned and sliced
1 Italian sweet sausage, skinned
3 to 4 tablespoons dry vermouth
2 tablespoons crisp croutons
1½ teaspoons salt
freshly ground pepper to taste
1 tablespoon unsalted butter

Remove the hens' giblets; clean, trim, chop, and set them aside. Rinse the hens' cavities, and rub well with the ½ lemon.

Heat the olive oil in a large frying pan. Add the rosemary, sage, celery, and mushrooms. Sauté for 5 minutes.

Break the sausage into 3 or 4 pieces and add them to the pan; then add the prepared giblets and the dry vermouth and cook another 3 to 4 minutes or until the wine has evaporated. Stir in the croutons. Add salt and pepper and remove from heat.

Fill the hens' cavities and neck pouches with the stuffing. Skewer the two openings shut. Any remaining stuffing may be placed in the hens' baking dish. Butter the hens' breasts.

Preheat oven to 190° C (375° F).

Bake 45 to 55 minutes or until tender. Baste 2 or 3 times during baking. Cut the birds in half with poultry shears, sprinkle with the juice of remaining ½ lemon, and serve. For 4.

Rock Cornish Hen with *Grappa*

galletto alla grappa

1 Rock Cornish hen, quartered

3 tablespoons unsalted butter

1 tablespoon olive oil

½ teaspoon salt

freshly ground pepper to taste

1 medium celery stalk, washed

1 medium carrot, scrubbed

1 medium onion, peeled

1 tart apple (Granny Smith, Baldwin)

2 medium potatoes, peeled

1 sprig fresh rosemary or 1 teaspoon dried rosemary

4 tablespoons *grappa*

Grappa is the powerful liquor, made from grape stems and skins, that reigns all across the arc of the Italian alps. With some slight regional variations in taste and name, it is the stuff, an old saying goes, a real *alpino* (alpine mountaineer) is made of. *Grappa* finds equivalents in *marc, aquavit, aguardiente, slivovitz,* and *tequila:* the alcohol may come from different sources, but the wallop is the same. Nonetheless, *grappa* (or *aquavit*), when used in cooking, gives a gentle, mellow flavor to food and sauce.

If you are using a conventional pan: brown the hen quarters on all sides in butter and oil. Sprinkle with salt and a generous amount of pepper.

Coarsely chop the celery and carrot; halve the onion and slice lengthwise; core and slice the apple; and, cube the potatoes.

Add the prepared vegetables and apple to the pan and sprinkle them with the rosemary. Stir, then simmer, covered, for 10 minutes.

Add 2 tablespoons of the *grappa* and recover immediately. When the *grappa* has finished evaporating, uncover the pot, stir and scrape loose the bits of browned hen clinging to the sides and bottom of the pan. Recover and simmer another 10 minutes.

Add one more tablespoon of *grappa,* stir and cover.

After 15 minutes, add the last of the *grappa.* Taste the sauce, and adjust the seasonings as necessary.

If you are using a pressure cooker: brown the hen pieces in the butter and oil in a six-quart pressure cooker. Add all the remaining ingredients. Seal the cooker, bring to a 15-pound pressure, and cook for 8 minutes. Bring down the pressure at once. Stir the sauce. Remove the hen to a hot platter. Boil the sauce down a bit, if you wish. Taste for seasonings, and correct if necessary. Pour the sauce over the hen and serve. For 2. Double for 4.

Rock Cornish Hen with Lemon

galletto al limone

2 tablespoons unsalted butter

2 tablespoons olive oil

1 Rock Cornish hen

flour for dredging

½ teaspoon salt

freshly ground pepper to taste

½ cup dry white wine

1 lemon

½ cup chicken broth (page 44)

½ stalk celery, washed and sliced (optional)

2 tablespoons chopped Italian parsley

Melt the butter with the olive oil in a sauté pan. Cut the hen into 4 pieces, dredge them in flour, and brown them thoroughly in the butter and oil. Add salt and pepper.

Add the wine and, when it has evaporated, add the juice of half the lemon and the celery if desired. Stir, and add the broth.

Cook another 10 to 15 minutes or until the hen is tender.

Slice the other half of lemon in rounds and add them to the pan.

Add the parsley, and cook another 2 minutes, turning the pieces back and forth to coat them well with both sauce and parsley.

For 2. Doubles easily for 4, but add only half again as much butter and oil.

Poor Gypsy's Chicken

galletto alla povera zingara

1 Rock Cornish hen (about 450 grams, 1 pound)

This is a formula originally worked out for pigeon and squab. American Rock Cornish hens are the perfect birds to receive a poor gypsy's touch of herbs, mushrooms, and mustard.

Cut off and discard the wing tips from the hen. Remove the giblets and reserve. Cut the hen in two along the breast bone. Open the hen, dry the cavity with paper towels, and pound the bird flat with a meat pounder.

Marinade

1 tablespoon olive oil

1 tablespoon lemon juice

½ teaspoon freshly ground pepper

½ teaspoon dried rosemary, crumbled

¼ teaspoon salt

2 or 3 dashes Tabasco, or to taste

Prepare the marinade by mixing well the olive oil, juice, pepper, rosemary, salt, and Tabasco. Place the hen on a plate, and baste it with the marinade, turning it over and over.

Preheat the broiler 10 minutes.

Spread

115 grams (about 4 ounces) fresh mushrooms, cleaned

1 tablespoon unsalted butter

salt to taste

freshly ground pepper to taste

1 tablespoon Dijon mustard

1½ teaspoons Tabasco sauce

1 tablespoon tomato ketchup

2 teaspoons lemon juice

½ teaspoon freshly ground pepper

Chop the mushrooms coarsely. Clean and chop the giblets. Melt the butter in a sauté pan and put in the giblets, mushrooms, and salt and pepper to taste. Cook for 4 minutes or until the mushrooms have released their moisture. Let cool.

Chop or grind the giblets and mushrooms to a paste. Stir in any pan juices, the mustard, Tabasco, ketchup, lemon juice, and ½ teaspoon additional pepper. Taste for salt, and adjust if necessary.

Place the hen halves, cavities up, in the broiler pan; brush with marinade and broil them 5 to 6 minutes or until well browned, brushing with marinade once or twice as they cook.

Turn and brown the hen's skin side, basting as you did before. When the skin is browned, turn again, spread the cavity with the mushroom mixture, and broil 3 to 4 minutes until the spread is cooked and beginning to crisp. Turn the skin side up, brush with remaining spread, and broil another 3 or 4 minutes.

For 2. Double for 4.

Turkey
tacchino

Today Italian cooks are adopting turkey for every use they can think of. No longer is it confined to the roasting pan: it is used for broth, cutlets, *polpette* (croquettes or meatballs, a name we abhor). It is rolled, sautéed, braised. Larger thighs are even cut and cooked as *osso buco*, a name until now reserved only for veal shank.

As a matter of fact, in many homes and restaurants, white meat of turkey is replacing veal in other dishes as well — such as the *saltimbocca* recipe that follows. "People like it just as much," a happy chef confided in us, "and some notice the difference only when they get the bill!"

Turkey, then, is not only fashionable and versatile, but, with the way food bills run on both sides of the Atlantic, it is less expensive than many cuts of meat, fish, or other fowl.

When you buy turkey for Italian recipes, look for fresh turkey. In any case, stay away from the "self-basting" variety: it slices miserably before cooking; moreover, when cooked the Italian way, the turkey remains moist, so any self-basting is redundant. When buying a whole fresh turkey, cut it into various pieces, cook what you need, and freeze the rest.

Frozen (nonself-basting) turkey breasts slice particularly well when partially defrosted, and the carcass yields a good broth.

Frozen turkey breasts precut into cutlets are also now available on the market, and they are a convenience when one does not need a whole breast.

Turkey Slices with Prosciutto

saltimbocca di tacchino

675 grams (1½ pounds) white meat of turkey, sliced thinly (about 8 slices)

½ lemon

1 fresh sage leaf for each slice turkey

1 thin slice prosciutto for each slice turkey (total weight about 115 grams or 4 ounces)

6 tablespoons unsalted butter

¼ cup dry white wine

Place the turkey slices between two sheets of wax paper or plastic wrap and pound them gently but firmly with the flat side of a meat pounder.

Grate the rind of the lemon half and sprinkle each slice of turkey with a bit of the grated rind. Place a sage leaf (only half if it is a large one) on each slice of turkey. Cover each slice with a slice of *prosciutto*. Pin the slices together with wooden picks.

Melt the butter in a sauté pan over medium heat. Add the turkey-*prosciutto* slices and cook 3 minutes. Turn the slices over and cook another 3 minutes. Turn back over; add the wine and the juice of the lemon to deglaze the pan. Stir the liquids with a wooden spoon, moving the meat around and about to make sure all bits clinging to the pan go into the sauce. Remove to a warm platter, pour the sauce over the *saltimbocca,* and serve at once. For 4.

Turkey and Beef Croquettes

polpette di tacchino e manzo

2 slices day-old Italian bread, crustless

¼ cup milk

1 small onion, peeled and minced

2 tablespoons unsalted butter

340 grams (about 12 ounces) turkey breast or 6 small turkey breast cutlets

170 grams (about 6 ounces) lean ground beef

1 frankfurter (German style, with natural casing)

8 sprigs Italian parsley

5 tablespoons grated Parmesan cheese

2 eggs, beaten separately

½ teaspoon salt

¼ teaspoon freshly grated nutmeg

flour

unseasoned bread crumbs

vegetable oil for frying

1 lemon, cut in wedges

Put the bread to soak in the milk.

Sauté the onion in butter until limp.

Send the turkey, beef, and frankfurter through a meat grinder, mixing them well. Or process the three meats in a processor until finely minced.

Squeeze the bread dry, shred it, and mix it into the meats.

Remove and discard most of the parsley stems. Chop the leaves and add them to the meats. Add the cheese, 1 beaten egg, salt, and the nutmeg. Mix well, then shape the meat mixture into 18 balls, each just a little larger than a golf ball.

Roll these *polpette* in the flour, dip them in the remaining beaten egg, then roll them in the bread crumbs. Fry *polpette* in hot vegetable oil until golden brown.

Serve with lemon wedges. For 4.

Turkey *Osso Buco*

osso buco di tacchino

2 turkey legs with thigh
flour for dredging
3 to 4 tablespoons olive oil
3 tablespoons unsalted
  butter
1 sprig fresh rosemary or 1
  teaspoon dried rosemary
3 or 4 fresh sage leaves or
  ½ teaspoon dried sage
  leaves
1 garlic clove, peeled
2 tablespoons chopped
  Italian parsley
grated zest of ½ lemon
1 cup dry white wine
1 cup chicken broth (ap-
  proximate) (page 44)

Separate thighs from drumsticks. Chop off and discard the bony, meatless ends. Chop each turkey leg into two or three cross sections about 2 inches long. If the skin of the turkey does not hold meat to the bone well, tie them in place with kitchen string.

Dredge pieces in flour and brown them thoroughly in oil and butter, either in a sauté pan with a good cover or in a pressure-cooking pan.

Mince the rosemary leaves, sage, and garlic with the chopped parsley and lemon zest. Add this mince to the turkey pan. Cook 2 to 3 minutes, and add the wine.

When the wine has evaporated, add salt and pepper.

Add the broth.

If you are using a pressure cooker, cover, bring to a 15-pound pressure, and cook 10 minutes. Allow pressure to fall by itself.

If you are using a conventional sauté pan, bring to a boil, cover, lower the heat, and simmer for 20 to 25 minutes or until the turkey is well done.

Once cooked, remove the turkey to a warm serving platter in a warm place.

If the sauce is too thin, simmer a while longer to reduce it. Taste for seasonings, and adjust to please. Pour the sauce over the turkey pieces. Serve with *risotto alla milanese.* For 4.

Christmas Turkey with Rice Stuffing

tacchino di Natale con ripieno di riso

Stuffing

giblets of 1 turkey
giblets of 3 chickens
5 tablespoons unsalted butter
1 bay leaf
½ teaspoon dried oregano
3½ teaspoons salt
freshly ground pepper
3 cups water
1⅓ cups extra-long-grain rice
5 large mushrooms, cleaned and sliced
2 sweet peppers (1 green and 1 red, if possible), cored and diced *or* 3 stalks celery, washed and diced
1 tablespoon grated Parmesan cheese

Turkey

1 5-kilo (11-pound) turkey, fresh or frozen (thawed, if frozen) but not self-basting
1 teaspoon salt
½ teaspoon freshly ground pepper
¾ teaspoon freshly grated nutmeg
5 tablespoons unsalted butter
2 tablespoons olive or vegetable oil
1 bay leaf
1 celery stalk, washed and chopped

Trim all the giblets, chop them coarsely, and sauté them in butter with the bay leaf and oregano for 5 minutes. Sprinkle with ½ teaspoon salt and freshly ground pepper to please. Taste, and adjust seasonings if you wish.

Bring the water to a boil, add the remaining 3 teaspoons salt and the rice. Bring back to a boil, stir, cover, and cook 10 minutes. Drain.

Add the rice to the giblets. Add the mushrooms and peppers (or celery) and the Parmesan cheese.

Stir and cook over medium heat for about 1 minute or until well mixed. Taste for seasoning again, and adjust if necessary.

The rice will still be a bit undercooked; and this amount of stuffing will seem a bit too little for the bird. However, the rice swells and cooks in the roasting and fills the cavity nicely.

Place the turkey, breast down, on a chopping board. Slit the skin along the back from neck to tail. Pull the skin open a bit and, with the point of a sharp knife, separate the meat from the ribs and breast bone, following the contour of the bone. When you reach the wing joint, snap it with your fingers, then cut through the joint, detaching the wing from the carcass but not breaking the skin.

Follow the same procedure for the legs of the bird: cut through the joint connecting the thigh to the carcass and that connecting thigh to drumstick, but leave the thigh meat and the drumstick attached to the skin. Remove the

1 onion, peeled and quartered
2 cloves
4 or 5 peppercorns
1 ½ cups dry white wine
1 ½ to 2 cups chicken broth (page 44)
2 tablespoons quick-mixing flour or instant mashed potato
juice of 1 lemon

thigh bone itself. Pull the carcass away, leaving skin, breast meat, wings, thighs, and drumsticks spread out, breast up on the cutting board. Sprinkle with salt, pepper, and nutmeg.

Thread a needle with strong cotton thread and, beginning at the tail, sew the skin back together along the original slit. Leave unsewn an opening large enough to spoon in the rice stuffing.

Stuff the bird, and complete the sewing of the opening. The stuffed turkey will look somewhat limp, but it will plump up with cooking.

Melt the butter and oil in a flat-bottomed roasting pan. Add the bay leaf, celery, onion, cloves, and peppercorns, and sauté until limp.

Preheat oven to 163° C (325° F).

Place the turkey in the roasting pan and brown it on all sides over medium heat. Add the wine, and continue cooking 5 minutes. Let the turkey cool off a bit, then lift it up, and put a rack under it, with the turkey breast up.

Cover the turkey with 2 layers of cheesecloth. Pour about ½ cup of the broth over the breast, and place the roasting pan in a moderate (163° C, 325° F) oven.

Roast for 3½ to 4 hours, basting from time to time with the remaining broth and pan juices.

After 3 hours, remove the cheesecloth.

When the turkey is cooked, remove it to a serving platter and let it rest about 20 minutes before carving.

Strain and degrease the pan juices and put them in a saucepan over medium heat. Stir in the flour or instant potato. Add the lemon juice, and stir and cook for 4 minutes. Adjust salt and pepper to your taste. If the sauce becomes too thick, add a bit of water. Serve with the roast turkey. For 16.

Turkey with Sausage Stuffing

tacchino ripieno con salsiccie

Stuffing

6 slices day-old Italian bread, crustless

½ cup milk (approximate)

3 rounded tablespoons coarsely chopped Italian parsley

310 grams (11 ounces) lean pork

225 grams (8 ounces) Italian sweet sausage

giblets of the turkey

3 eggs

1 teaspoon salt

2 tablespoons grated Parmesan cheese

freshly ground pepper

1 teaspoon freshly grated nutmeg

100 grams (3½ ounces) sliced *mortadella*

100 grams (3½ ounces) cooked ham, sliced and cut in narrow strips

Turkey

1 5-kilo (11-pound) turkey, fresh or frozen (thawed, if frozen) but not self-basting

1 carrot, scrubbed

1 onion, peeled

1 celery stalk or tops of 2 stalks, washed

1 bay leaf

4 teaspoons salt

Soak the bread in the milk.

If using a food processor, put the steel blade in place, add the parsley, and process on/off. Scrape down the sides, process on/off again until the leaves are minced. (Or mince by hand.)

Cut the pork in cubes and skin the sausages. Place in the food processor and process on/off until coarsely chopped. Skin the turkey gizzard, clean the heart and liver, and put all in the food processor.

Squeeze the bread of its milk and shred it into the food processor. Add two of the eggs, salt, cheese, pepper, and nutmeg, and process on/off about 4 times to chop and mix well. (Or chop the meats and sausage well; then mix by hand with the eggs and cheese and seasonings.)

Fry a bit of the above mixture, taste for seasonings, and adjust to taste.

Beat the last egg, make a very thin omelet, salting and peppering to taste, and cut the omelet in thin strips.

Remove the neck from the turkey and place it in a soup pot or pressure-cooking pan. Add the carrot, onion, celery, or leaves, bay leaf, 1 quart water, 4 teaspoons salt, and the peppercorns. Bring to a boil, scoop off the froth, and let simmer while you semibone the turkey.

Preheat oven to 163 ° C (325 ° F).

Semibone the turkey (see pages 196 to 197). Place the bones in the soup pot or pressure cooker. Cover. If you are using a pressure

5 peppercorns

1 tablespoon unsalted butter

½ cup olive oil (approximate)

½ cup dry white wine, vermouth, or dry sherry

cooker, bring it to a 15-pound pressure, cook 25 minutes, reduce the pressure, and uncover. If you are using a conventional pan, cover, bring to a low boil, lower the heat, and simmer an hour or two. Use this broth for basting during the roasting of the turkey.

Sew the turkey skin about ⅓ of the way, starting at the tail.

Beginning at the tail end, place the *mortadella* slices so they overlap each other and cover the cavity. Spread the slices with about half the stuffing. Cover the stuffing with the strips of ham.

Add the last of the stuffing, spreading it evenly over the ham.

Place the strips of omelet down the center of the stuffing.

Close the rest of the cavity with even stitches.

Butter the roasting rack and place it in the roasting pan. Place the turkey in the rack, breast upward. Butter the bird's breast and cover it with kitchen cheesecloth. Sprinkle with olive oil.

Roast in a moderate (163° C, 325° F) oven 4½ hours or until the meat thermometer registers 82° C (180° F). During the roasting, baste every half hour or so with turkey broth. After 2 hours of roasting, remove the cheesecloth. After 3 hours, baste with the wine as well as the broth and pan juices.

When the turkey is cooked, remove it to a warm platter in a warm place and let it sit for at least ½ hour before carving. For 16.

Rolled Stuffed Turkey Breast in Aspic

rollato di tacchino ripieno in galantina

Turkey

2½ kilos (5 pounds) boneless turkey breast, fresh or frozen (thawed if frozen)

2 small garlic cloves, peeled

2 sprigs fresh rosemary or 2 teaspoons dried rosemary

10 juniper berries, crushed
  handful Italian parsley leaves

5 fresh sage leaves or 1 teaspoon dried sage

225 grams (½ pound) fresh *mozzarella* cheese, grated or shredded

285 grams (10 ounces) *capocollo*, thinly sliced

6 sprigs Italian parsley

5 tablespoons olive oil

freshly ground pepper

½ cup dry white wine (approximate)

If you are using a fresh or thawed turkey breast (thaw all day in the top shelf of the refrigerator or on a counter in a cool place) and are boning it yourself, cut away and discard all visible fat. Remove the skin by peeling back with one hand while cutting between skin and flesh with the point of a very sharp boning knife. Discard the skin. Cut off and save for another use (or discard, if you wish) any neck bone still clinging to the breast. With the boning knife, follow the curve of the ribs, cutting the meat away from them. The breast comes away easily in two large pieces.

Lay the two pieces flat on the counter and cut off any irregular bits to make them nearly rectangular. Use the cutoff scraps to cover any thin places on the breast. Place a piece of plastic or wax paper over the turkey meat, and pound the meat gently but firmly to widen, lengthen, and thin it a bit.

Place garlic, rosemary, juniper, parsley leaves, and sage in a food processor or on a cutting board and mince well.

Spread the mince thinly over both pieces of turkey.

Sprinkle the *mozzarella* over the mince.

Place the *capocollo* on top of the turkey in order to cover it, but leave a border of about 1 inch on all sides.

Roll each of the turkey pieces into a salami-like roll, skewer the long side, then tie neatly with kitchen string. Remove the skewer.

Place the parsley sprigs in the bottom of a large baking dish (or in two small dishes). Cover with olive oil. Put the turkey rolls on the parsley, add freshly ground pepper, and turn the rolls around and around to coat with oil and pepper.

Place in a hot (200° C, 400° F) oven and bake for 1 hour or until slightly golden and the turkey meat is cooked. Baste with the wine 3 or 4 times during baking.

Remove the turkey rolls to a work platter, reserving the juices from the pan for the aspic. Remove the strings from the turkey rolls, and cool completely in the refrigerator (2 to 3 hours or overnight; turkey rolls keep well in the refrigerator 3 to 4 days).

At least 2 hours before serving time, make the aspic.

Aspic

¼ cup turkey cooking juices

2 packets unflavored gelatine

3 cups water

2 teaspoons salt, or to taste

¼ to ⅓ cup dry sherry

Pour the reserved turkey juices into a cup and chill thoroughly. Remove and discard any fat or oil that rises to the top.

Mix the gelatine with the turkey juices, add the water, and heat and stir until the gelatine is completely dissolved. Add salt, and taste; correct salt if necessary.

Add ¼ cup sherry, and taste; increase sherry if you desire.

Pour all but 1 cup of this aspic mixture into a shallow, flat-bottomed, sided cookie sheet to chill completely.

Chill the remaining cup of aspic until it is syrupy.

To assemble: cut the two turkey rolls into very thin slices and place them on your serving platter. (Garnish the edges of the platter as you wish with fresh parsley, watercress, celery leaves, etc.)

Paint the turkey slices with the syrupy aspic, put the platter to chill for 10 minutes or so until the aspic has hardened, and repeat the painting process until all the slices glisten. Chill thoroughly.

Cut the pan of hardened aspic into tiny cubes and place them around and over the glazed turkey-roll slices in the platter.

Keep chilled until serving time. The aspic, if made in this fashion, resists melting under warm room or garden conditions.

This is an ideal platter for parties. For approximately 20.

Chicken
pollo

Chicken Marengo
pollo alla Marengo

Here we wish to set history straight. On June 14, 1800, Napoleon was waging war with the Austrians in the fields around Marengo, a Piedmont village. The scenario goes that in the protracted and confused battle, the Austrians had the upper hand and Napoleon's chef had difficulty with food supplies. So he scavenged around nearby farms and came back with chicken and mushrooms — but no tomatoes or shrimp. By adding a few more flavorings and herbs, the chef provided a respectable dish. The battle then swung to France's favor and Napoleon named the chef's chicken after his victory: Marengo.

We would like to think that the chef was promoted immediately. We would also like to suggest a scenario of our own: fifteen years later, on June 18, the chef again found himself in similar circumstances. He scavenged, shook pots and pans, and produced another impromptu dish. But, alas, "Chicken Waterloo" never made history.

Chicken Marengo

pollo alla Marengo
(*continued*)

1 small chicken (about 1 kilo, 150 grams, or 2½ pounds)

flour for dredging

4 tablespoons olive oil

1 teaspoon salt, or to taste

freshly ground pepper

¼ teaspoon freshly grated nutmeg

1 sprig fresh rosemary or 1 teaspoon dried rosemary

3 fresh sage leaves or ½ teaspoon dried sage leaves

3 sprigs Italian parsley

1 bay leaf

¼ cup dry white wine

¼ cup brandy

1 tablespoon quick-mixing flour

1 cup chicken broth (page 44)

285 grams (10 ounces) fresh mushrooms, cleaned and sliced

2 to 3 tablespoons lemon juice

2 tablespoons minced Italian parsley

Remove the giblets and save for another use.

Cut the chicken in 8 to 10 pieces and flour them. Brown them in olive oil over a relatively high heat. When the first side is browned, turn the pieces and sprinkle with some of the salt, pepper, and nutmeg. When the other side is browned, transfer the chicken pieces, with only the oil that clings to them, to another skillet over medium heat.

Add remaining salt, pepper, and nutmeg. Tie the rosemary, sage, parsley, and bay leaf in a little bundle in cheesecloth and add it to the chicken.

Add the wine and the brandy and let them evaporate a bit.

Mix the flour with the broth and add it to the chicken.

Stir the pan well, lower the heat, and simmer for 20 minutes.

Add the mushrooms, and cook 5 minutes more.

Add 2 tablespoons lemon juice. Remove the bundle of herbs. Taste for seasonings, and correct if necessary. Sprinkle in the minced parsley, cook 1 minute more, and serve. For 4 generals.

Stuffed Chicken Breasts

petti di pollo farciti

4 chicken breasts, boned
and skinned (8 pieces)

4 slices *Fontina* or Muenster cheese

1 tablespoon chopped Italian parsley

1 tablespoon capers,
rinsed

flour for dredging

3 tablespoons unsalted
butter

2 tablespoons olive oil (approximate)

salt to taste

freshly ground pepper to
taste

4 tablespoons very dry
sherry

Cut off and discard any fat clinging to the chicken.

Place the chicken pieces between sheets of wax paper or plastic wrap and pound them with the flat side of a meat pounder. Lift the paper, overlap any pieces that may have split in pounding, replace the paper, and pound those overlapping pieces gently to make them stick together.

Cut or fold the cheese to cover half of each piece of chicken breast.

Mince the parsley and capers together and spread on the cheese.

Fold each chicken piece to enclose the stuffing, pressing the edges together to seal.

Dredge the stuffed chicken in flour, pat well, and let rest a few minutes.

Sauté the chicken in butter and olive oil 3 minutes on each side or until golden brown. Sprinkle with a little salt and pepper, and remove to a warm plate in a warm place.

Add the sherry to the pan. Stir and cook over medium heat about 1 minute or until a sauce has formed. Pour over the chicken breasts. For 4.

Chicken Legs in Wine Sauce

coscie di pollo al vino

4 chicken legs with thighs (about 800 grams, 1¾ pounds)

flour for dredging

1 tablespoon olive oil

1 tablespoon unsalted butter

1 small onion, peeled

1 medium carrot, scrubbed

1 celery stalk with leaves, washed

1 teaspoon salt, or to taste

freshly ground pepper to taste

½ teaspoon paprika

1½ cups dry wine (red or white)

2 tablespoons chopped Italian parsley

Separate thighs from drumsticks and dredge all the chicken pieces in flour.

In a sauté pan or pressure-cooking pan, sauté chicken in the oil and butter until browned.

Mince the onion, carrot, and celery together and add to the chicken. Continue cooking, uncovered, until the mince is limp. Add salt, pepper, paprika, and wine.

When the wine has evaporated, cover the pan.

In a sauté pan, simmer about 25 minutes or until the chicken is cooked. Stir 2 or 3 times while the chicken simmers. Place the chicken on a serving platter, strain the sauce over the chicken, sprinkle with parsley and serve.

In a pressure cooker, bring the pressure up to 15 pounds, cook 7 minutes, then bring the pressure down immediately. Remove the chicken pieces to a warm serving platter in a warm place. Cook the sauce down about 5 minutes before straining it over the chicken. Sprinkle the chicken with parsley and serve. For 4.

Batter-Fried Chicken

pollo fritto

Batter

1 recipe yeast batter diluted with ¼ cup water (pages 25 to 27)

¼ teaspoon white pepper

Chicken

2 1-kilo (2-pound) frying chickens

5 tablespoons lemon juice

1 teaspoon salt

¼ teaspoon white pepper

1 tablespoon Tabasco sauce

1 rounded tablespoon chopped Italian parsley

2 garlic cloves, peeled and thinly sliced lengthwise

leaves of 2 sprigs fresh rosemary, minced or 2 teaspoons dried rosemary

¼ cup dry white wine

flour for dredging

vegetable oil for frying

2 lemons, cut in wedges

Mix batter. Add the pepper, and let rest in a warm place (such as an oven with a pilot light) for at least an hour.

Cut the chickens in small pieces; remove and set aside (for broth or other uses) the wing tips, end of drumsticks, backs, necks, and giblets.

Make a marinade of all the remaining ingredients except the flour, oil, and lemon.

Place chicken pieces and marinade in a snugly fitting dish or sturdy plastic bag and turn it around and about in order to coat all the meat. Let rest for 2 hours, turning two or three times.

Remove chicken from marinade, drain on absorbent toweling, pat dry, and dredge in the flour.

To fry: put ample vegetable oil (3 to 4 inches) in each of two pans. Bring one of the pans to low frying heat (183° C, 360° F) and the other to higher frying heat (190° C, 375° F).

Stir the batter and dip the chicken pieces in it.

Place as many pieces of chicken as will fit comfortably in the first pan, turning them back and forth to let the batter swell and begin to turn golden. Remove and place in the second and hotter pan to finish cooking to a deep brown, very crisp stage.

Drain well on absorbent toweling. Serve hot (or cold, they are ideal for a picnic) with wedges of fresh lemon. For 8.

Chicken, Hungarian Style

pollo all'ungherese

1 small chicken (no more than 1 ½ kilos, 3 pounds)
flour for dredging
4 tablespoons unsalted butter
3 tablespoons olive oil
1 medium onion, peeled
⅝ cup whole milk
½ lemon
¾ cup basic tomato sauce (page 40)
1 chicken bouillon cube
1 teaspoon paprika
6 to 8 drops Tabasco sauce
1 to 1½ teaspoons salt
freshly ground pepper to taste
5 sprigs Italian parsley

Cut the chicken into 8 or 10 pieces, reserving the giblets for another use.

Dredge chicken pieces in flour and sauté them in butter and oil in a sauté pan or pressure cooker until browned on all sides.

Mince the onion and add it to the chicken. Continue cooking until the onion is limp.

Mix the milk with the juice of the lemon half and add to the chicken. Add the tomato sauce, bouillon cube, paprika, Tabasco, salt, and pepper.

In a sauté pan, stir the sauce well, bring to boiling, cover the pan, lower the heat, and simmer the chicken for about 20 minutes or until tender. Stir 2 or 3 times as the chicken cooks. Mince the parsley leaves with a bit of the stem and mix with the grated rind of the lemon. Stir parsley and lemon rind into the pan. Cook another 5 minutes.

In a pressure cooker, seal the cover, bring the pressure to 15 pounds, and cook 10 minutes. Lower the pressure immediately, remove the cover, and stir in the grated lemon rind and minced parsley. Cook, uncovered, another 5 minutes or until the flavors have blended and the chicken is completely cooked.

Taste for seasonings and adjust. For 4.

Chicken Legs and Peas

coscie di pollo con piselli

2 chicken legs with thighs
2½ tablespoons olive oil
1 small onion, peeled
1 small garlic clove, peeled
½ cup dry white wine
1 small bay leaf
1 chicken bouillon cube
2 cloves
⅛ teaspoon ground cinnamon
2 to 3 peeled plum tomatoes, fresh or canned
1 285-gram (10-ounce) package frozen peas, thawed
salt to taste
freshly ground pepper to taste

Separate drumsticks from thighs, and cut off and discard any visible fat.

Brown the chicken pieces in the olive oil over medium-high heat, turning frequently so that they do not stick to the pan.

Mince the onion and garlic together and add to the pan when the chicken is well browned. Continue cooking until the mince is limp.

Add the wine, bay leaf, bouillon cube, cloves, and cinnamon, and cook until the wine has evaporated.

Press the tomatoes through a coarse sieve or pass them through a food mill into the pan. Stir, cover, and, when the sauce boils, lower the heat and cook 15 minutes.

Stir the pan, turn the chicken pieces over, add the thawed peas, and taste the sauce. Add salt and pepper to please.

Recover the pan, cooking another 8 to 10 minutes or until the peas are tender. Serve with hot Italian bread. For 2.

Baked Chicken

pollo al forno

3 frying chickens, cut in 8
  pieces each

3 teaspoons salt (approximate)

freshly ground pepper to
  taste

3 cloves garlic, peeled

½ cup olive oil (approxi-
  mate)

2 level tablespoons tomato
  paste, dissolved in ½ cup
  warm water

1½ cups red wine vinegar

2 bay leaves crumbled

10 fresh basil leaves,
  chopped, or 1 teaspoon
  dried basil

Preheat oven to 177° C (350° F).

Cut away and discard any chicken fat you can.

Mix the salt and pepper together and rub a generous amount on each piece of chicken.

If you have a large frying or sauté pan, use it; otherwise, use two frying pans simultaneously to brown all the chicken at once and not over-crowd any pan.

Brown the garlic in the olive oil. Remove the garlic, and let the pan(s) cool for a minute or two. Add the chicken to the pan(s), and brown thoroughly on all sides. As the pieces brown, re-move to drain on absorbent paper toweling.

When all the chicken is browned, place in a baking dish just large enough to hold them comfortably.

Dilute the tomato paste in the warm water, then add it to the wine vinegar and the herbs, and pour all over the chicken.

Bake in a moderate (177° C, 350° F) oven for ½ hour, basting 3 to 4 times. Serve with hot Ital-ian bread. For 10 to 12.

Duck

anitra

Grilled Duckling

anitra alla griglia

1 garlic clove, peeled and
  quartered
2 sprigs fresh rosemary or
  2 teaspoons dried rose-
  mary
12 juniper berries, crushed
2 tablespoons soy sauce
1 tablespoon Worcester-
  shire sauce
1 teaspoon Tabasco sauce
3 tablespoons *grappa*
  (page 188) or vodka
1 lemon
1 1- to 1¾-kilo (2- to 3-
  pound) duckling

Make a marinade with the first seven ingredients, plus the juice of the lemon. Save the
empty lemon halves.

Remove the giblets and neck from the duck
and set them aside for another dish. Cut off and
discard (if the butcher has not done so) the oil
sacks above the duck's tail. Cut off any extra fat
at the cavity opening.

Rinse the duck thoroughly, and rub the cavity with one half of the lemon whose juice you
used in the marinade. Place the other half in the
cavity.

Put the duck in a plastic bag or a covered
dish large enough to hold it comfortably. Add
the marinade and cover (or seal the bag, and
place it on a platter) at room temperature 2
hours before it is time to grill. Turn the duck
from time to time to ensure a good soaking.

Get a grill going with ample hot coals.

Tie the wings and legs of the duck tightly to
the body and place the duck on a spit. Put the
marinade in a bowl or jar for use during cooking.

Keep a spray bottle of water handy so that, as
the duck's fat falls on the coals and ignites, the
flames can be brought under control. This hap-
pens at the beginning of the grilling, and the
spraying prevents the duck from being too
blackened by smoke.

Allow the duck to rotate slowly over the hot
coals for approximately 40 minutes. Baste often
with the marinade.

At the end of cooking, the duck's juices will

run clear when the meaty portions are skewered or pierced with a fork; the skin will be very dark and crisp.

Cut the duck into 4 pieces with poultry shears, brush once more with any remaining marinade, and serve. For 4.

Duck with Almonds

anitra alle mandorle

Duck

1 2-kilo (about 4½-pound) duck

85 grams (3 ounces) almonds, shelled, slivered, and toasted

140 grams (5 ounces) or 2 small bunches scallions

2 lemons

¼ cup dry white vermouth

½ chicken bouillon cube dissolved in ¾ cup chicken broth (page 44)

Preheat oven to 200° C (400° F).

Remove giblets and neck from the duck's cavity, and save for later use. Pierce the upper thighs, breast, and skin around the cavity with a fork.

Place the duck on a rack in a shallow roasting pan in the hot (200° C, 400° F) oven for 25 minutes. Remove the duck from the oven and the pan. Pour off and discard the fat in the pan.

Cut the duck in pieces: the drumsticks at the ball joint, the wings at the joint, the breast meat from the breast. Cut each half breast in half again lengthwise. Remove as much fat from the pieces as you can.

Place the toasted almonds in the bottom of the roasting pan.

Wash the scallions and cut off and discard the roots and all but 2 inches of the green. Slice scallions in thin circles, and add to the almonds.

Place the duck pieces over the scallions.

Grate the lemons, and sprinkle the grated rind over the duck.

Add all but 2 tablespoons of the juice of the lemons to the pan.

Add the vermouth and half the bouillon broth to the pan.

Place the duck in the oven, lower the heat to 190° C (375° F), and roast 30 to 40 minutes or until duck juice runs clear when the leg is pierced with a fork. Baste at least 3 times while roasting.

Sauce

duck's liver
duck's neck meat
1 tablespoon unsalted butter
½ teaspoon salt, or to taste
freshly ground pepper
1 teaspoon fresh rosemary leaves or ½ teaspoon dried rosemary
6 juniper berries, crushed
1 tablespoon wine vinegar
¼ cup dry red wine

Meanwhile, prepare the sauce: clean and chop the duck's liver, remove as much meat from the neck as you easily can, and put it with the liver and butter in a sauté pan. Begin to cook over brisk heat. Add salt, pepper, rosemary, and juniper berries, and cook 5 minutes. Add the vinegar, and cook until evaporated. Add the wine, and cook 5 minutes more.

Remove the sauce from heat and process, blend, or send through a food mill to reduce to a smooth consistency.

When the duck is cooked, place on a warm platter. Surround the duck with the nuts and scallions.

Strain the pan juices into the sauce you have made, mix well, and taste. If the sauce is too thick, add the remaining chicken bouillon broth. Or you may add hot water if the sauce has enough salt or seems rich enough. It is a rich sauce in any case. Heat the sauce well and serve in a sauce boat. For 4.

Omelets

Frittate

Along with a quick dish of pasta with a simple sauce, *frittate* could easily be called the leading Italian "fast food." While we translate *frittate* as omelets, they are a bit different from French omelets in that they are usually served round (not folded over), their fillings are blended and mixed with the eggs, and they tend to be more flat than fluffy. But the translation still stands in view of the fact that they are mostly eggs, are cooked in pans that should be reserved for them, and are very versatile.

Frittate, nowadays, are generally served as second courses for light meals; but for centuries they were the filling for the working man's luncheon loaf of bread.

The pan for making *frittate* can be a well-seasoned iron skillet, a teflon or silverstone coated pan, or a well-seasoned, heavy aluminum omelet pan.

If this is your first try with Italian *frittate* and your iron or aluminum pan is new, the seasoning process is simple. Fill the pan with fresh vegetable oil almost to the brim; place the pan over medium heat; bring to a boil; remove from heat; and let stand at least 8 hours. Pour off and discard the oil and wipe the pan dry with paper toweling. When using your pan, never wash it, just wipe it clean with paper toweling. If things stick to the bottom (it does happen sometimes!), sprinkle salt in the pan and scrub with dry paper toweling, then wipe clean.

A coated frying pan needs no seasoning, but follow the manufacturer's cooking instructions regarding heat during cooking.

A pan 10½-inches in diameter works well with 6 large eggs, allowing the depth of the eggs to be no more than ¾ inch.

For fillings, you may use herbs such as basil, chives, parsley, or a mixture of all three; you may use asparagus, artichokes, chard, green beans, mushrooms, onions, potatoes, tomatoes and onions, spinach, zucchini, or invent something yourself. Cheese and ham also lend themselves to *frittate*. The actual weight or measure of any *frittate* filling frequently depends on the cook's choice and what is on hand. For example, 2 artichokes or 2 onions or 2 potatoes or 2 zucchini go well with 6 eggs and turn into a *frittata* for 4. The above vegetables are cooked in olive oil directly in the proper pan, and the eggs are poured on top of them. If you are using spinach, chard, asparagus, or green beans, you should blanch them first in lightly salted water, drain well, and add to beaten eggs; or start the eggs in unsalted butter, and then add the drained blanched vegetables.

For a cheese *frittata,* the cheese is usually mixed into the beaten egg and then poured into the proper pan — which already holds hot butter or olive oil.

Frittate may also be made in small sizes and stacked in layers with a simple sauce between the layers, such as the Tomato and Basil Sauce (page 40). Rolled *frittate* frequently are made with the addition of a little flour: then they are called *crespelle,* the equivalent of French *crêpes.* Stacked *frittate* with sauce are small enough to be given the diminutive, *frittatine.*

Our two earlier books carried a total of fifteen recipes for the assorted *frittate.* We will not repeat them here; but following are four recipes, great favorites, whose assemblage and cooking cover the subject.

Zucchini Omelet

frittata di zucchine

1 medium or 2 small zuc-
chini, washed and sliced
in thin rounds
3 tablespoons olive oil
½ teaspoon salt, or to taste
6 large eggs
2 tablespoons grated Par-
mesan cheese

Put the zucchini rounds and olive oil in the *frit-tata* pan and cook over medium heat until the zucchini is wilted and beginning to turn golden. Sprinkle with a bit of the salt. Lower the heat.

Beat the eggs lightly with the cheese and then pour it over the zucchini, stirring gently to distribute the slices evenly.

When the edges of the *frittata* begin to set, slip the spatula around the edge of the pan, tilt the pan, and let some uncooked egg slip down under. Cook until the bottom of the *frittata* is solid and golden. Shake the pan a couple of times as the *frittata* cooks to make sure it slides easily and is not stuck. If it sticks, put your spatula to work and loosen the eggs from the bottom. When the bottom is cooked, you may turn it in any of three ways:

Flip it like a pancake by tossing it right up out of the pan (a little practice is recommended);

Flip it with a spatula if the "filling" isn't too loose; or

Slide it out onto a plate just slightly larger than the pan, turn the pan over to cover the plate, then turn the *frittata* back into cooking position in the pan.

Cook the second side as you did the first. Slip the *frittata* out onto the plate you used earlier or onto a serving plate. Sprinkle with the last of the salt. For 4.

Little Omelets with Sauce

frittatine al sugo

1 recipe Tomato and Basil Sauce (page 40)

6 large eggs

1½ tablespoons all-pur-pose unbleached flour

½ teaspoon salt

1½ tablespoons water

3 tablespoons unsalted butter

1 tablespoon olive oil, if needed

3 tablespoons grated Par-mesan cheese

While the sauce is simmering, the *frittatine* may be mixed, cooked, and placed on a large platter prior to stacking. For *frittatine* a smaller omelet pan is easier to work with than the 10½-inch pan usually used with 6 eggs. We recommend about 8 inches in diameter.

Beat the eggs well, then mix in the flour, salt, and water.

Melt 2 tablespoons butter in your omelet pan over medium high heat. Pour in enough beaten egg to make a thin round 5 to 6 inches in diameter. As soon as the underside is golden and cooked, turn the omelet over. As soon as the second side is cooked, remove the *frittatina* and place it on a warm platter in a warm place.

If your sauce is ready, spread the *frittatina* with a bit of sauce. If not, proceed with the cooking and layer with the sauce at the end.

Continue cooking little *frittate* until all the batter is used. Add the last of the butter and the olive oil as needed to keep the pan slippery.

When all the *frittatine* are cooked, layer them on the serving platter with a tablespoon or two of sauce between every two omelets. Cover the completed stack with the remaining sauce. Sprinkle with Parmesan cheese and serve. For 4.

A pleasant variation on this recipe is to roll each cooked *frittatina* and place it in the simmering sauce. Serve when all the *frittatine* have been in the sauce for a few moments.

Cheese Omelet

frittata al formaggio

6 large eggs

3 tablespoons unsalted
  butter

225 grams (½ pound) fresh
  mozzarella cheese,
  shredded or whole milk
  mozzarella, cubed

½ teaspoon salt, or to taste

1½ tablespoons minced
  Italian parsley or minced
  fresh basil

freshly ground pepper

Beat the eggs lightly.

Melt the butter in the omelet pan, add the eggs, then sprinkle with the *mozzarella.*

Add the salt.

As the eggs start to set around the edges, go around with a spatula to make sure they do not stick. Lift the edges here and there, tilting the pan to let some of the uncooked egg slip down underneath.

Sprinkle with the parsley or basil.

When the underside is cooked and golden, turn (page 217) and cook the second side.

Slide the *frittata* onto a warm serving plate, sprinkle with a bit of pepper, and serve. For 4.

Omelets with Ham and Three Cheeses

*frittate con prosciutto
e tre formaggi*

¼ cup fresh *ricotta*

2 tablespoons Parmesan
  cheese

60 grams (2 ounces) fresh
  mozzarella cheese,
  grated

60 grams (2 ounces)
  cooked ham, diced

1 tablespoon cream

5 large eggs, well beaten

2 tablespoons unsalted
  butter

salt to taste

Mix the three cheeses with the ham, and add the cream to make a soft filling.

Pour one-quarter of the beaten egg into a hot, buttered omelet pan. When the underside is well browned and the top is beginning to set, place one-quarter of the filling down the center of the omelet, fold the sides up over the filling, and continue cooking a moment or two longer. Cook the remaining egg and add the last of the filling to make three more omelets. Serve hot. For 4.

Seafood

Pesce

When it comes to fish, it is hard for us to draw a line on the number of offerings in any one book. We love fish. We love the Italian perspective on fish: the extreme care not to overcook, over-sauce, or overseason, any one of which destroys texture and hides original flavor; the extra effort to buy really fresh fish; and the care in keeping frozen fish frozen and in thawing it properly.

Perhaps you will find the recipes that follow surprisingly simple. A lot of Italian cooking rules are simple, but achieve sophisticated results.

The choice of fish, on the other hand, can be complicated: the Atlantic and Pacific Oceans offer such a host of marvelous fish, to say nothing of fresh-water varieties, that it is virtually impossible to put a complete fish selection in a single chapter or under a single heading. Hence we have concentrated on giving normally found-on-the-market fish the Italian treatment. We have matched ocean cousins to Mediterranean sea species where possible and types of ocean fish to types of sea fish.

We will continue to recommend *baccalà,* dried salt cod. It can be the backbone of any collection of fish recipes. Once inexpensive and universal, it has become hard to find in some areas. We prefer the boxed salt cod to that wrapped in plastic. The soaking of cod must be thorough. And if you do not find the dried cod recipe you are looking for in this book, we modestly urge you to look at our other two books, which star *baccalà* in their fish chapters.

Generally speaking, there are five basic ways of preparing fish in the Italian manner:

In Padella: pan-cooked with butter or butter and olive oil. Small fish or fish filets weighing about 225 grams (½ pound) are dipped in milk, then in flour, and sautéed quickly over relatively high heat. Porgy, rainbow trout, sole, perch, and whiting fit this treatment, as do filets of fresh and frozen haddock, cod, hake, flounder, and others of your choice.

In Bianco: poached in barely boiling salted water to which you have added aromatic vegetables, white wine, or wine vinegar. Large fish are poached 12 to 14 minutes per pound; smaller fish 9 minutes per pound. Salmon leads the list of poachable fish, which also includes bass, carp, eel, haddock, perch, pike, porgy, salmon trout, and freshwater trout. The largest of the fish to be poached should be put in the water when it is cold. Smaller fish should have the water and flavorings boiled about 20 minutes to ½ hour ahead of time and barely simmering when the fish goes in. Both sizes of fish should be wrapped in kitchen cheesecloth with a long knot at each end for gentle and easy removal of the fish from water to platter. Poached fish are easily skinned while still hot, and the flesh is better tasting if you leave the head and tail on the fish while cooking.

Alla Griglia: grilled over hot coals or broiled in the oven. Angler or monkfish, bluefish, halibut, mullet, trout, swordfish steaks, tuna steaks, shrimp, and scallops head the list of fish easily grilled. They are firm of flesh and react nicely to marinating before being cooked. Mackerel, eel, and large sardines are ideal because the grilling eliminates the oils, leaving a delicate flesh to be savored. Large porgy and red snapper are also perfect for grilling. The larger specimens need a hotter fire to begin and then a longer, lower heat to complete the cooking. Smaller and more oily fish or steaks call for a very hot fire and rapid cooking. Marinating for 30 minutes before grilling adds to the fish's flavor. Marinades differ according to the cook's choice, but the basic components are olive oil and lemon juice, with the addition of herbs, such as bay or rosemary, sage or oregano.

Al Cartoccio: wrapped and sealed in roasting paper along with aromatic vegetables or herbs and even other fish, such as mussels or shrimps, and baked in a hot oven. This is probably the most simple and satisfying of all the techniques — not a drop of natural juices goes wasted, flavorings have maximum opportunity to do their job, and individual servings remain very much intact. Filets of larger fish, such as sand shark, do well *al cartoccio* as do the smaller fish John Dory or scup, mullet, porgy, and sea bream. Once you have chosen your flavorings and fish, wrap them in roasting paper or aluminum foil, seal carefully, and place in a hot oven set from 200° to 220° C (400° to 425° F). Cook from 12 to 16 minutes, letting the size of the fish be your guide. And never hesitate to invent a flavoring, because this method of cooking really lets you be creative.

Al Forno: roasted or baked, however you wish to call it, this is the method for big fish, either in the form of large filets or whole and stuffed. The oven should be hot (200° to 220° C, 400° to 425° F), and the timing depends on the dressed weight of the fish; it will be about 8 to 10 minutes per pound. The main thing is to cook the interior of the fish thoroughly.

A Short Guide to Seafood

Fish	
Anchovy	*Acciuga*
Anglerfish or frog fish	*Rospo, pescatrice, coda di rospo*
Bass: Black sea bass of the Atlantic	Like *branzino* (Mediterranean term; also called *spigola* in the Adriatic area)
White sea bass of the Pacific	Like *spigola*
Fresh water bass of the Great Lakes or Mississippi valley	Can be treated like *branzino* but is more delicate, so watch timing
Bonito	*Tonnetto*
Carp	*Carpa*
Cod	*Baccalà*
Rock cod	Like *Cernia*
Stockfish	*Stoccafisso,* cod, sun-dried without salt

Dogfish	*Gattuccio*
Eels	*Anguille*
Conger eel	*Gronco*
Flounder	*Sogliolone*
Haddock and Hake	*Merluzzo,* a name also given to cod, members of the *Merluzzo* family
John Dory	*Pesce San Pietro*
Mackerel	*Sgombro,* maccherello
Monkfish	*Rana pescatrice,* anglerfish in England
Mullet	
Grey mullet	*Cefalo,* not unlike bass
Red mullet	*Triglia,* found in the Adriatic, the Mediterranean, and English waters
Striped mullet	Like *cefalo,* also called black mullet in Florida
Perch	*Pesce persico*
Pike	*Luccio*
Porgy	*Orata,* similar to sea bream and scup; also called *marmora.* White bream is called *sarago*
Skate	*Razza*
Salmon	*Salmone*
Salmon trout	*Trota salmonata,* also called sea trout and sometimes known as weakfish
Sardine	*Sardina*
Shark	*Pescecane*
Sand shark	*Palombo*
Sole	*Sogliola*
Sturgeon	*Storione*
Swordfish	*Pescespada*
Trout	*Trota.* Rainbow trout is *trota iridea*

Tuna	*Tonno*
Turbot	*Rombo*
Umbrine	*Ombrina,* resembles perch or very large sea bass
Whiting	*Nasello*

Shellfish

Crab	*Granchio*
Crab, Venetian or Adriatic	*Granzeola*
Lobster	*Aragosta*
Shrimp	*Gamberetti,* Jumbo shrimp are *gamberi,* prawns are *scampi*
Freshwater shrimp, crayfish	Also known as *gamberi*

Mollusks

Clams	*Vongole*
Cuttlefish	*Seppie*
Mussels	*Cozze, muscoli, mitili*
Oysters	*Ostriche*
Octopus	*Polpo*
Scallops	*Cape sante, conchiglie, pellegrine,* and *conchiglie di San Giacomo*
Squid	*Calamaro*

Baked Fish Filets

filetti di pesce al forno

1 kilo (2 pounds) filets or steaks of firm-fleshed fish

1 teaspoon salt (approximate)

white pepper to taste

3 tablespoons olive oil (approximate)

1 slice day-old Italian bread, crustless

15 sprigs Italian parsley

½ garlic clove, peeled

2 anchovy filets, drained or rinsed and drained

1 rounded tablespoon capers, rinsed and drained

1 or 2 lemons, cut in wedges

This is a recipe for filets or steaks of the larger, more firm fish such as fresh cod, turbot, halibut, haddock, hake, and whiting.

Preheat oven to 200° C (400° F).

Sprinkle the fish with salt and pepper on both sides. Oil a baking dish just large enough to hold the fish comfortably and place the fish in it.

Break the bread in small chunks. Cut off and discard parsley stems. Process these and all the remaining ingredients except the lemons in a food processor or blender until well minced. (Or mince well by hand.) Spread the mince on the steaks. Dribble the steaks with additional olive oil.

Bake 15 minutes in a hot (200° C, 400° F) oven. Serve with lemon wedges. For 4.

Poached Fish Filets

filetti di pesce in bianco

Fish

675 grams (1½ pounds)
  frozen fish filets, thawed
1 teaspoon salt
2 lemons

This is a simple way of cooking frozen fish filets such as turbot, halibut, haddock, and cod (but not sole, which is too thin and tender).

Let the fish filets thaw slowly on the lowest shelf of the refrigerator, either overnight or during the day, depending on cooking time.

Place the filets in a large frying pan in one layer. Add the salt and enough water to cover. Bring to a boil, reduce the heat to simmer, and cook until the fish flakes.

Place the cooked fish on a warm serving platter to drain. Pour off any water that accumulates on the platter after 4 minutes.

Dress fish with juice of 1 lemon. Surround the fish with wedges of the second lemon.

Sauce

2 tablespoons minced Italian parsley
1 tablespoon capers, rinsed, drained, and chopped
6 tablespoons olive oil
½ cup black Sicilian olives (packed in brine)
  or
4 to 6 tablespoons *maionese* (pages 30 to 32)
  or
4 to 6 tablespoons *salsa verde* (pages 33 to 34) made with lemon

If you are using the parsley and capers, mix them together with the olive oil and dress the fish with the mixture. Add the olives to the platter, and let the fish stand about half an hour in the refrigerator before serving.

If you are using the maionese *or* salsa verde, baste the fish with the lemon juice a couple of times while it cools in the refrigerator for about half an hour. Serve with the sauce of your choice on the side. For 4.

Fish Soup
zuppa di pesce

A *zuppa di pesce* is rarely considered a first course but usually stars on its own as a main dish, followed by green salad and fruit. It is truly a special festive dish. Because its main ingredients are so varied, *zuppa di pesce* is usually made for a group of 6 to 8 and served either with hot crusty Italian bread or with slices of fried Italian bread in each bowl. Either way, the cooking time is short in order to preserve the texture of the fish. This soup should be made with the whole fish, since heads, tails, and bones increase the flavor of the broth. But for those who cannot find whole, cleaned fish or who do not care for the appearance of the heads, it is possible to eliminate the "whole," at the price of a slight loss in taste.

There may easily be as many recipes for fish soup as there are Italian fishing ports. The following recipe is a composite we have worked out for Atlantic fish. The guidelines to our choice of fish are those any native Italian cook would hold to: use as many different kinds of fish as possible, including rock fish and eel; choose fish for variety in both texture and flavor; use a large pot with a close-fitting cover so that once a boil is reached and the cover goes on the fish cooks by steaming and poaching; when adding fish to the pot, add the sturdiest fish first and end with the most delicate.

Serve fish soup as soon as it is cooked, with large napkins (for use after peeling one's own shrimp), and provide finger bowls with warm water and a slice of lemon so guests can tidy up before the salad.

The choice of bread is up to you. One of us prefers hot Italian bread, the other sliced Italian bread fried in olive oil.

If, after all the fish has been consumed, there is any broth left over, we suggest straining and freezing it and using it as *brodo di pesce,* the ultimate in fish broth, for another day.

Fish

About 3 kilos (6½ pounds) varied fish, including some or all of the following:

225 grams (½ pound) squid, cleaned (pages 251 to 252) and cut in rings

1 small whiting (about 340 grams, ¾ pound), cleaned but with head and tail intact or the same amount fresh cod filet

1 small red snapper (about 225 grams, ½ pound), cleaned but with head and tail left on

225 grams (½ pound) halibut steak, cut in chunks

2 small porgies (about 450 grams, 1 pound), cleaned but with head and tail left on

1 mullet (about 450 grams, 1 pound), cleaned but with head and tail left on

450 grams (1 pound) monkfish steaks, cut in chunks

225 grams (½ pound) medium shrimp, with shells

450 grams (1 pound) mussels, scrubbed clean

Flavorings

½ cup olive oil

2 garlic cloves, peeled

(*continued*)

Place the olive oil in a big soup pot; add the garlic and pepper pod; sauté them until golden and deep brown — respectively — and then discard.

Add the squid pieces, and cook 4 minutes or until their color has turned to pink and lavender.

Add the wine, and cook until it has evaporated.

Add the tomatoes, half the parsley sprigs, the celery leaves, and the Tabasco sauce (if you are using it).

Bring the pot to a boil, then cover it, lower the heat, and simmer 15 minutes.

Add the whiting and, when the pot bubbles, add the red snapper. When the pot bubbles again, add the halibut and the porgies and mullet. When the pot comes up to a boil again, add the monkfish and fish broth (or water) to cover.

Bring the pot to a boil again, lower the heat and cover again, and cook about 5 minutes or until the larger fish have cooked.

Add the shrimps and mussels, and cook 4 minutes longer or until the shrimp are bright coral in color and the mussels open.

Taste for salt, and add as needed (but remember that all fish add some salt to the water, and if you are using fish broth it also adds salt).

Serve fish, fish chunks, mussels, and shrimps evenly distributed in soup bowls. Strain broth

2 hot red pepper pods,
seeded or 1 teaspoon
Tabasco sauce
2 cups dry white wine
3 cups peeled plum toma-
toes, fresh or canned
10 sprigs Italian parsley
leaves of 1 celery stalk
3 to 4 tablespoons salt, or
to taste
fish broth (page 47) or
water to cover

into a soup tureen, and add some to each bowl.
Serve remaining broth on the side.

Sprinkle each bowl with a bit of chopped
parsley (the last 5 sprigs), and serve. For 8 to 10,
depending on appetites.

Bonito

tonnetto al cartoccio

1 1-kilo (2-pound) bonito,
   cleaned but with head
   and tail intact

1 teaspoon salt, or to taste

freshly ground pepper to
   taste

1 large piece of aluminum
   foil or roasting paper

2 lemons

3 or 4 peeled plum toma-
   toes, preferably fresh
   and very ripe

2 tablespoons chopped
   Italian parsley

4 tablespoons olive oil

1½ dozen mussels

Preheat oven to 200° C (400° F).

Sprinkle the cavity of the fish with some of the salt and pepper.

Place the fish on the foil or paper and bring it up and around the fish. Squeeze 1 of the lemons and put about half the juice in the fish cavity. Sprinkle the remaining salt and pepper over the fish. Add the last of the first lemon's juice.

Cut the second lemon in rounds and place them along the length of the fish.

Pass the tomatoes through a sieve or food mill and put some on each lemon slice, the rest around the fish. Sprinkle with parsley. Put the mussels around the fish.

Sprinkle the olive oil over all. Seal the foil or paper perfectly so that none of the juices or any of the vapor can escape. Place the sealed-up fish in a shallow baking dish and bake in the hot (200° C, 400° F) oven for 30 minutes.

Place fish in its packet on a serving platter. Open the packet at table, slice the fish along the spine, and remove first one filet and then the other. Serve filets with the sauce in the packet. For 3 to 4.

This same treatment is good for any 1-kilo (2-pound) fish, such as porgy, mullet, bass, trout, or red snapper and also for filets or steaks of perch, John Dory, sand shark, swordfish, and salmon. When cooking filets, count on about 12 minutes oven time and place 2 filets to a person in individual packets. Whole fish weighing 675 grams (1½ pounds) stay in the oven 15 to 20 minutes. And, finally, since no two fish weigh the same, we find it is a good idea to keep a record of cooking times that have worked well for you so that you can time your next fish in a packet to perfection.

Deep-Fried Cod Filets

filetti di baccalà fritti

1 kilo (2 pounds) dried cod, soaked, skinned, and boned
1 recipe yeast batter for frying (pages 25 to 26)
vegetable oil for frying
2 lemons, cut in wedges

Dried salt cod comes either whole (often found in Italian specialty stores complete with skin and bones) or cut in filets and then dried (found in boxes or in plastic in supermarkets).

Either way you buy it, salt cod must be soaked for 12 to 24 hours under slowly running water or in water that is changed from time to time. At the end of the soaking, the flesh is plump and moist, the salt only a trace for flavoring. Sometimes you can find salt cod already soaked and ready to be boned, which can save you time. Ask around any Italian shopping area; there is always at least one grocer who clings to the old ways of preparing cod for the Friday customer.

Cut the soaked cod into pieces about 5 inches long and 1½ inches wide, and pat dry on paper toweling.

When the batter has risen, stir it well and begin dipping the pieces of fish in it.

Bring two saucepans of vegetable oil to high heat, one of them at about 177° C (350° F) and the other about 190° C (375° F).

Place a piece of fish in the first of the saucepans and let it fry until the outside is hardened and the filet has risen to the surface. Remove with a pair of tongs and place in the second, hotter pan. Fry until golden brown. Remove to paper toweling to drain.

Continue frying a filet or two at a time, first in the warm pan and then in the hotter pan. When all the pieces are fried, serve immediately with wedges of lemon.

For 4 to 6 — but you may find that this traditional Roman dish is rather addictive and that eaters become almost gluttonous when confronted with *baccalà fritto*.

Eels

anguille

In a popularity contest in this country, eels would place out of the running. And that is a shame, because under any rubric from taste to nutrition the meat ranks at the top. It is flavorful and practically boneless. In all of Italy's regions, eels are highly regarded. They are a gastronomic specialty of the Po river delta and a must in Campania for the Christmas holidays. In Rome, no one waits for a special reason to serve eel; in the Veneto, eels are considered a most delicate morsel to accompany rice or *polenta*. The irony for the Venetians, who are particularly proud of their eels, is that in recent years they have had to augment the native supply with eels airshipped from Newburyport, Massachusetts.

Eels are considered ugly, but are not, especially if compared with some of the other fish of the sea. Eels are also thought to be mean, but are gentle creatures and mind their own business. The one vicious eel is the Moray — but even so its meat is held in the highest esteem in Italy.

Eels are considered slippery, and that they are, but only when alive.

Eels are thought to be fatty, but actually their fat is skin-deep and most of it strips off when the eels are skinned. When eels are roasted, broiled, or barbecued, the skin stays on: heat melts the fat away, the skin turns crisp, and Italian gourmets (or mere eel lovers) fight over it.

A good eel is a live eel, and the creatures cooperate by being practically indestructible. We recommend that you let your fishmonger do the dispatching and the skinning. But if you should find yourself the proud possessor of a few live eels, follow these steps or you will find yourself in a very slippery, frustrating situation:

Put the eels in a clean, empty bucket. Add a cup or two of salt, and cover the bucket. Shortly the eels will go to sleep and in 15 to 30 minutes, depending on their attachment to life, they will have given up the ghost. Get hold of a rag or an old newspaper and some sand or wood ashes and rub the eels with it. Or just rub the eels under clear running water until they are no longer slippery. Make an incision on their belly up to the gills and clean them as you would any fish. If they are to be cooked with the skin on, cut off the head and tail. If they are to be skinned, make a partial incision around the head, leaving a small strip of skin intact. Lift an inch or so of skin from the body near the head. Bend the head back (the backbone should snap) and hold the portion of the skinned body with one hand. With the other hand, pull down the skin resolutely toward the tail. The skin will strip as easily as pulling off a sock.

Wash the skinned eel under running water, pat it dry, and you are ready to cook.

Venetian Eels and Peas

bisato e bisi

800 grams (about 1¾ pounds) eels, skinned (page 234)

flour for dredging

5 sprigs Italian parsley

1 garlic clove, peeled

⅓ cup olive oil

1½ cups peeled plum tomatoes, fresh or canned, seeded

285 grams (10 ounces) frozen tiny peas or equivalent tiny fresh peas, shelled

salt

freshly ground pepper

Cut the eels in 2- to 3-inch pieces and dredge them in flour.

Mince the parsley leaves and garlic together and sauté them briefly in oil. (If you have a top-of-the-stove Italian earthenware casserole, use it for this dish.)

Add the eels, brown them briefly on all sides, and add the tomatoes cut in chunks.

Add salt and pepper, bring to a boil, then lower the heat, and simmer for 15 minutes, stirring occasionally and breaking up whatever tomato solids remain.

Remove the eels to a serving dish. Add the peas to the tomato sauce and cook at a low boil about 5 minutes or until the peas are tender. Pour sauce and peas over the eels. Serve with slices of hot Italian bread. For 4.

Marinated Eels

anguille marinate

1 kilo (approximately 2 pounds) eels

⅓ cup olive oil

2 lemons

⅓ cup dry white wine

12 fresh sage leaves (dried sage will not work)

1 teaspoon salt (approximate)

freshly ground pepper

3 tablespoons unseasoned bread crumbs

Skin the eels (page 234), or have them skinned, and cut them in 3-inch pieces. Place the pieces in a dish that will accommodate them snugly.

Mix all but 3 tablespoons of the oil with the juice of 1 lemon and the wine, and pour over the eels.

Coarsely chop half the sage leaves and sprinkle them over the eels. Add salt and pepper. Turn and baste the eels, then let rest for at least 1 hour, turning occasionally.

Put the reserved oil in a skillet or sauté pan large enough to hold the eels in one layer. Add the remaining sage leaves, and sauté until they are limp.

Add the eels and sauté 2 minutes, turning frequently. Raise the heat, add the marinade, sprinkle in the bread crumbs, and let the sauce thicken.

Place the eels on a serving plate and pour the sauce over them. Cut the remaining lemon into wedges and serve with the eels. For 4.

Eels on Skewers

spiedini d'anguille

800 grams (about 1¾ pounds) eels
1 garlic clove, cut in half
¼ cup olive oil
juice of 1 lemon
4 tablespoons wine vinegar or 2 tablespoons vinegar and 2 tablespoons dry white wine
1 tablespoon fresh rosemary leaves (about 1 sprig) or 1 teaspoon dried rosemary
10 bay leaves
1 teaspoon salt, or to taste
freshly ground pepper
1 dozen fresh mushrooms (approximate), cleaned
1 dozen cherry tomatoes

If the eel is to be cooked in a skillet, remove the skin (page 234). If using an outdoor or indoor grill (which is the best way), leave the skin on.

Cut the eels in 2-inch pieces.

Rub a deep dish with the garlic clove and discard the clove. Mix the oil, lemon juice, and vinegar together, and put this dressing in the dish. Arrange the eels in the dish and sprinkle them with the rosemary leaves, 2 crumbled bay leaves, salt, and pepper. Marinate the eels for at least an hour, turning and basting them from time to time.

Arrange the eels on skewers alternately with the mushrooms, cherry tomatoes, and pieces of bay leaf.

If you are using a skillet, barely coat it with oil; when it is hot, arrange the skewers in it. Cook, turning and basting frequently with the marinade, for 10 to 15 minutes or until the eel pieces are cooked. The flesh flakes like fish flesh.

If you are cooking on a grill, place the eels on skewers on the grill 4 to 5 inches above the coals. Grill until cooked, about 8 minutes, depending on the eels' size. Baste and turn frequently. Serve on toasted Italian bread slightly moistened with marinade. For 4.

Baked Grouper

scorfano al forno

In the Mediterranean, the *scorfano rosso* is used as one of the solid fish in soups and stews. Its Atlantic cousin, the grouper, is used a great deal for frozen fish filets, bearing no name whatsoever. But if you are lucky enough to live where grouper is sold, either in filets from the larger fish or whole if small, here are two recipes that are also equally good with sea bass or red snapper.

1 2-kilo, 700-gram (6-
  pound) grouper or 2 filets
  of the same weight
1 sprig fresh rosemary or 1
  teaspoon dried rosemary
3 small bay leaves
2 garlic cloves, peeled
1 ½ teaspoons salt, or to
  taste
freshly ground pepper
½ cup olive oil
1 teaspoon dried oregano
5 sprigs Italian parsley
1 tablespoon wine vinegar
¾ cup plain tomato juice
100 grams (3 ounces)
  black Sicilian olives

Have the fish cleaned, but leave the head and tail on for a more flavorsome dish.

Preheat oven to 200° C (400° F).

Mince the rosemary, bay leaves, and garlic together and sprinkle the mince throughout the cavity (or over the filets). Add 1 teaspoon of the salt and a generous sprinkling of pepper.

Put the oil in a dish just large enough to hold the fish. Add the oregano to the oil. Place the parsley sprigs down the center of the dish. Put the fish on top of the parsley and sprinkle with ½ teaspoon salt and a little more pepper.

Add the vinegar and tomato juice to the dish, and baste the fish three or four times.

Surround the fish with the olives.

Bake in a hot (200° C, 400° F) oven 45 minutes to 1 hour, cover the dish with aluminum foil for the first ½ hour, then remove the foil, baste thoroughly, and continue baking another 15 to 30 minutes. Taste the now diminished sauce for salt, adding more if desired.

Serve the fish with the olives surrounding it and its sauce poured over it. For 6.

Grouper with Tomato Sauce

scorfano coi pomodori

2 teaspoons salt, or to taste

freshly ground pepper

1½ kilos (3¼ pounds) grouper filets

225 grams (½ pound) peeled plum tomatoes, fresh or canned

3 tablespoons olive oil

2 tablespoons chopped Italian parsley

2 bay leaves

¼ teaspoon dried marjoram

2 tablespoons unsalted butter

1 tablespoon all-purpose unbleached flour

Preheat oven to 200° C (400° F).

Salt and pepper the fish filets generously.

Cut the tomatoes in small chunks and put them in a baking dish with the olive oil, parsley, bay leaves, and marjoram.

Add the fish filets to the dish, and turn them back and forth in the oil to coat them well.

Bake in the hot (200° C, 400° F) oven 15 to 20 minutes, turning the filets once. Remove from oven. Place fish on an oven-proof platter.

Pour the sauce from the baking through a food mill into a sauté pan. Mash the butter with the flour and add it to the sauce; cook and stir 4 minutes. Taste for seasoning, and adjust as you wish. Pour the sauce over the fish, and return the fish to the oven for 10 minutes. Serve immediately. For 4.

Baked Stuffed Haddock

merluzzo ripieno

1 large haddock, cleaned
salt to taste
115 grams (4 ounces)
  mushrooms, cleaned
4 stalks celery, washed
2 to 3 tablespoons olive oil
2 to 3 slices day-old Italian
  bread, crustless, cubed
1 to 2 teaspoons salt, depending on size of fish
freshly ground pepper
10 sprigs Italian parsley
2 lemons

Preheat oven to 220°C (425°F).

If you are cooking for a crowd and want a spectacular dish, buy a very large haddock and have the fish man leave the head and tail on the fish; if you are serving 4, choose a 2-pound fish without head and tail.

With a very sharp knife and working from the inside of the fish, cut the flesh away from the spines on both sides of the backbone. Sever the bone just under the head, and lift it out. This should remove most of the bones but most likely not every single one. Be careful not to cut all the way through and pierce the back skin. Open up the fish and sprinkle it with a small amount of salt.

Slice or process the mushrooms into thick slices.

Cut the celery stalks in half lengthwise and slice them as you did the mushrooms.

Put the olive oil in a sauté pan and brown the bread cubes. Add the mushrooms and celery, sautéing until the mushrooms give up their natural juices. Sprinkle with a small amount of salt and pepper.

Remove the bread-celery-mushroom mixture from the heat. Coarsely chop the leaves of half the parsley and stir them into the celery mixture.

Put this stuffing on half the fish, fold the other half over it, and secure with small skewers. Sew the fish shut with kitchen needle and string. Remove skewers.

Place a piece of aluminum foil in the bottom of a baking dish just large enough to hold the fish. Place the last of the parsley sprigs on the foil. Put the fish on top of the parsley.

Bake 20 to 25 minutes (or about 10 minutes

per pound of total fish) in a hot (220° C, 425° F) oven.

With two spatulas remove the fish from the baking dish and put it on a warm platter. Remove the string.

Sprinkle with the juice of half a lemon. Serve with wedges of remaining lemon. For 4 to 8, depending on the fish.

Boiled Lobster
aragosta lessa

1 large live lobster (1 kilo, 800 grams, or about 4 pounds)

abundant salted water in your largest pot

1 onion, peeled and quartered

1 carrot, peeled

3 bay leaves

10 sprigs Italian parsley

10 peppercorns

½ cup wine vinegar

extra parsley, celery leaves, hearts of lettuce, watercress, lemons, olives, capers or hard-cooked eggs, for decoration

1 recipe *maionese* (pages 30 to 32)

This is a recipe for the occasional big lobster. Prepared ahead of time, chilled thoroughly, partially removed from its shell, the dish can be rather spectacular. Heavy or large lobsters should cook 19 to 21 minutes per kilo (9 to 10 minutes per pound) after the water has returned to a boil.

For the nicest results, tie the lobster to a straight stick or wooden spoon to keep the tail straight during cooking.

Bring the water to a boil, add all the flavorings (including the vinegar), and put the lobster in to cook. When the water comes back to a boil, cook 30 minutes, or 40 minutes, for a 2½-kilo (5-pound) lobster.

Remove the lobster from the pot and, when cool enough to handle, remove the tail carefully.

With very sharp scissors, cut open the shell on the underside of the tail and extract and save the meat. (Remove the dark digestive tract that runs along the center.)

Cut the tail meat in ½-inch rounds.

Empty the body and discard the entrails, but save any coral (roe).

Remove the claws and extract the meat from them. Leave the legs attached to the now-empty body.

Place the body on a platter surrounded by parsley, celery leaves, or lettuce. Fill cavity where tail was attached with parsley or watercress.

Place the meat of the claws in position at the top of the body. Make a line of tail-meat slices to replace the tail. Place any remaining slices of tail meat decoratively around the edge of the platter. Add olives or capers or hard-cooked egg slices, as you wish, to complete the platter. Serve with *maionese* on the side and wedges of lemon. For 6 to 8, depending on how substantial the rest of the meal will be.

Skewers of Monkfish, Mushrooms, and Tomatoes

spiedini di rana pescatrice

1 kilo (2 pounds) monkfish in 3 slices, about ¾ inch thick

2 green sweet peppers, cored and cut in 1½-inch squares

225 grams (½ pound) large brown mushrooms, washed, stems removed

1½ dozen cherry tomatoes, washed, hulls removed

½ cup olive oil

½ cup dry white wine

2 tablespoons snipped fresh or freeze-dried chives

1 tablespoon chopped Italian parsley

1 teaspoon fresh rosemary leaves or ½ teaspoon dried rosemary

½ teaspoon dried oregano

freshly ground pepper

Trim the fish slices of the central bone and the skin. Cut the fish in 1½-inch squares.

Place a piece of green pepper at one end of a skewer. Add a mushroom, tomato, piece of fish, tomato, mushroom, fish, tomato, mushroom, fish, mushroom, tomato, and finally a second piece of green pepper. Send another skewer up alongside the first to hold all the pieces well.

Repeat on other skewers; the aim is to get 3 pieces fish on each skewer and begin and end with the pepper, which is sturdy enough to protect the other pieces.

Place the skewers on a platter.

Put oil, wine, herbs, and pepper in a jar, shake well, and pour over the skewers. Let marinate, basting from time to time, for at least ½ hour.

Grill skewers on open grill or in a preheated broiler, turning as one side is cooked, about a total of 6 minutes. Baste with any remaining marinade, and serve when the fish is cooked, the tomatoes and mushrooms just barely cooked, and the peppers still green and crisp. Makes about eight 9-inch skewers. For 4.

Red Mullet, Genoa Style

triglia alla genovese

juice of ½ lemon

1 1-kilo (2-pound) red mullet, cleaned but with head and tail intact

½ garlic clove, peeled and thinly sliced lengthwise

2 basil leaves, chopped coarsely or ¼ teaspoon dried basil

½ teaspoon salt, or to taste

olive oil

2 to 4 teaspoons *pesto* (pages 36 to 39), or to taste

Squeeze the lemon juice into the fish cavity.

Place the garlic and basil and salt in the cavity and fold the fish shut. Skewer the opening.

Brush the fish with olive oil, and place it on a very hot oiled grill.

After about 8 minutes, brush the top side of the fish with more oil, turn the fish, and grill about 8 minutes or until cooked on the second side.

Remove the fish to a work platter, take off the head and tail, and filet the fish.

Dress filets with *pesto* and serve immediately. For 2.

Poached Salmon

salmone in bianco

4 liters (4 quarts) water (approximate)

1 medium onion, peeled

tops of 4 or 5 celery stalks, washed

2 carrots, scrubbed

2 bay leaves

¼ teaspoon dried dill weed or ½ teaspoon minced fresh dill

10 sprigs Italian parsley

8 teaspoons salt

8 peppercorns

½ cup wine vinegar

1 kilo 225 grams (about 2½ pounds) fresh salmon (weight does not include head or tail), wrapped in cheesecloth

1 recipe *maionese* (pages 30 to 32)

Put the water, vegetables, herbs, salt, peppercorns, and vinegar in a large saucepan with a well-fitting cover. Bring to a boil and simmer for at least ½ hour.

Add the salmon, slowly bring to a boil, lower the heat to just barely boiling, cover, and cook 15 minutes. Remove the fish from the pan, place it on a work platter, remove the cheesecloth, and skin the fish while it is still hot. Remove the bones and place the two filets on a serving platter.

Serve chilled or at room temperature with the *maionese*. For 6.

Most of the fish markets we have been in recently tend to prepare the salmon without the head; therefore, the weight in this recipe is listed that way. The timing is 8 minutes for 450 grams (1 pound) headless fish.

Grilled Salmon Steaks

salmone alla griglia

This recipe is exactly like that for grilled swordfish (page 253). Just substitute 4 salmon steaks for the 2 swordfish steaks, and proceed accordingly.

Salmon Trout with Rice and Shrimp

trota salmonata con riso e gamberi

1 onion, peeled and thinly sliced lengthwise

1 large carrot, scrubbed and sliced

5 sprigs Italian parsley

3 bay leaves

2 celery stalks with leaves, washed

2 garlic cloves, peeled

¾ cup white wine vinegar

6 to 8 teaspoons salt

10 peppercorns

1 2- to 2½-kilo (4- to 5½-pound) salmon trout (also called sea trout or weakfish), cleaned and wrapped in cheesecloth

4 tablespoons olive oil

2 cups extra-long-grain rice

4 tablespoons unsalted butter

1 kilo (2 pounds) medium shrimp, peeled and deveined

black olives

1 recipe *maionese* (pages 30 to 32)

A fish this size is best cooked in a fish poacher but, if you do not have one, you can use a roasting pan on top of the stove.

Place enough cold water in the fish poacher to cover the fish, plus 2 cups extra, about ¾ full. Add half the onion slivers; the carrot, parsley, bay leaves, and celery; 1 garlic clove; and the wine vinegar, salt, and peppercorns. Taste after the salt has dissolved, adjusting as necessary. Bring all this to a boil, cover, lower the heat, and let simmer at least ½ hour.

Place the fish in the poacher, bring back to a boil, lower the heat until the water barely ripples, cover, and cook exactly 8 minutes to the pound, about 35 minutes.

When the fish has cooked about 10 minutes, mince the remaining onion and garlic together. Sauté in olive oil in a saucepan or pressure-cooking pan. Add the rice, and cook until it crackles.

Add 2 cups of the fish-cooking liquid and cover the pan. If you are using a normal saucepan, cook 14 minutes. If using a pressure cooker, bring the pressure to 15 pounds, cook 8 minutes, bring the pressure down immediately, uncover, and stir the rice.

In a third pan, sauté the shrimps in the butter until the color is bright coral. Add 3 tablespoons of fish bouillon from the poacher, and cook 3 minutes more.

Place the cooked fish on a work platter and

peel off its skin. If the fish came with its head on, leave it on.

Place the rice around the edge of your serving platter. Put the fish in the middle of the rice. Surround the fish decoratively with shrimp and olives. Serve with the *maionese*. For 8.

Fried Scallops

conchiglie di San Gia-como fritte

1 recipe egg batter (page 27)

1 kilo (2 pounds) sea scal-lops, cleaned and dried

juice of 1 lemon

4 to 5 tablespoons olive oil

1¼ teaspoons salt, or to taste

white pepper to taste

2 tablespoons chopped Italian parsley

vegetable oil for frying

1½ to 2 lemons, cut in wedges

Mix up the egg batter and let it rest for 30 minutes. Stir well before using.

Place the scallops in a dish in one layer and dress them with the lemon, oil, salt, pepper, and parsley. Toss well and let rest for 30 minutes. Dip a few at a time in prepared batter.

Bring a pan with at least 3 inches of vegetable oil to frying temperature (190° C, 375° F) and fry the scallops as they are removed from the batter. When the scallops are golden and crisp, remove them from the frying oil, drain on paper towels, and place in a warm serving dish. When all the scallops are fried, serve with lemon wedges. For 4.

Poached Scallops with Mayonnaise

conchiglie di San Giacomo con maionese

675 grams (1½ pounds) sea scallops, cleaned and dried

2 cups fish broth (page 47)

2 tablespoons olive oil

1 tablespoon white wine vinegar

½ to ¾ teaspoon salt, or to taste

white pepper to taste

1 to 2 tablespoons chopped Italian parsley

½ cup fresh *maionese* (pages 30 to 32), or to taste

If any of the scallops are very large, cut them in half.

Bring the fish broth to boil, place the scallops in the broth, and cook 7 minutes without quite letting the broth boil again.

With a slotted spoon or spatula, lift the scallops out of the broth, drain well, and place in a serving dish.

Dress with oil, vinegar, salt, pepper, and parsley. Toss well. Serve with *maionese*. For 4.

Scallops, Florentine Style

pellegrine alla fiorentina

Vegetables

675 grams (1½ pounds) fresh spinach or 2 285-gram (10-ounce) packages frozen chopped spinach

1 teaspoon salt

2 tablespoons unsalted butter

¼ teaspoon freshly grated nutmeg

3½ cups freshly cooked mashed potatoes or 1 5-serving packet instant Idaho mashed potatoes

2¾ cups milk

¾ teaspoon salt

⅛ teaspoon white pepper

2 tablespoons unsalted butter

1 tablespoon grated Parmesan cheese

Scallops

1 kilo (2 pounds) sea scallops, cleaned and dried

2 tablespoons unsalted butter

1 tablespoon olive oil

2 tablespoons snipped fresh or freeze-dried chives

½ garlic clove, peeled and minced

(continued)

Wash fresh spinach well, discard the heaviest of the stems, and cook the remainder in the water that clings to the leaves. Add the salt, and cook and stir until just tender. Drain well. Squeeze dry. (Or cook the frozen spinach in the least possible amount — about 2 tablespoons — of boiling salted water until just tender. Drain well and squeeze out all remaining water.)

Place cooked spinach in a saucepan with the butter. Sprinkle with nutmeg, and heat and stir until the butter has melted and coated the spinach.

If you are using fresh mashed potatoes, season them with the salt, pepper, butter, and cheese. Add as much milk as needed to make smooth whipped potatoes.

If you are using instant potatoes, heat up the milk, salt, pepper, and butter until almost boiling. Beat in the instant potatoes until smooth. Stir in the cheese; remove from heat.

For the scallops: melt the butter in the olive oil in a sauté pan large enough to hold all the scallops in one layer. Add the chives and minced garlic and parsley. Add the scallops. Pour the white wine over the scallops; add salt and pepper. Bring to a boil, cover, lower the heat, and cook 4 minutes.

Preheat oven to 230° C (450° F).

Divide the spinach equally into 6 oven-proof au gratin dishes. Using a pastry bag with a wide

1 tablespoon minced Italian
  parsley
½ cup dry white wine
½ teaspoon salt, or to taste
⅛ teaspoon white pepper
2 tablespoons quick-mixing
  flour
⅔ cup whole milk
⅓ cup medium (all-pur-
  pose) cream
6 tablespoons grated Par-
  mesan cheese

nozzle, pipe the mashed potatoes around the edge of the spinach. (You can arrange it with a spoon or fork, but the pastry bag is better.)

Take the scallops from their pan, reserving the juices, and place them on the spinach.

Add flour to the scallop pan, mix with a whisk, add the milk and cream, and bring to a boil slowly, whisking all the time. Taste for salt and pepper, and correct to please. Cook at least 4 minutes.

Pour the sauce over the scallops in each dish. Sprinkle with Parmesan cheese.

Bake in a hot (230° C, 450° F) oven for 5 minutes or until slightly golden here and there. Let stand a few minutes before eating or you will burn your tongue and miss the combination of flavors and textures.

Each of the main ingredients of this dish may be prepared ahead of time, with the whole assembled about 15 minutes before serving. For 6.

Baked Sea Bass

branzino al forno

1 1½-kilo (3-pound) sea
  bass, cleaned but with
  head and tail intact
1 cup dry white wine
1 shot cognac
leaves of 5 sprigs Italian
  parsley, minced
1 small onion, peeled and
  minced
1 garlic clove, peeled and
  minced
1½ to 2 teaspoons salt
white pepper to taste
2 pounds mussels
2 tablespoons unsalted
  butter

Place the fish in a stainless steel or oven-proof glass baking dish. Add the wine, cognac, and minced aromatic vegetables. Turn the fish over and over to moisten it well. Add the salt and pepper and let it marinate 1 hour.

Preheat oven to 190° C (375° F).

Clean the mussels and place them around the bass. Cut the butter in small pieces and place them on and around the fish. Baste with the marinade.

Bake in the oven for ½ hour or until the fish is cooked. Remove fish and mussels to a hot platter. Strain the pan's liquids and serve with the fish. For 4 to 6.

Poached Sea Bass

spigola in bianco

1 2-kilo (4-pound) sea bass, cleaned but with head and tail intact

3 to 4 liters (3 to 4 quarts) water

3 teaspoons salt

1 carrot, scrubbed

1 garlic clove, peeled

5 sprigs Italian parsley

1 bay leaf

5 peppercorns

½ lemon, cut in wedges or slices

1 cup dry white wine

1 recipe *maionese* (pages 30 to 32) or *salsa verde* (pages 33 to 34)

Rinse the fish thoroughly. Wrap it in kitchen cheesecloth. In a fish poacher or other suitable pan, bring the water with all the rest of the ingredients to a boil and simmer for ½ hour.

Add the fish to the pan; bring up the heat until the water is barely boiling; and cook, partially covered, at just under a boil for 20 to 24 minutes.

Remove the fish from its pan to a hot platter. Remove the cheesecloth, bone and skin the fish, and divide into 4 filets.

Serve hot with *maionese* or *salsa verde*. For 6.

Shrimp and Scallops

gamberi e cape sante

450 grams (1 pound) scallops

450 grams (1 pound) large shrimp

1 garlic clove, peeled and quartered

4 to 5 tablespoons olive oil

¾ teaspoon salt

freshly ground pepper, white if possible

1 tablespoon capers, rinsed and drained

5 to 6 sprigs Italian parsley, chopped

10 drops Tabasco sauce

2 tablespoons brandy

juice of 1 lemon

Wash the scallops thoroughly. If they are very large, cut them in half. Peel, clean, and rinse the shrimps. Pat both fish dry with paper towels.

Cook the garlic in olive oil over medium heat until golden, then discard. Let the oil cool a moment or two.

Add scallops and shrimp, raise the heat, and sauté for 4 minutes, turning occasionally. Sprinkle with salt and pepper, and sauté 2 minutes more.

Mince the capers and parsley leaves together to make at least 3 full, rounded tablespoons, and add to the pan along with the Tabasco. Cook 1 minute.

Add the brandy and lemon juice. Cook and stir 2 minutes. Taste for salt, and adjust to please. Serve hot. For 4 generous servings.

Baked Red Snapper

pesce al forno

2 to 4 red snappers, depending on sizes available; total weight about 2 kilos (4½ pounds)

4 tablespoons olive oil (approximate)

1½ to 2 teaspoons salt, or to taste

freshly ground pepper

5 sprigs Italian parsley

4 bay leaves, or 1 sprig fresh rosemary (or 1 teaspoon dried) and 1 garlic clove, peeled and minced

juice of 1 lemon or ¼ to ½ cup dry white wine

1 lemon, cut in wedges

Have the fish cleaned, but leave the heads and tails on.

Preheat oven to 200° C (400° F).

Put the olive oil in a baking dish large enough to hold the fish comfortably. Sprinkle a bit of salt and pepper into the oil.

Place the parsley sprigs to cover the oil.

Sprinkle the cavities of the fish with salt and pepper. Place ½ bay leaf in each cavity and the remaining bay leaves in the baking dish; or sprinkle the cavities with half the rosemary and garlic mince and put the rest of the mince around and about in the oil.

Put the dressed fish in the baking dish and place in a hot (200° C, 400° F) oven. After cooking 10 minutes, baste with the oil in the dish and add the lemon juice or wine. Cook another 10 minutes, basting with the oil and lemon in the dish. Cook another 5 minutes (or until the fish is cooked through at the fleshiest part) and remove the fish to a serving platter.

Moisten the fish with some of the baking-dish juices. Add the last of the salt and pepper. Serve with lemon wedges. For 4.

This same method can be used with bluefish or almost any fish weighing not more than 1 kilo (2.2 pounds, to be exact). The parsley sprigs keep the fish from sticking to the pan. Rosemary can be substituted for the bay leaves, as above; or you can make a mince of capers, parsley, and a small clove of garlic. Or, if you prefer, try oregano or fresh sage. Flavoring fish, however, must be done with a gentle hand.

Squid

calamari

Two of the most familiar mollusks in the Italian kitchen are squid and cuttlefish — two cousins whose larger cousin goes under the name of octopus. The delicate flesh of the squid and cuttlefish lends itself to sauces for pasta and rice; by itself it is a prize for any menu, whether fried, stuffed, stewed, or served as a salad. (Many of our favorite recipes have already appeared in *The Romagnolis' Table* and *The Romagnolis' Meatless Cookbook.*)

By and large, you can obtain fresh squid in most fish markets, and frozen squid from California and Taiwan is often found in supermarkets, sometimes already cleaned. The fresh ones sometimes are cleaned by the fish market, but most of the time we do it ourselves. It is not hard.

With a sharp knife, remove the tentacles (the richest part of the mollusk) by cutting between them and the eyes. Push out and discard the mouth or beak, which is hidden in the center of the tentacles. Cut the tentacles in half, if large, and put all the pieces to dry on paper toweling.

Hold the body or mantle of the squid under running water and with one hand squeeze the lower body. With the other hand pull off and discard the head. With it will go most of the innards. Peel off and discard the mantle's thin membrane. From the body pull out and discard the transparent quill-like bone. (If you are preparing cuttlefish, follow the same procedure; you will see the bone is opaque white.) Rinse the body well and place to dry on toweling.

Squid or cuttlefish may be cut in rings or squares or left whole for stuffing. Octopus, on the other hand, is a tougher mollusk and must be beaten well to tenderize before cooking. The tentacles are then either dipped in batter and fried or boiled in salted water and served with oil and lemon juice.

Fried Squid

calamari fritti

1½ kilos (3 pounds) fresh or frozen small squid, cleaned (page 251)
flour for dredging
vegetable oil for deep frying
salt to taste
2 lemons, cut in wedges

Cut the tentacles of the squid in half, the bodies in rings.

Put about ½ cup of flour in a heavy plastic or sturdy paper bag and shake the squid to coat them thoroughly with flour.

Bring frying oil to 190° C (375° F) and fry a handful or so of squid pieces at a time. Do not overcrowd the pan. Turn the squid with a slotted spoon as they become golden.

Remove to drain on absorbent paper as soon as the squid are golden brown and crisp. Sprinkle with salt. Serve with lemon. For 3 or 4.

Squid, Venetian Style

seppie alla veneziana

1 kilogram (2 pounds) squid, fresh or frozen
1 medium onion, peeled
1 garlic clove, peeled
6 tablespoons olive oil
½ cup dry white wine
1 teaspoon tomato paste
½ cup warm water
salt to taste
3 tablespoons minced Italian parsley
¼ teaspoon flour (optional) worked into
½ teaspoon unsalted butter (optional)

Clean the squid (page 251), cut the bodies in ½-inch rings and the larger tentacles in half lengthwise.

Mince the onion and garlic together and sauté them in olive oil until translucent. Add the squid, and cook over moderate heat until the tentacles open up and curl and all the pieces change to a pink and purple color.

Add the wine, stir, cover, and simmer for 10 minutes.

Dilute the tomato paste in warm water, add to the squid, raise the heat, and cook another 10 minutes, uncovered, or until tender. Taste for salt, and add to please. Stir in the parsley.

If the pan sauce is excessively liquid by the time the squid are done, either scoop the squid out onto a warm plate and let the sauce boil down or add the optional flour and butter and cook gently, stirring, until the flour cannot be tasted and the sauce has thickened (about 4 minutes). For 4.

Baked Swordfish with Potatoes

pescespada al forno con patate

unsalted butter

2 450-grams each (1 pound) swordfish steaks, fresh, if possible, or frozen and thawed

4 medium potatoes, peeled and thinly sliced

4 tablespoons chopped Italian parsley

4 small onions, peeled and thinly sliced lengthwise

1 sprig fresh rosemary or 1 teaspoon dried rosemary

1½ teaspoon salt, or to taste

freshly ground pepper to taste

3 tablespoons olive oil

juice of 1½ lemons

Preheat oven to 220° C (425° F).

Butter a baking dish large enough to hold the 2 steaks.

Make 2 small cuts in the skins of each steak to prevent curling during baking.

Put a layer of potato slices in the bottom of the dish. Sprinkle the potatoes with 2 tablespoons of the parsley. Place the swordfish on top of the potatoes. Sprinkle with onions, remaining parsley, rosemary, salt, and pepper. Dribble olive oil over everything.

Bake for 20 to 25 minutes, basting three times during baking. When the swordfish is done and its flesh has turned from pink to white, add the lemon juice and baste again thoroughly. Taste for salt in the sauce, and adjust if necessary. For 4.

Grilled Swordfish

pescespada alla griglia

2 450-gram (1-pound) 1-inch-thick fresh swordfish steaks

6 tablespoons unsalted butter

4 tablespoons chopped Italian parsley

1½ teaspoons salt

freshly ground pepper to taste

juice of 1½ lemons

Preheat broiler 15 minutes, or start a grill going about ½ hour before cooking time.

Make 2 cuts in the skin of each steak to prevent curling during grilling.

Mash the butter and chopped parsley together. Put 1 to 1½ tablespoons of the parsley-butter on each steak. Place the swordfish on the hot grill or in the hot broiler and cook it 7 minutes.

Remove the steaks to a serving platter and sprinkle with salt, pepper, and lemon juice. Serve immediately. For 4.

Sautéed Swordfish

pescespada in padella

3 to 4 tablespoons olive oil

2 sprigs fresh rosemary or 2 teaspoons dried rosemary

2 450-gram (1-pound) swordfish steaks, 1 inch thick

½ medium-sized sweet onion, peeled and sliced in thin rounds

juice of 1 ½ to 2 lemons

1 ½ teaspoons salt, or to taste

freshly ground pepper

Heat the olive oil over moderate heat in a pan large enough to hold the fish steaks. Add half the rosemary. Add the fish.

Put the onion rings on either side of the steaks. Sprinkle with salt; add a generous amount of pepper and the juice of 1 lemon. Cook for 3 minutes, then turn the fish. Add a bit more salt and pepper and as much additional lemon juice as you wish.

Continue cooking about 5 more minutes or until the fish, when cut, has lost its pink color.

Remove from heat, and serve. For 4.

Broiled Turbot

rombo alla griglia

1 recipe parsley butter (page 29)

4 fresh basil leaves, chopped or ½ teaspoon dried basil

2 large (450-gram, 1-pound) filets of turbot (See note below)

1 lemon

½ teaspoon salt, or to taste

white pepper to taste

Preheat broiler for 10 minutes.

Make the parsley butter and add the basil to it.

With a large piece of aluminum foil, shape a shallow boat to hold the 2 pieces of fish. Butter the foil lightly with about half the herbed butter. Place the filets in the boat, dotting with the remaining herbed butter; or, if you wish, save just a small bit for after the fish is broiled.

Place the fish in its boat in the broiler and broil it at least 7 minutes or until the fish is cooked through, the butter melted, and the herbs scattered.

Remove the fish from its foil and slide it on to a hot serving platter. Dot with any remaining butter.

Cut the lemon in half; sprinkle juice of one half over the fish, and cut the other half in wedges.

Sprinkle the fish with salt and pepper and serve immediately with wedges of lemon. For 4.

Note: This method also works easily and well with fresh cod, hake, halibut, bluefish, flounder, salmon, and swordfish.

Vegetables and Salads

Verdure ed insalate

It was only three or four centuries ago that the Americas sent Europe, and Italy, their first tomatoes, potatoes, red peppers, and beans. How Italy and Europe had managed without these in their fields and markets is hard to imagine.

The uses Italy alone has found for these once exotic ingredients are varied, extensive, and, we think, glorious. Like the arrangements of the colorful market stalls up and down the peninsula, the vegetable dishes are grand blends of color and imagination.

But Italy, like many other countries, no longer depends solely on the fresh market. Frozen vegetables — peas, green beans, tiny onions, squash, to say nothing of the ubiquitous chopped spinach — are also enjoyed.

And yet the Italian tradition of seeking the freshest and earliest of each season's produce is held to as much as possible; and cooking times are regulated to preserve color, texture, and flavor. Vegetable dishes are as thoughtfully made as any dishes of meat, fish, or poultry. They are called *contorni* — that is, they go with and often play a major part in second courses; they do not merely stand apart as "side dishes."

Apple and Onion Rings

anelli di mele e cipolle

1 tart apple
1 medium-sized sweet onion, peeled
2 tablespoons unsalted butter
⅛ teaspoon salt, or to taste
⅛ teaspoon freshly ground pepper
¼ teaspoon ground cinnamon
1 tablespoon sugar
juice of ¼ lemon

Core the apple without quartering it, and cut it into rings about ¾ inch wide.

Cut the onion in round slices slightly thinner than the apple rings.

Melt the butter in a large skillet and in it sauté the onions until they are barely limp. Remove onions from skillet and set aside.

In the same skillet arrange the apple rings in one layer and sauté over medium heat, so that the rings are light brown on the outside yet firm inside. Add the salt and pepper, the cinnamon, and the sugar. As soon as one side of the apple rings begins to turn color, turn them with a spatula and put the onion rings back in the skillet.

Tilt the skillet back and forth. (If need be — depending on the quality of the apples — add another teaspoon of butter.) When the second side of the apples is beginning to brown, turn them over again, onion rings and all, and cook for a minute at high heat.

Add the lemon juice, and tilt the skillet so that butter and lemon blend into a sauce. Remove from the fire and arrange on a serving plate or around the meat they are to accompany. Apple and onion rings are especially good with pork and boiled beef. For 2. For more multiply the ingredients accordingly.

Artichokes with Peas

carciofi con piselli

1 large artichoke, cleaned and trimmed (pages 4 to 5) and cut in ¼-inch wedges
juice of 1 lemon
1 small onion, peeled and minced
2 slices *prosciutto* or ham, cut in strips
2 to 3 tablespoons olive oil
⅓ package (85 grams, 3 ounces) frozen tiny peas
½ cup chicken broth (page 44)
salt to taste
freshly ground pepper to taste

Put the artichoke wedges to soak in water to cover, to which you have added the juice of a lemon.

Sauté the minced onion and the *prosciutto* in the olive oil until the onion is limp and translucent, about 5 minutes. Drain and dry the artichoke wedges, add them to the onion and ham mixture, and cook about 8 minutes, turning a couple of times.

Add the peas and the broth, raise the heat to boil the broth, then lower it, simmering it until the peas and artichokes are tender, about 6 more minutes. Serve hot.

For 1. For more multiply ingredients accordingly. But use only as much oil as is needed to sauté nicely.

Golden-Fried Artichokes

carciofi fritti dorati

4 medium artichokes
2 lemons
¾ cup all-purpose unbleached flour
½ teaspoon salt
3 medium eggs
vegetable oil for frying

Clean and trim the artichokes (pages 4 to 5) and cut them in thin wedges. Put the wedges in cold water with the juice of one lemon.

Mix flour and salt in a small bowl. Beat the eggs in a second small bowl.

Bring the vegetable oil, at least 3 inches deep, to 190° C (375° F), hot enough to make a drop of egg sizzle instantly on contact.

Dredge a handful of artichoke wedges in the salt-flour mixture; dip them one by one into the beaten egg, then drop them into the hot oil.

Place only as many pieces in the oil as will fit comfortably, so that you can turn them easily from side to side.

When the artichokes are a toasty brown, remove them, and let them drain on paper toweling. Serve hot with the second lemon, quartered. For 4 as a side dish.

Artichoke Casserole

parmigiana di carciofi

Sauce

1 medium onion, peeled, halved, and thinly sliced lengthwise

3 tablespoons olive oil

4 cups peeled plum tomatoes, fresh or canned, put through a food mill

1 teaspoon salt, or to taste

6 fresh basil leaves, minced or 1 teaspoon dried basil

½ teaspoon sugar (optional)

Artichokes

1 recipe *Carciofi fritti dorati* using 4 artichokes (pages 4 to 5)

340 grams (12 ounces) whole milk *mozzarella* cheese, coarsely grated or shredded

⅓ cup grated Parmesan cheese

⅓ cup unseasoned bread crumbs

1 ½ tablespoons unsalted butter

In a skillet, cook the onion slivers in olive oil until wilted and translucent. Add the plum tomatoes, salt, and basil. Bring to a boil, lower the heat, and cook, uncovered, 25 minutes or until the sauce has thickened. Taste, and, if the tomatoes seem too pungent (some have more acidity, no matter what the brand), add the sugar and cook another 5 minutes.

Meanwhile, prepare the artichokes (pages 4 to 5) and golden-fry them.

When the sauce and artichokes are ready, place 3 to 4 tablespoons of sauce in the bottom of an oven-proof casserole. Add a layer of fried artichokes, another layer of sauce, then a sprinkling of *mozzarella*. Repeat until all the ingredients are used, finishing with top layers of sauce and *mozzarella*.

Mix the Parmesan with the bread crumbs, and top the casserole with the mixture. Dot with butter.

Bake at 190° C (375° F) for 30 minutes or until the top is lightly golden and crusty. Let cool 15 minutes before serving. For 6 to 8 as a second course or main dish.

Artichoke Pie

torta di carciofi

4 medium artichokes

1½ lemons

1 onion, peeled, halved, and thinly sliced length- wise

3 tablespoons olive oil

1 teaspoon salt

3 slices day-old Italian bread, crustless

½ cup milk

2 large eggs

5 tablespoons grated Par- mesan cheese

½ pound *ricotta*

340 grams (12 ounces) puff pastry (pages 320 to 323)

2 tablespoons unsalted butter (approximate)

Clean and trim the artichokes (pages 4 to 5) and cut them into thin wedges. Place in a bowl of cold water with the juice of 1 lemon.

Sauté the onion slivers in the olive oil until limp and translucent.

Drain the artichokes, and add them to the onions with ½ teaspoon of the salt; continue cooking about 8 minutes or until tender. Add the juice of the remaining half lemon, cook and stir another minute, then set aside to cool.

Shred the bread into the milk in a mixing bowl. Let stand a few minutes. Add the eggs, the Parmesan cheese, and the last of the salt. Beat with an egg beater until smooth. Add the *ricotta,* and beat again. Fold in the cooled arti- chokes and their sautéeing juices.

Preheat oven to 200° C (400° F).

If you are using your own puff pastry (pages 320 to 323): divide it into three equal pieces. Roll one piece to cover the bottom and sides of a cake pan about 8 inches in diameter and 2 inches deep. Butter and flour the pan, and place the first piece of pastry in it. Prick the pastry here and there with the tines of a fork. Fill with the *ricotta*-artichoke mixture. Roll the second and third pieces of pastry to cover the filling and put them in place, one on top of the other. Go around the edges of the pan with a pastry cutter to crimp the bottom crust together with the top two.

If you are using commercially prepared puff pastry: roll out one sheet to cover the bottom and sides of a 7″ × 10″ baking dish. Butter and flour the dish, and place the rolled pastry in it. Prick the crust here and there with a fork. Add the filling.

Roll out the other two sheets of pastry to cover the filling and put them in place, one on top of another. Go around the edge of the dish with a pastry cutter to seal the crusts together.

Roll out the leftover pastry cuttings; make an artichoke cutout for decoration.

Pierce the top crusts with a fine skewer or cake tester.

Brush the top with melted butter and gently press the decoration in place. Bake on the lower rack in a hot oven for 1 hour 10 minutes or until puffed and golden brown. Let cool 15 minutes before serving. For 6 to 8.

Asparagus or Easter Pie

torta di pasqua

1 285-gram (10-ounce) package frozen cut asparagus or same amount fresh, root end broken off and discarded

3 slices day-old Italian bread, crustless

½ cup milk

3 large eggs

½ teaspoon salt

¼ teaspoon freshly grated nutmeg

5 tablespoons grated Parmesan cheese

340 grams (12 ounces) *ricotta*

450 grams (1 pound) puff pastry (pages 320 to 323)

2 tablespoons unsalted butter (approximate)

Shred the bread into the milk to soak. Let stand about 5 minutes.

Cook the asparagus in boiling salted water until just barely tender. Drain well and let it dry on paper toweling; then cut in 1-inch long pieces (if using fresh variety).

Add the eggs, salt, nutmeg, and Parmesan cheese to the bread and milk. Beat with an egg beater until smooth. Fold in the *ricotta* and beat again; then taste for seasonings, adjusting if necessary. Fold in the drained asparagus.

Preheat oven to 200° C (400° F).

If you are using your own puff pastry (pages 320 to 323): cut it into three pieces, one slightly larger than the other two. Roll the largest piece to fit the bottom and sides of a two-quart casserole about 8 inches in diameter. Butter and flour the casserole, and lay the pastry in it. Prick the pastry with the tines of a fork or point of a cake tester. Put the *ricotta* filling on this layer of pastry. Roll the second and third pieces of pastry to cover the *ricotta,* one above another, and the edges in order to seal the top to the bottom. Roll any scraps together, and cut out teardrop-shaped pieces to put around the edge as a design. Brush the top of the pastry with melted butter. Place the design pieces on top, brushing them with butter. Pierce the top layers of pastry with a cake tester. Chill 10 minutes.

Place in the hot (200° C, 400° F) oven for 1 hour 10 minutes. Use the lower rack in the oven to make sure the bottom crust bakes evenly. Let cool 15 minutes before serving.

If you are using frozen commercial puff pastry: your baking dish should be 7″ × 10″ (approximately)

and at least 3 inches deep. Thaw the pastry 10 minutes, roll it out, and use one sheet for the bottom layer and the other two for top layers. Trim, decorate, and bake as above. For 6 to 8.

Avocado, Asparagus, and Artichoke Salad

insalata di avocado, asparagi, e carciofi

450 grams (1 pound) thin
   asparagus
4 artichokes
½ lemon
½ teaspoon salt
3 peppercorns
1 bay leaf
2 ripe avocados
225 grams (½ pound) fresh
   ricotta
3 tablespoons olive oil
1 tablespoon lemon juice
¼ teaspoon salt, or to taste
white pepper

Break off and discard the root ends of the asparagus stalks, then boil the asparagus in a wide saucepan in salted water to cover for 5 minutes or until tender but still crisp. Drain thoroughly and spread on absorbent toweling.

Prepare the artichokes (pages 4 to 5) and cut them into wedges. Boil until tender in water with the half lemon, salt, peppercorns, and bay leaf. Drain thoroughly and spread on paper toweling.

Cut the avocados in half, remove and discard the pit, and peel the halves.

Fill the avocado halves with *ricotta* and put them in the center of a serving plate. Arrange the asparagus stalks and artichoke wedges around the avocado.

Shake the olive oil with the lemon juice, salt, white pepper. Dribble dressing over the entire serving plate. For 4.

Belgian Endive– Cress Salad

insalata d'indivia belga e crescione

4 heads Belgian endive
1 large bunch watercress
½ garlic clove, cut in half (optional)
4 tablespoons olive oil
salt
freshly ground pepper
2 tablespoons red wine vinegar

Trim the endive by cutting it in half lengthwise and taking out the small core at the base. Wash in cold water, drain, and cut it into bite-size pieces.

Break off the most sturdy of the cress stems and discard. Wash and drain the rest.

If using garlic, rub the salad bowl with it and discard. Put the endive, cress, and olive oil in the bowl and toss the greens well.

Add salt and pepper to taste. Add the vinegar; toss again. Serve immediately. For 4.

Brussels Sprouts and Onions

cavolini di Bruxelles e cipolline

225 grams (½ pound) fresh Brussels sprouts or frozen equivalent
225 grams (½ pound) small onions or frozen equivalent
3 tablespoons unsalted butter
½ beef bouillon cube dissolved in ¼ cup hot water
¼ teaspoon dried marjoram
¼ teaspoon freshly grated nutmeg
freshly ground pepper
85 grams (3 ounces) cooked ham, cut in julienne strips

Clean the sprouts carefully, discarding ragged outer leaves. Cut off the stems and core or scoop out the center of the core with the point of a knife.

Boil in salted water 8 minutes.

Peel and trim the onions; boil in salted water until tender (small frozen ones no longer than 5 minutes).

Drain the onions and sprouts thoroughly.

Melt the butter in a sauté pan, add the bouillon, the vegetables, the herbs, and pepper (this last to please). Cook 2 to 3 minutes. Add the ham strips, mix well, and serve. For 4.

Stuffed Cabbage

cavolo ripieno

Stuffing

- 340 grams (12 ounces) tur-key breast or 6 small tur-key-breast cutlets
- 170 grams (6 ounces) ground beef
- 5 sprigs Italian parsley
- 2 slices day-old Italian bread, crustless
- ¼ cup milk
- 1 frankfurter (German type, with natural casing)
- 5 tablespoons grated Par-mesan or *Romano* cheese (to taste)
- 1 egg
- grated rind of ½ lemon
- ¼ teaspoon freshly grated nutmeg
- ½ teaspoon salt
- freshly grated pepper
- 1 small onion, peeled and minced
- 2 tablespoons unsalted butter

Cabbage

- 1 Savoy cabbage
- 3 cups chicken-beef broth (pages 45 to 46)

Sauce

- 1 cup light *besciamella* (pages 41 to 42)
- 1 teaspoon Dijon mustard
- 1 teaspoon English mus-tard

Coarsely chop the turkey meat. Mince the beef. Mix the two meats together in a large mixing bowl. Chop the parsley leaves, and add them to the meats. Squeeze the bread dry after it has soaked in milk a few moments and shred it into the meats. Mince the frankfurter, and add it to the meats.

Now add cheese, egg, lemon rind, nutmeg, salt, and a generous amount of pepper.

Sauté the onion in butter until limp, and add both to the mixing bowl. Mix thoroughly.

To check for seasonings, cook a little bit of the mixture in the onion pan and check the taste. Add extra salt and pepper to please.

To assemble: with a very sharp knife, cut out as much of the core on the underside of the cab-bage as you can without detaching leaves.

Place the cabbage in a big pot of boiling salted water. Bring back to a boil and cook 10 minutes.

Drain, cool, and place on a large piece of kitchen cheesecloth.

Gently loosen the outer leaves one by one from the top until you have almost opened the vegetable and it resembles a green rose.

As you work closer to the center, the smaller leaves become difficult to open. Slice out a bit of this center ball of leaves and scoop out a hole about as big as a large egg.

Fill the hole with stuffing. Tuck small bits of stuffing between as many leaves as you can. Fold each leaf back in place.

When the filling is all used, fold the outer leaves in place and tie the stuffed cabbage in-side the cheesecloth.

Bring the chicken-beef broth to a boil.

Put the cabbage into a casserole just deep and wide enough to hold it. Pour the broth over the cabbage, cover the casserole, and cook 1½ hours in a moderate (177° C, 350° F) oven.

Remove the cabbage from the casserole and let it cool 10 minutes before removing the cheesecloth. Cut into wedges. Serve topped with hot mustard-flavored *besciamella*. For 6 to 8.

Carrots and Mushrooms

carote e funghi

450 grams (1 pound) carrots, peeled

340 grams (12 ounces) mushrooms, cleaned

4 tablespoons unsalted butter

½ teaspoon salt

4 tablespoons chopped Italian parsley

juice of 1 lemon

white pepper to taste

Cut the carrots in julienne strips.

Bring abundant salted water to a boil, add the carrots, and, when the water comes back to a boil, cook 2 minutes. Drain immediately.

Slice the mushrooms and cook them 2 minutes in the butter. Add the salt. Add the cooked carrots, parsley, lemon juice, and pepper. Stir and cook 1 minute. Toss well, and serve. For 4 to 6.

Baked Eggplant

melanzane al forno

1 450-gram (1 pound) egg-
plant

salt

1 medium onion, peeled
and quartered

3 sprigs Italian parsley

4 fresh basil leaves

85 grams (3 ounces) *pro-
sciutto* or cooked ham,
cut in strips

4 tablespoons olive oil

2 cups canned peeled plum
tomatoes (6 to 7 toma-
toes with juice)

1 teaspoon vinegar

¼ teaspoon sugar

freshly ground pepper

flour for dredging

vegetable oil for frying

salt to taste

2 slices (85 grams, 3
ounces) *Emmenthal* or
Groviera or Muenster
cheese

4 tablespoons coarse un-
seasoned bread crumbs

2 teaspoons grated Parme-
san cheese

Clean the eggplant and cut it into thin rounds about ⅛ inch thick. Sprinkle with salt and place them upended in a colander for half an hour to drain out their bitterness.

Mince the onion, parsley, basil, and *prosciutto* by hand or in a food processor (with steel blade on/off 6 to 7 times) until almost pastelike. Sauté the mince in olive oil about 4 minutes or until limp.

Push the tomatoes through a sieve or food mill directly into the sauté pan. Add vinegar, sugar, and pepper. Simmer about 20 minutes or until the mixture reaches saucelike consistency.

Rinse the salt from the eggplant slices and pat them dry with absorbent toweling. Dredge in flour and fry in vegetable oil (at 190°C, 375°F) until golden on both sides. Drain on absorbent toweling, and sprinkle lightly with salt.

Preheat oven to 200°C (400°F).

Chop the sliced cheese into tiny cubes.

Butter a casserole or au gratin dishes. Place 1 to 2 tablespoons of the tomato sauce in the bottom of the dish(es).

Put a layer of fried eggplant slices to fit the bottom of the dish. Add a bit of sauce. Sprinkle with ½ the cheese cubes. Make a second layer of eggplant, add more sauce and the last of the cubed cheese.

Make a third layer of eggplant, cover with the last of the sauce, and sprinkle with the bread crumbs and Parmesan cheese. Bake in a hot (200°C, 400°F) oven for 10 minutes. For 4.

Fennel Baked with Cheese

finocchio ai formaggi

1 fennel bulb
¼ teaspoon freshly grated nutmeg
¼ teaspoon salt, or to taste
freshly ground pepper
115 grams (4 ounces) *Groviera* or Swiss cheese
½ recipe *besciamella* (pages 41 to 42)
½ beef bouillon cube, crumbled
2 tablespoons grated Parmesan cheese
1 tablespoon unseasoned bread crumbs
2 tablespoons unsalted butter

Depending on the size of the fennel or your appetite, one fennel bulb is sufficient for 2 to 3 servings. An average bulb weighs about 700 grams (1½ pounds) before trimming.

Preheat oven to 200° C (400° F).

Cut off and discard the stems of the fennel where they join the bulb proper.

Cut the bulb in 16 even wedges. Slice off most of the core at the bottom of each wedge.

Cook the fennel sections 4 to 5 minutes in boiling salted water until tender but still crisp. Drain well.

Sprinkle the fennel with nutmeg, salt, and pepper, and toss.

Cut the *Groviera* in 14 slices, approximately the same size as the fennel sections.

Butter 2 or 3 individual au gratin dishes or 1 larger casserole. Arrange the fennel sections in the dish(es), alternating with the cheese slices, so that each slice overlaps another slightly.

Make the *besciamella* sauce, and flavor it with the bouillon cube. Pour the *besciamella* over the fennel and cheese to cover. Sprinkle with Parmesan cheese and bread crumbs. Dot with the butter.

Bake in a hot (200° C, 400° F) oven 10 to 12 minutes or until lightly toasted on top. Serve hot. For 2 or 3.

Bean and Celery Salad

insalata di fagioli e sedano

450 grams (1 pound) fresh shell beans, shelled

2½ liters (2½ to 3 quarts) cold water

1 fresh sage leaf

1 garlic clove, peeled

1½ teaspoons salt

4 celery stalks, washed

3 tablespoons olive oil

1½ tablespoons wine vinegar

8 drops Tabasco sauce

8 drops Worcestershire sauce

⅛ teaspoon salt

freshly ground pepper

1 tablespoon snipped fresh or freeze-dried chives

Put the beans in cold water, add sage and garlic, cover, bring to a boil, lower the heat, and cook gently for 18 minutes. Add salt at the 10-minute mark.

Cut the celery in half lengthwise and then into small dices. Add to the boiling beans and cook about 7 minutes longer or until the beans are tender and the celery partially cooked but still crisp.

Drain the beans and celery thoroughly. Dress with olive oil, vinegar, Tabasco, and Worcestershire sauce. Sprinkle with salt and pepper. Toss with the chives and serve tepid or cold. For 4.

Green Beans, Florentine Style

fagiolini alla fiorentina

450 grams (1 pound) fresh green beans (preferably very young and under 3 inches long)

4 tablespoons olive oil

1 small onion, peeled and sliced

1 teaspoon fennel seeds, mashed to a powder and sieved

salt to taste

freshly ground pepper to taste

2 tablespoons tomato paste

4 tablespoons hot water

If your beans are not the tiny first-of-the-crop size, cut off the tops and ends and slice diagonally into 1-inch pieces. Cook in boiling salted water about 5 minutes or until tender but still crisp to the bite. Drain thoroughly.

Sauté the onion in olive oil until limp, then add the beans, mashed fennel seeds, salt, and pepper.

Dilute the tomato paste in hot water, add it to the beans, stir well, lower the heat, and cook, covered, 8 to 10 minutes or until the beans are thoroughly cooked and flavored. Serve hot. For 4.

Lima Beans, Tuscan Style

fave alla toscana

285 grams (about 10 ounces) frozen lima beans

1 teaspoon salt

2 or 3 slices (60 to 85 grams or 2 to 3 ounces) thickly sliced *prosciutto* or very lean smoked bacon

1 tablespoon olive oil

½ medium onion, peeled and cut lengthwise in slivers

¼ cup dry white wine

1 rounded tablespoon chopped Italian parsley

freshly ground pepper

This is the Tuscan way of doing fava beans. Since they are not easily found in non-Italian markets, we will use the method with frozen fordhook lima beans.

Cook beans with a teaspoon salt, in water to cover, until nearly tender, 7 to 10 minutes. If using the six-quart pressure cooker, bring the pressure up to 15 pounds, cook 1½ minutes, then bring the pressure down immediately.

Drain beans thoroughly and set aside.

Cut off almost all of the fat from the *prosciutto* or bacon. Cut the slices in thin strips.

Place *prosciutto* or bacon and olive oil in a frying pan and cook 3 minutes. Add the onion slivers and continue to cook until onion is limp.

Add the dry white wine and deglaze the pan.

Add the beans, and stir and cook until the beans are tender. Add the parsley and a generous sprinkling of pepper, and stir and cook 1 minute. For 3 or 4 as a side dish.

New Year's Day Lentils

lenticchie del primo d'anno

5 sprigs Italian parsley

2 celery stalks with leaves, washed

1 garlic clove, peeled

1 medium onion, peeled

2 slices lean salt pork or pancetta, cut in small pieces

4 tablespoons olive oil

1 tablespoon tomato paste

450 grams (1 pound) lentils, washed

6 to 7 cups water (approximate), hot

1 teaspoon salt, or to taste

freshly ground pepper

Mince the parsley, celery, garlic, onion, and salt pork by hand or in the food processor (on/off for about 5 seconds) until almost pastelike. In a large saucepan, sauté the mince in the olive oil until golden. Add the tomato paste, and mix well. Add the lentils. Stir and cook a minute or two until they sizzle. Add the hot water, bring to a boil, cover, lower the heat, and simmer for 45 minutes to one hour, stirring occasionally. When the lentils are nearly cooked, taste for salt. Add freshly ground pepper, 5 or 6 twists of the mill.

Serve with Italian sweet sausages. For 8 to 10.

Onions and Peppers

cipolline con peperoni

2 sweet peppers (1 red and 1 green), cored and cut in tiny squares

2 tablespoons olive oil (approximate)

285 grams (10 ounces) small white onions, frozen

3 tablespoons chopped Italian parsley

¼ celery stalk (about 3 inches long), washed and chopped

salt to taste

white pepper

Sauté the peppers in the olive oil about 10 minutes or until they are almost cooked. Add the onions, stir, and continue cooking about 5 minutes or until the onions are tender. Season with chopped parsley, celery, salt, and pepper. Cook another moment, and serve. For 4.

You may use fresh onions, but they take longer to peel and prepare; the frozen store easily, cook up much faster, and are more uniform in size.

Peas, Piedmont Style

piselli alla piemontese

675 to 900 grams (1½ to 2 pounds) tiny fresh peas, the first of the crop

60 grams (2 ounces) sliced pancetta or lean salt pork

1 small onion, peeled

10 sprigs Italian parsley

1 tablespoon olive oil

1 cup chicken broth (page 44) (approximate)

salt to taste

freshly ground pepper to taste

Shell the peas and soak them in cold water for ½ hour.

Mince finely together by hand or food processor the *pancetta,* onion, and parsley.

Put the mince in a frying pan with the olive oil and cook a few minutes over medium heat until the onion bits are limp.

Drain and add the peas. Add the broth to cover.

Raise the heat, stir, cover, and cook 5 minutes. Uncover, and taste the peas for salt. Add salt, if the *pancetta* has not contributed enough. Add pepper, several twists of the mill.

Continue cooking 5 to 10 minutes or until the peas are tender. Serve hot. For 4 to 6.

Pepper Casserole

peperoni in casseruola

8 large basil leaves

6 sprigs Italian parsley

1 garlic clove, peeled

5 tablespoons olive oil

2 medium onions, peeled and finely sliced

3 sweet peppers (red, green, or yellow)

1 small zucchini

115 grams (4 ounces) mushrooms, cleaned

1 chicken bouillon cube

3 tablespoons wine vinegar

¼ to ½ teaspoon salt, or to taste

freshly ground pepper to taste

2 potatoes, peeled

Mince the herbs with the garlic and put the mixture in a flameproof casserole along with the olive oil and sliced onions. Sauté over medium heat until the onions are limp.

Core the peppers and cut them into 1-inch square pieces. Slice the zucchini into thin rounds. Cut the mushrooms in half.

Add the vegetables to the onions. Break up the bouillon cube, adding it to the vegetables. Add the vinegar, salt, and pepper, and stir well. Cover the pan with a tightly fitting cover, lower the heat, and cook 15 minutes.

Slice the potatoes in very thin rounds, and add them to the casserole at the 15-minute mark. Stir, cover, and cook another 15 minutes or until the peppers are cooked but still firm to the bite. Taste for seasonings, and adjust if necessary. Serve as a main dish. For 6.

Rice and Asparagus Salad

*insalata di riso
ed asparagi*

Salad

1 cup extra-long-grain enriched rice, cooked in salted water

450 grams (1 pound) fresh asparagus

2 celery stalks, washed

225 grams (½ pound) large mushrooms, cleaned

Dressing

1 large egg, room temperature

½ teaspoon Dijon mustard

½ teaspoon salt

⅛ teaspoon white pepper

¾ cup olive oil

juice of 1 lemon

2 tablespoons heavy cream

2 tablespoons brandy

1 tablespoon chopped Italian parsley

When the rice is cooked, rinse it briefly in cold water, drain, and let it cool completely.

Break off and discard the root end of the asparagus stalks. Slice the stalks diagonally in 1-inch pieces, leaving the tips whole. Cook in 1 inch of boiling salted water for 3 to 5 minutes or until tender but still bright in color and slightly crisp. Drain immediately and let cool.

Peel the celery stalks of any tough strings and cut them into thin slices. Cut the mushrooms vertically into slices.

For the dressing, combine the egg, mustard, salt, pepper, and 2 tablespoons of the olive oil in a blender. Blend, covered, at high speed until thick and creamy. Add the remaining olive oil in a slow trickle, and continue to blend until the mixture is very thick. Blend in the lemon juice, then, at medium speed, the cream and, finally, add the brandy.

Put the rice, asparagus, celery, and mushrooms in a salad bowl. Toss gently. Add the dressing and toss again. Sprinkle with chopped parsley. Chill at least ½ hour. For 6.

Roast Potatoes and Tomatoes

patate araganate

1 kilo (2 pounds) potatoes, peeled and sliced

3 large onions, peeled and cored, cut in rings

675 grams (1½ pounds) fresh plum tomatoes, peeled and cut in chunks

4 to 5 tablespoons olive oil

salt to taste

1 teaspoon dried oregano

¼ cup unseasoned bread crumbs

3 tablespoons grated Parmesan or Romano cheese or a mixture of the two

Preheat oven to 190° C (375° F).

Prepare the vegetables.

Barely moisten with olive oil the bottom of an oven-proof casserole.

Put in it a layer of potato slices, then one of onion rings; place a few chunks of tomato over the onions.

Sprinkle with salt and a hint of oregano and trickle olive oil all around.

Continue layering, finishing with a layer of tomatoes.

Sprinkle with bread crumbs and cheese and add a last trickle of olive oil.

Roast in the oven at 190° C (375° F) for about 50 minutes or until the potato slices are tender. For 4 to 6.

Roast Red Potatoes

patate rosse al forno

1 kilo (2 pounds) red potatoes

¼ cup olive oil

1 teaspoon salt, or to taste

freshly ground pepper

1 tablespoon chopped Italian parsley

Preheat oven to 200° C (400° F).

Wash potatoes well and cut out potato eyes, but leave as much peel as possible. Quarter the potatoes and place them in a baking dish large enough to hold them all in one layer.

Sprinkle with olive oil and salt and pepper. Turn the potatoes over and stir them about to be sure they are coated with olive oil.

Roast at 200° C (400° F) for 25 minutes or until tender, turning a couple of times with a spatula. Remove from the oven, sprinkle with parsley, and place in a warm serving dish. For 6.

Stuffed Tomatoes with Roast Potatoes

pomodori ripieni e patate arroste

4 large ripe tomatoes
½ cup olive oil
1 teaspoon salt, or to taste
freshly ground pepper to taste
¼ cup extra-long-grain rice
1 small garlic clove, peeled
2 tablespoons chopped Italian parsley
10 large fresh basil leaves
¼ teaspoon dried oregano
2 potatoes, peeled

Preheat oven to 200° C (400° F).

Neatly cut the tops off the tomatoes about ¼ of the way down, saving the tops. Scoop out the insides, and push them through a sieve, saving the juice.

Sprinkle the insides of the tomatoes with a drop or two of olive oil and salt and pepper to taste.

Cook the rice in a cup of boiling water with ¼ teaspoon salt for 8 minutes. Drain and place in a bowl.

Mince the garlic, parsley, basil, and oregano together; add to the rice, along with 3 table-spoons olive oil and ¼ cup tomato juice. Fill the tomatoes with the rice mixture and cover each with its own top.

Cut four ½-inch slices from one of the pota-toes and cut the rest into bite-size chunks. Oil a baking dish, and arrange the potato slices in it evenly spaced. Put the tomatoes on the rounds, and fill the spaces with the remaining chunks of potatoes. Dribble the remaining olive oil over everything. Sprinkle with salt.

Bake in the hot (200° C, 400° F) oven for 45 minutes, basting once or twice or until the po-tatoes are done, the rice tender.

Serve the tomatoes and potatoes hot as a side dish; or serve the tomatoes alone at room tem-perature as an *antipasto*. For 4.

Mixed Spring Vegetables

padellata primaverile

450 grams (1 pound) fresh early peas or 285-gram (10-ounce) package frozen tiny peas

225 grams (½ pound) scallions

225 grams (½ pound) small new carrots, peeled

3 slices prosciutto or blanched lean salt pork

3 tablespoons unsalted butter

¾ cup beef broth (page 43), hot

225 grams (½ pound) mushrooms, cleaned

1 tablespoon chopped Italian parsley

salt to taste

freshly ground pepper

If using fresh peas, shell them. If using frozen peas, thaw them. Cut off and discard the root ends and tops of the scallions and wash the remaining pieces. Cut the carrots in quarters.

Cut the *prosciutto* into ¼-inch strips. Melt the butter in a large saucepan. Add the *prosciutto,* and cook over medium heat until the fat has become translucent.

Add the peas, scallions, and carrots to the ham. Cook and stir 5 minutes.

Add the broth, cover the pan, and cook about 5 minutes or until the carrots are tender.

Add the mushrooms, and cook 5 more minutes.

Add the parsley, taste for salt (the ham should have added enough), and add more if necessary. Add pepper, and serve. For 6.

Vegetable Platter

verdure all'agro

450 grams (1 pound) carrots, peeled

450 grams (1 pound) Swiss chard

450 grams (1 pound) broccoli

1 cauliflower

⅓ cup olive oil (approximate)

2 lemons

Cut the carrots into 3-inch-long julienne strips. Wash the chard well and cut the stems in 3-inch lengths; wash the broccoli and cut the heads in flowerets. Cut the cauliflower in flowerets.

Bring a big pot of water to a boil; add 1 teaspoon salt per quart of water. Cook the carrots 6 minutes or until just tender. Lift them out of the boiling water, drain thoroughly, and place on a serving platter.

Put the chard leaves in, then remove them when the pot comes back to a boil.

Put the chard stems in, and cook about 4 minutes or until tender. Drain well and place on the platter with the other vegetables.

Cook the broccoli and cauliflower in the water, removing them as soon as they are tender but still a bit crisp.

Arrange the vegetables in pleasing alternations of color. Drain off any accumulated water. Dress with the olive oil and the juice of one lemon. Serve with the remaining lemon, cut into wedges. Serve warm or cold. For 12.

Desserts

Dolci

The grand list of Italian desserts is still made up of the traditional rich butter and sugar and egg combinations of yesterday: oldies and goodies which keep reappearing on feast days. By and large these are not everyday affairs.

What is new on the sweet scene is the availability of mixes and ingredients to speed up home preparation and a plethora of new cooking-oriented magazines and articles. Today, the cook can avoid the lengthy preparation of *pasta sfogliata,* puff pastry, by buying it frozen or preparing it in large batches at home and then freezing it. The advent of home freezers and related gadgetry has made a host of new Italian cooks expert on a number of desserts formerly prepared only by commercial pastry cooks and ice cream makers. Closely kept secrets of the trade are now available to every family.

Thus, a certain amount of expertise has moved back into the family kitchen and is put to work for parties and holidays. That is what this section is mostly about: making traditional pastries by modern methods. Our previous books, *The Romagnolis' Table* and *The Romagnolis' Meatless Cookbook,* provide the handmade versions of some of these recipes.

Ice Cream, Ices, and Fruit

Gelati, sorbetti, e frutta

It is quite possible, although we have not run a research project on it, that every city and town in Italy has its own major ice-cream producer, unexcelled for kilometers around in the production and sale of superlative, rich, calorie-laden ice cream. In the attempt to reproduce such glory in the kitchen and evoke memories of summer nights when only an ice cream could soothe, we modestly offer this recipe for the home ice-cream machine.

Once the mixture is made, follow the instructions of the machine maker to a T, since the proper amounts of salt and ice for the temperature of the room will confirm a smooth texture. The flavor is gained as follows:

Vanilla Ice Cream

gelato alla vaniglia

5 cups milk

1 vanilla bean, about 4
  inches long

10 large egg yolks

2 cups sugar

½ teaspoon salt

1 liter (1 quart) medium
  (all-purpose) cream (or
  half heavy cream and
  half light cream)

4 teaspoons vanilla extract

Bring the milk with the vanilla bean in it just to the scalding point, then let cool.

Beat the egg yolks with the sugar and salt until very pale in color, very fluffy in texture.

Pour the scalded, cooled milk through a sieve into the egg-sugar mixture. Stir until well mixed.

Place the mixture over medium heat. Cook, stirring slowly with a wooden spoon and always in the same direction, until the mixture coats the spoon and has reached about 85 °C (185 °F) on the thermometer but has not boiled. Do not let it boil or it will curdle and the texture will be less smooth. (If, however, all this richness does curdle, allow it to cool, place it in the food processor with the steel blade in place, and process until smooth. The texture will be good — though not superlative — and you will not have to throw anything out.)

Allow the mixture to cool.

When the egg-milk mixture has cooled, add the quart of cream. Add the vanilla, and stir gently until well mixed.

Place the cream mixture in the ice-cream machine, and follow the instructions of the manufacturer for freezing.

Once the cream has become almost solid it must be hardened off in the freezer. Either place the container of the ice-cream machine in the freezer or pour the almost solid mixture into suitable freezing containers, leaving an inch or so at the top for final expansion. Tap the mixture down briefly with the back of a spoon. Let vanilla ice cream harden off for about 2 hours. Yield: 1 gallon.

Chocolate Ice Cream

gelato al cioccolato

4 cups milk

1 vanilla bean, about 4 inches long

10 egg yolks

2 cups sugar

½ teaspoon salt

8 squares unsweetened chocolate

1 liter (1 quart) medium (all-purpose) cream (or half heavy cream and half light cream)

2 teaspoons vanilla extract

Bring the milk with the vanilla bean to scalding, then let cool.

Beat the egg yolks with the sugar and salt in a large (four-liter or four-quart) saucepan until pale in color and very fluffy, rather like frosting.

Pour the cooled, scalded milk through a sieve into the egg-sugar mixture, and mix well with a spoon.

Bring the saucepan almost to scalding (85 ° C, 185 ° F), the point at which the mixture coats the spoon but has not boiled.

Melt the chocolate in a small double boiler and add it to the warm custard mixture. Stir gently to mix in the chocolate. Add the vanilla and the quart of cream. Let the saucepan cool completely in a sink full of cold water or in a large pan of cold water.

Freeze in a home ice-cream machine, and then place in quart-size containers for hardening off.

Chocolate ice cream is best when allowed to harden off for at least 24 hours in the freezer. Yield: about 1 gallon.

Grapefruit Sherbet with Pomegranate Seeds

sorbetto di pompelmo con melagrano

4 grapefruit, preferably
   pink and with thin skins
1¼ cups sugar
⅓ cup water
3 egg whites
¼ teaspoon cream of tartar
pinch of salt
seeds of ½ pomegranate

Fresh Grapefruit Method

Squeeze the grapefruit well. Pour the juice through a sieve, measure, and reserve 3 cups of juice.

Bring the sugar and water to a boil, and continue to boil to the hardball stage, when the candy thermometer reaches 121° C (250° F).

While the sugar-water mixture boils, beat the egg whites with the cream of tartar and salt until they hold a peak. Pour the hot syrup slowly into the egg whites, continuing to beat as you pour. Keep on beating for a total of 5 minutes or until the egg whites are stiff and glossy.

Stir the egg whites into the grapefruit juice.

Pour into a shallow metal pan and freeze until almost firm. Remove from the freezer, place in a mixing bowl, and beat briefly until smooth, fluffy, and blended. Pour into 8 chilled dishes and finish freezing. Remove from the freezer 15 minutes before serving and sprinkle with pomegranate seeds. For 8.

Frozen Grapefruit

1 170-gram (6-ounce) can frozen unsweetened grapefruit juice concentrate

½ cup water

1 cup sugar

2 large egg whites at room temperature

¼ teaspoon salt

seeds of ½ pomegranate

Method

Mix the grapefruit juice concentrate with 2 parts (cans) water, stir well, and pour through a sieve into a three-quart stainless-steel bowl.

Boil the water with the sugar until it reaches the hardball stage — 121° C (250° F) on a candy thermometer.

While the syrup boils, beat the egg whites with the salt until they hold stiff peaks.

Pour the sugar syrup slowly into the beaten egg whites, and continue beating until firm glossy peaks can be made. Stir the egg whites into the grapefruit juice.

Freeze the mixture in the freezer about 2½ hours, stirring every half hour. When the mixture is nearly frozen stiff, remove it from the freezer and beat it with a handheld electric beater at the lowest speed.

Pour into 6 to 8 chilled individual custard cups and return to the freezer until 15 minutes before serving time. Remove from the freezer and sprinkle with pomegranate seeds. For 6 to 8.

Lemon Sherbet

sorbetto di limone

1 cup lemon juice
juice of 1 orange
1 cup water
2 cups sugar
grated rinds of 2 lemons
2 egg whites
¼ teaspoon salt

Strain lemon and orange juice through a fine sieve into a three-liter (three-quart) stainless-steel bowl.

Boil sugar and water together with the lemon rinds until the hard-crack stage is reached, when the candy thermometer registers 149° C (300° F). Let cool.

Mix the syrup and lemon and orange juices together, and place in the freezer for about 2 hours. Remove the bowl, and whip with an electric beater. Freeze 1 more hour.

Beat the egg whites with the salt until they hold firm peaks. Remove the juice mixture from the freezer, whip it again, and mix the egg whites into the ice at the lowest speed of the handheld electric beater.

Pour into 6 chilled individual custard cups and return to the freezer until 15 minutes before serving time. For 6.

Raspberry Sherbet

sorbetto di lampone

1 285-gram (10-ounce) packet frozen raspberries
1 cup sugar
½ cup water
juice of 1½ lemons
2 egg whites
⅛ teaspoon salt

Thaw the raspberries at room temperature, and press them through a sieve into a stainless-steel bowl.

Boil the sugar and water over medium heat until the syrup reaches the hard-crack stage; a candy thermometer will register 149° C (300° F). Let the syrup cool.

Mix raspberry juice, syrup, and lemon juice. Place the bowl in the freezer (it should be hovering around 0° C, 32° F). Stir the mixture every half hour for 3 hours.

Beat the egg whites with the salt until stiff peaks are formed.

Remove the raspberry mixture from the freezer (it should be almost frozen by now), and beat it well. Fold in the egg whites, and return to the freezer.

If you have a home ice-cream maker, use it according to its freezing directions. Harden the sherbet in the freezer. For 6.

Lime Ice

granita di limetta

3 cups sugar

4 cups water

½ teaspoon grated lime peel

1¾ cup lime juice (about 8 limes)

drop of green vegetable food coloring (optional)

Bring sugar, water, and lime peel to a boil, and boil to the hard-crack stage (when the candy thermometer reaches 149° C, 300° F). Remove from heat and let cool, then refrigerate until very cold.

Strain the lime juice into the cold syrup through a sieve. Add the vegetable coloring if you wish.

Freeze in a three-liter (three-quart) stainless-steel bowl for about 2 hours or until partially frozen. Stir well with a fork, and continue freezing, stirring every half hour until almost solid. Then beat with an electric beater and return to the freezer to harden.

Or freeze according to directions for the home ice-cream freezer.

Makes 1½ quarts, approximately, or about 10 to 12 servings.

Melon Ice

granita di melone

1 450-gram (1-pound) bag frozen mixed melon balls or the fresh equivalent

⅛ teaspoon salt

½ cup sugar

¼ cup water

¼ cup lime juice or 3 tablespoons lemon juice

Semi-thaw the melon balls, and sprinkle them with salt.

Bring the sugar and water to a boil, and boil to the hard-crack stage (when a candy thermometer reaches 149° C, 300° F). Let cool.

Place the melon balls in a food processor, and process on/off until reduced to a fine mash. Pour in the cooled syrup as you process. Add the lime or lemon juice, and process on/off until mixture is smooth.

Pour the melon mixture into a stainless-steel bowl and place in the freezer for 15 minutes. Beat with a handheld electric beater or whisk. Freeze another 15 to 30 minutes, and the *granita* should be ready to serve. Use the day it is made, since that is when the flavor is at its best. For 4 to 6.

Strawberry Ice

granita di fragole

1 cup water
2 cups sugar
1 quart very ripe fresh
  strawberries
juice of 2 lemons
juice of 1 orange

Fresh Strawberry Method

Bring the water and sugar to a boil, and boil for 5 minutes. Let cool.

Wash the berries thoroughly and hull them. Reserve 5 or 6 of the biggest and prettiest berries; puree the rest by putting them through the finest disc of the food mill or by mincing them with the steel blade of a food processor. Add the lemon and orange juice to the strawberries.

Pour the berry mixture into a large stainless-steel bowl, add the cooled syrup, mix well, and place in the freezer. The actual freezing time is 2 to 4 hours and depends on how cold the freezer really is. As the *granita* starts to freeze, stir it well two or three times. When it is almost solid, beat it with a handheld electric beater or fork. Slice the reserved berries, mix them into the *granita,* and pour into chilled individual dessert glasses. Freeze another 15 minutes to ½ hour. For 10 to 12.

1 560-gram (20-ounce)
  package or bag frozen
  whole strawberries (without sugar)
1 cup sugar
½ cup water
grated rinds of 2 lemons
¼ cup lemon juice

Frozen Strawberry Method

Thaw the strawberries at room temperature. Squeeze them through 2 layers of kitchen cheesecloth into a stainless-steel bowl.

Bring the sugar and water with the lemon rind to a boil, and boil to the hard-crack stage (when the candy thermometer reaches 149° C, 300° F). Cool.

Add the sugar-water syrup to the strawberry juice. Stir in the lemon juice. Place in freezer for 1 hour, stir, and put back in the freezer. Stir again after ½ hour. Repeat until the *granita* is almost firm. For 6.

Chocolate Cream Mold

semifreddo di cioccolato

85 grams (3 ounces) unsweetened chocolate

6 tablespoons unsalted butter, softened

½ cup sugar

4 large eggs at room temperature, separated

¼ teaspoon salt

½ cup Italian brandy

½ layer Pan di Spagna (pages 302 to 303) or Torta Margherita (page 306), (optional)

whipped cream, flavored with vanilla and sugar to taste (optional)

In the top of a double boiler, melt the chocolate over hot, but not boiling, water. When the chocolate is melted, remove the whole double boiler from the heat.

Add the butter a tablespoon at a time to the chocolate, beating the buttered chocolate slowly and constantly. Continue beating while you add the sugar until the sugar and butter have both melted into the chocolate and the whole has increased in bulk. Then beat in the egg yolks, one at a time.

Beat the egg whites with the salt in a separate bowl until stiff.

Remove the top of the double boiler from its bottom, and slowly fold the egg whites into the chocolate. Fold in 4 teaspoons of the brandy.

Place a tablespoon or so of the chocolate mixture in the bottoms of 8 ramekins (small custard dishes).

If using the cake, cut it into ½-inch or 1-inch cubes, dribble with the remaining brandy, and place in the ramekins. Fill the ramekins with the remaining chocolate mixture. Chill in the refrigerator for 2 hours.

Serve as is or top with a tablespoon or two flavored whipped cream. For 8.

Almond Filled Peaches

pesche ripiene alle mandorle

4 ripe freestone peaches
½ cup slivered almonds
½ cup sugar
yolks of 2 medium eggs
½ cup coarsely chopped amaretti (Italian macaroons)
butter for the baking dish and approximately 2 tablespoons for the peaches
¼ to ½ cup dry Marsala wine

Preheat oven to 190° C (375° F).

Cut the peaches in half. Remove and discard the pits. Scoop out a bit of pulp from each cavity and place the pulp in a mortar or in a food processor with the steel blade in place.

Add ½ the almonds and process on/off until the almonds are in small bits. Add half the sugar, the egg yolks, and the *amaretti,* and process on/off 3 times. Or grind the almonds with the peach pulp in the mortar until the almonds are reduced in size. Add the sugar, egg yolks, and *amaretti,* and mix well.

Generously butter a baking dish large enough to hold the 8 peach halves.

Fill the peach halves, cover them with the remaining almonds, and place in the baking dish. Place a quarter tablespoon butter on each peach. Sprinkle the peaches with the remaining sugar and dribble the Marsala over all.

Bake about 40 minutes in a medium (190° C, 375° F) oven until the filling is golden and crusty. Baste with more Marsala (or with that in the dish) during the baking, if the peaches seem to be drying out. Let the peaches cool at room temperature about ½ hour before serving. For 4.

Flamed Peaches

pesche al brandy

4 large ripe peaches
2 to 3 tablespoons lemon juice
1 tablespoon unsalted butter
½ cup sugar
2 tablespoons brandy

Blanch the peaches briefly, peel them, then cut them in eighths. Sprinkle with the lemon juice, and stir gently to coat all the pieces with lemon.

Melt the butter in a flameproof serving dish, add the sugar and the peaches, and stir over fairly high heat for just a few moments in order to coat the peaches well with butter and sugar. Do not cook them.

Warm the brandy in a large spoon or ladle, ignite it, and pour it over the peaches to flame them. Serve immediately. For 4.

Stuffed Pears

pere ripiene

4 ripe Bartlett pears
½ cup mixed crushed walnuts and almonds
5 tablespoons sugar
1 small egg
1½ cups sweet white wine (approximate)

Preheat oven to 200° C (400° F).

Peel and cut in half the pears. Scoop out the cores and discard them. Scoop out a bit more of the center, put it in a mortar or a food processor, and mash it up.

Add the nuts, 3 tablespoons of the sugar, and the egg. Process on/off or mash a bit more until everything is well amalgamated.

Butter a baking dish just large enough to hold the pear halves. If they roll about or tilt, cut off a small slice of pear to flatten the part that sits in the dish.

Fill the pears with the nut mixture. Sprinkle with the remaining sugar. Pour wine over the pears and into the bottom of the dish.

Bake 1 hour in a hot (200° C, 400° F) oven or until the pears are tender, the filling toasted, and the wine almost evaporated. Serve hot or cold (stuffed pears keep well in the refrigerator). For 4.

Pear and Cheese Mold

*torta di formaggio
con le pere*

285 grams (10 ounces, approximate) Muenster cheese

3 tablespoons unsalted butter, softened

225 grams (8 ounces) farm cheese (also known as farmer cheese and pressed cheese, similar to a mild, dry *ricotta*)

1 tablespoon heavy cream

1 or 2 Bartlett pears

An old Italian saying goes, "Do not let the farmer know how good cheese is with pears," presumably because, exposed to such a sumptuous taste, his life of honest labor would be corrupted by gluttony. This cheese-and-pear *torta* would do just that, even if its form is more to emphasize than to alter the tastes of the two basic ingredients. So, if you wish to impress your gluttonous friends, here is the way.

Process, with the steel blade, the Muenster cheese with the butter (or cream it with a fork) until you have a smooth, stiff, but spreadable mixture. Set aside.

Process (or cream) the farmer cheese with the heavy cream in the same way until you have a smooth, soft texture.

Peel, core, and cut one pear in small slivers or chips and fold them into the Farmer's cheese mixture.

Line a small mold with plastic wrap (a 6-inch steel or Pyrex bowl will do). Line the wrap with a layer of the Muenster cheese mixture, using about ⅔ of the total. Fill the center of the mold with the farmer cheese–pear mixture, topping this with the last of the Muenster.

Cover the bowl or mold with plastic wrap and refrigerate for at least an hour. Unmold, unwrap, and serve, cut in thin slices like a small cake.

To make an even greater impression: peel and cut the second pear in eighths. Cut out the cores and slim the wedges to ¼-inch thickness. Save the trimmings.

Line your mold with the plastic wrap and then with ⅔ of the Muenster cheese mixture. Press the pear wedges into the cheese, curved side pressing against the side of the mold. Fill the center with the farmer cheese mixture. Top with the remaining Muenster mixture, and cover with the saved pear chips, pressing them in to hold firmly. Cover the mold and refrigerate 1 hour. Unmold, place on a serving platter, flat side down, and cut in thin slices like a cake. For 8.

Filled Watermelon

cocomero ripieno

1 ripe round (Florida) watermelon, chilled
2 cups seedless green grapes, washed
1 cup sugar, or more to taste
2 cups dry white wine
2 cups light rum
½ cup Campari
3 lemons
3 sprigs fresh mint

Wash the outside of the melon and dry thoroughly. Set the melon on its base (blossom end) and, with a very sharp knife, draw and then cut a scalloped or zigzagged design all the way around the melon about ¼ of the way down from the top (stem end). Remove the top and set aside.

Using a melon-ball cutter, scoop out the insides of both parts of the melon, discarding the seeds as you scoop. Not all of the melon will be perfect balls, but do the best you can. Place the melon balls in a bowl.

When the large part of the melon is about ⅔ empty, put balls and pieces back in the melon, alternating with green grapes.

Mix the sugar, wine, rum, Campari, and juice of 2 lemons together. Adjust the sugar to taste. Pour the mixture over the melon balls. Cut the third lemon in thin slices, and decorate the top of the melon. Add the mint sprigs.

If your melon has no stem to use as a handle, take a length of heavy white cotton kitchen string, and make three or four loops. Make a small hole where the stem was and push one end of the loops through the hole. Make a tidy large knot to hold the loops in place, thus creating a handle for the top.

Set the lid on top of the filled part and chill the melon 2 to 4 hours before serving. For 20.

Cakes and Pastry

Crostata

Perhaps the most familiar of all Italian pastries is the *crostata,* or fruit pastry tart, made with a sweet pastry crust and fresh or preserved fruits. Here are two basic apple tarts, one "imperial" apple tart and a family favorite of oranges and chocolate.

Crostata Dough for Food Processor

pasta frolla

115 grams (4 ounces) unsalted butter, chilled and cut in small pieces
⅔ cup sugar
¼ teaspoon salt
2 cups flour
2 large eggs
1 teaspoon lemon extract

Put everything in the food processor bowl except the eggs and lemon extract. Process on/off with the metal blade until the consistency of coarse meal is reached.

Beat the eggs and lemon extract lightly together and add to the dough. Continue processing until the mixture forms a ball. Remove it from processor, firm it with the hands, and wrap in plastic wrap. Chill at least ½ hour before use.

Roll ⅔ of the dough to fit the bottom of a 10-inch *crostata* pan or tart or quiche pan. The last third of the dough may be rolled out, cut in strips with a pastry cutter, and used as a lattice for the *crostata.*

Apple Tart I

crostata di mele I

1 recipe *crostata* dough
(page 295)

3 baking apples (Cortland,
Northern Spy, or Bald-
win)

juice of 1 lemon

6 very crisp cookies
(American "Brown Edge
Wafers" or 6 crumbled
meringhe, pages 325 to
327)

4 *amaretti* (Italian macaroons)

½ cup Italian brandy or
Apple Jack

3 tablespoons sugar

3 heaping tablespoons
crab-apple jelly

Make the pastry dough according to directions, wrap it in plastic or wax paper, and chill for at least ½ hour.

Preheat oven to 190° C (375° F).

Peel the apples and cut them in thin slices. Moisten the slices with lemon juice as you go along to help them keep their color and to heighten their flavor.

On a floured surface, roll out the dough to fit the bottom and sides of a 10-inch *crostata* or tart or quiche pan. Roll the dough around the rolling pin, lower into the pan, and prick with the tines of a fork here and there.

Crumble all the cookies by placing them between two sheets of wax paper and rolling over with a rolling pin (or process them). Sprinkle the cookie crumbs over the pastry dough.

Place the apple slices on top of the cookie crumbs, overlapping in circles, starting with the outside and working toward the middle until the entire surface is covered.

Sprinkle with brandy and then with the sugar.

Bake 40 minutes in the 190° C (375° F) oven. Let cool.

Warm the jelly in a small saucepan until melted, then paint the apple slices with it. Let cool. Serve the day the tart is made. For 10.

Apple Tart II

crostata di mele II

1 recipe *crostata* dough
(page 295)

5 to 7 baking apples (Bald-
wins, Cortlands, Northern
Spys)

4 tablespoons sugar

½ teaspoon ground cinna-
mon

2 teaspoons lemon juice

½ cup crisp cookie crumbs
(*meringhe*, pages 325 to
327)

grated rind of ½ lemon

1 tablespoon unsalted butter

When your pastry dough is ready, roll it out on a floured surface to a size that will fit the bottom and sides of a 9- to 10-inch *crostata* or tart or quiche pan. Prick with a fork.

Preheat oven to 230° C (450° F).

Peel, core, and slice the apples into a large bowl. Once the bottom of the bowl is covered, sprinkle with a bit of sugar, cinnamon, and lemon juice. Continue slicing and sprinkling until all the apples are ready. Stir carefully.

Cover the bottom *crostata* crust with crumbled cookies, add the apples and lemon rind, and dot with butter.

With the last of the dough, roll out a top crust, place it over the apples, crimp around the edge, and cut little half-moon slits in it.

Bake in a hot (230° C, 450° F) oven for 15 minutes, lower the temperature to 200° C (400° F), and bake until the crust is golden brown. For 10.

Imperial Apple Tart

*crostata imperiale
di mele*

Crostata Dough

1 ½ cups all-purpose un-
bleached flour

9 tablespoons unsalted
butter, chilled and cut in
½-inch cubes

pinch of salt

⅔ cup sugar

2 large eggs

grated rind of 1 lemon

Filling

5 Golden Delicious apples

115 grams (4 ounces) al-
monds, blanched,
peeled, toasted, and
chopped

4 tablespoons sugar

1 ½ tablespoons unsalted
butter

140 grams (5 ounces)
crab-apple jelly

1 tablespoon brandy

Put the flour, butter, and salt in a food-proces-sor bowl and process with the steel blade on/off (or mix in a bowl with a pastry blender) until the butter is blended and the mixture is the tex-ture of coarse meal.

Add sugar, eggs, and lemon rind and process (or blend) until a ball of dough is formed (about 2 to 3 minutes); or mix by hand until well blended and doughy. Wrap the dough in wax paper or plastic wrap and let rest ½ hour.

Preheat oven to 200° C (400° F).

Peel the apples, cut in half, remove the cores. Cut as if to slice thinly the rounded side of the apple halves, but do not cut all the way through. Each half will thus open up like the leaves of a book.

Place the dough in a 10-inch tart pan and pat it down. With your fingers push the dough to the edge of the pan and up the side. Trim the edges. Sprinkle the dough with the toasted al-monds. Place 8 of the apple halves around the edge of the tart, curved side up; put one half in the center; and break up the final half, placing a quarter of it on each side of the center. Sprinkle with the sugar.

Dot with the 1½ tablespoons butter.

Bake in a hot oven (200° C, 400° F) for 45 to 55 minutes or until the edge of the pastry crust is toasted and the apples are cooked and tender.

Remove from the oven. Heat the jelly in a small pan until melted and bubbling. Add the brandy and paint the apples and crust with the melted jelly. Cool and serve. For 10.

Orange and Chocolate Tart

crostata di arancie e cioccolato

6 oranges

1 recipe *crostata* dough (page 295)

⅔ cup plus 1 tablespoon sugar

3½ tablespoons unsalted butter

1 jigger orange liqueur

115 grams (4 ounces) dark semisweet chocolate

30 grams (1 ounce) unsweetened baking chocolate

¾ cup medium (all-purpose) cream

1 teaspoon vanilla extract

¾ cup *ricotta*

With a very sharp knife or vegetable peeler, cut off all the zests of the oranges, peeling around in a spiral as you would an apple. Put the zests in a bowl or pitcher large enough to hold them, and let stand under cold running water for an hour or so.

Make the *crostata* dough and set it to chill.

Preheat the oven to 177° C (350° F).

Butter a 9-inch *crostata* or quiche pan. Roll out the dough on a floured surface and fit it to the pan. Cut a piece of waxed paper to fit the inside of the dough and place it over the bottom. Cover the paper with pastry weights, and bake in a moderate (177° C, 350° F) oven for 15 minutes. Remove the pan from the oven, remove the weights and waxed paper, and return the dough to the oven for another 8 minutes or until toasty and well baked. Let cool.

Drain the orange zests, pat them dry, and cut them in the thinnest possible strips — like pine needles — with kitchen scissors. Place in a small saucepan and add ⅔ cup sugar, the butter, and the orange liqueur. Cook over low heat (but do not allow to boil) until the zests have absorbed almost all of the liquid.

Place the cooked crust and pan bottom on a serving platter.

Fill the crust with the orange zest mixture.

Cut the sweet and bitter chocolate into bits and melt them over boiling water in a double boiler. Dribble the melted chocolate in circles or loops over the orange zests.

Place the *crostata* in the refrigerator for an hour. Just before serving time, whip the cream with the remaining tablespoon of sugar and the vanilla extract. Whip the *ricotta* separately, then fold it into the cream. Place the mixture in a pastry bag with a star tip, and make small rosettes around the edge of the *crostata* crust and here and there on the chocolate. For 16. It is very rich.

Italian Pound Cake

10 tablespoons unsalted butter

1 cup sugar

8 large eggs at room temperature

½ teaspoon salt

1⅔ cups all-purpose unbleached flour

1 teaspoon vanilla extract

Preheat the oven to 200° C (400° F).

Cream together (or process on/off with the steel blade) the sugar and butter until soft and fluffy.

Separate the eggs. Beat the yolks until thick and pale yellow in color. Beat the yolks into the butter-sugar mixture. Beat the whites, adding salt, until they hold a stiff peak. Fold the whites into the yolks and sugar.

Sift the flour three times and fold into the egg mixture. Fold in the vanilla.

Pour into a buttered and floured bread pan (about 9″ long, 3″ wide, and 4″ deep).

Bake in a hot oven (200° C, 400° F) 55 minutes or until the cake is golden brown and risen high and a cake tester comes out clean. Remove cake from pan when cool, and cut as desired or serve plain. For 10 at least.

Italian Chocolate Layer Cake

1 recipe Italian pound cake (page 300)

225 grams (8 ounces) unsalted butter, chilled

2 cups confectioners' sugar

2 egg yolks

115 grams (4 ounces) unsweetened chocolate, melted and cooled

3 tablespoons chopped toasted almonds

2 jiggers rum

170 grams (6 ounces) semisweet chocolate, melted and cooled

Cut your pound cake in 4 or 5 horizontal layers.

Place a piece of waxed paper to cover a cookie sheet. Place 1 layer of cake on the paper.

Cream butter and sugar well. Add the egg yolks one at a time, creaming well after each addition.

Add the unsweetened chocolate and the almonds and rum. Mix well.

Spread the prepared layer with ⅓ (if you have 4 layers) or ¼ (if you have 5 layers) of the chocolate cream. Add another layer, spread with cream, and another and another. When all the cream is used and the top layer on, cover the cake top and sides with the semisweet chocolate.

Cool the cake until the top layer is solid. Keep in the refrigerator until serving time, up to 48 hours. Slice very thin. For 20.

Cakes and Pastry

Sponge Cake
pan di Spagna

10 large eggs at room temperature
1 teaspoon salt
3 cups sugar
1 teaspoon lemon extract
grated rinds of 1 lemon and 1 orange
2¼ cups all-purpose unbleached flour
1 teaspoon cream of tartar

Pan di Spagna is a traditional cake used for making *zuppa inglese* or served by itself for dessert with just a sprinkling of confectioners' sugar. The name means "bread of Spain," but many feel it was originally *pan di spugna* or "sponge bread." Whatever you wish to call it, it is a light, airy cake with a delicate crust.

This recipe for *pan di Spagna* is larger than most, designed to be made for major feasts. It serves 20 to 30 people (depending on how hungry your guests are), keeps well, and freezes well; and, according to a lovely lady in Venice, when used in *zuppa inglese* (pages 304 to 305) or in *la bomba mocha* (pages 307 to 308), it "will soothe the most recalcitrant of daughters-in-law."

Preheat oven to 177° C (350° F).

Butter and flour 2 spring-form pans 10 inches in diameter and 2½ inches deep or 6 layer cake pans 8 inches in diameter.

Separate the eggs into two large (four- to five-quart) bowls, one a copper bowl (if possible) for the egg whites.

Beat the whites, adding the salt partway along, until stiff. Continue beating, and add 1 cup sugar, a heaping tablespoon at a time. Stop beating when the whites make glossy, stiff peaks.

Beat the yolks (you do not have to wash the beater), gradually adding the remaining sugar. Add the lemon extract and the lemon rind and continue to beat until the yolks are thick and creamy, the sugar virtually dissolved.

Gently fold about ⅓ of the whites into the yolks.

Pour the yolk-white mixture into the remaining whites and fold in carefully.

Sift the flour with the cream of tartar 3 times, then fold it into the eggs. This is a long slow process and you should be careful to get your spatula all the way down to the bottom of the bowl.

Pour the dough into the buttered and floured pans.

Bake the larger pans for 60 minutes, the smaller ones about 30 minutes, in a moderate (177 ° C, 350 ° F) oven. Test with a cake tester; when it comes out clean and the tops are toasty, the cakes are done. Let cool before removing from pans.

Use plain, sprinkled with confectioners' sugar, or in *zuppa inglese* (pages 304 to 305) or *la bomba mocha* (pages 307 to 308). The two large ones, layered, serve 20 to 30; three of the small layers serve 10 to 12.

Zuppa inglese

Zuppa inglese, literally translated, means "English soup"; but this dessert has nothing at all to do with soup. It is layers of sponge cake soaked (*inzuppati* — that is where the *zuppa* or soup comes in) with liqueur, spread with pastry cream, and then chilled. *Zuppa inglese* can also be made with pieces of *pan di Spagna* lining a mold, as charlottes are made with ladyfingers in French cuisine.

Rosolio, a red Italian liqueur made of rose essence and spices, contributes color and flavor.

Sponge Cake

2 large (10-inch) *Pan di Spagna* (pages 302 to 303)

Cut each layer of *pan di Spagna* horizontally into 2 discs.

Pastry Cream

½ cup sugar
8 egg yolks
½ cup flour
5⅓ cups milk
2 teaspoons vanilla extract
2 30-gram (1-ounce) squares unsweetened chocolate, melted
1 teaspoon grated lemon rind
¾ to 1 cup Rosolio (approximate)
½ cup rum (approximate)
½ cup Italian brandy (approximate)
½ cup grated unsweetened chocolate (approximate)

To make the pastry cream: place the sugar, egg yolks, and flour in a stainless steel saucepan and, with a whisk or spoon, beat and stir until the mixture is smooth and all the sugar dissolved.

In a second stainless steel saucepan, scald the milk. Over medium heat, slowly pour the milk into the egg mixture, stirring constantly and always in the same direction (to prevent curdling). Continue to stir and cook until the mixture starts to boil and thicken. Add the vanilla.

Pour half the mixture back into the saucepan you used for scalding the milk.

With both pans over medium heat, add the chocolate to one pan, the lemon rind to the other. Lower the heat, and continue to cook and stir, always in the same direction, for at least 4 minutes or until both mixtures are the consistency of pudding.

Remove from heat, place a piece of plastic wrap on the surface of the cream, and allow it to cool before spreading on the *pan di Spagna* layers.

Assembling zuppa inglese: place 1 layer crust side down, on a serving plate, and sprinkle with half the Rosolio. Spread with half the chocolate cream. Place a second layer of cake, crust side down, on top of the cream and sprinkle it with rum. Spread with a layer of lemon cream. Add a third layer, crust side down, and sprinkle it with brandy. Spread with the remaining chocolate cream. Sprinkle the cut side of the fourth and final layer with the last of the Rosolio, and place the layer, crust side up, on top of the other three. Spread with the last of the lemon cream. Sprinkle with grated bitter chocolate. Chill at least an hour or up to a day before serving. *Zuppa inglese* improves with time spent chilling. For 20.

Margherita Cake

torta Margherita

6 tablespoons unsalted butter
4 large eggs at room temperature
1 teaspoon vanilla extract
1¾ cups confectioners' sugar
6 egg yolks at room temperature
1 teaspoon honey
½ cup potato flour
¾ cup cake flour

Preheat oven to 177° C (350° F).

Melt the butter over low heat, and put aside to cool.

Put the whole eggs and the vanilla into a large (four-liter or four-quart) copper bowl or in the upper part of a stainless-steel double boiler. Beat with a whisk or with a handheld electric mixer at slow speed for a moment or two.

Stir the confectioners' sugar into the eggs a bit at a time, beating after each addition until it is well absorbed.

Add the egg yolks, one at a time, continuing to beat as each is added until it has been well blended in.

Put the bowl over hot but not boiling water, and beat three minutes or until the egg mixture is frothy and warm to the touch.

Remove from the heat, add the honey, and beat 8 minutes or until the mixture is cool.

Sift the flours gradually into the eggs, continuing to beat at low speed until the mixture is very soft and rather fluffy.

Add the cooled, melted butter and beat 30 seconds.

Place in a buttered and floured 9-inch spring-form pan. Bake in a moderate oven (177° C, 350° F) about 40 minutes or until a cake tester comes out clean.

Serve topped with a sprinkling of confectioners' sugar. For 10. Or cut in 3 layers and use in assembling *la bomba mocha* (pages 307 to 308).

Almond-Chocolate Cream Cake

la bomba mocha

Almond-Chocolate Cream

140 to 170 grams (5 to 6 ounces) slivered almonds

1 teaspoon almond extract

225 grams (2 sticks or ½ pound) unsalted butter, cut in small pieces and softened

2 cups confectioners' sugar, sifted or sieved

3 egg yolks

¾ cup coarsely grated semisweet chocolate (or chocolate chips)

½ cup cold, very strong coffee

Sponge Cake

3 8-inch-wide layers *Pan di Spagna* (pages 302 to 303) or *Torta Margherita* (page 306)

½ cup rum

Toast the almonds in the oven until nicely browned and roasted.

Mash the almonds almost to a powder, using either a sharp knife, a mortar with a pestle, or the food processor with its steel blade. Put the almonds in a small bowl and mix in the almond extract.

In a large bowl, cream the butter by hand or with an electric mixer until soft and fluffy. Add the sugar gradually, and continue beating until well absorbed. Add the egg yolks one by one, beating after each addition. Fold in the almonds and then the chocolate bits. Finally, fold in the cold coffee. The consistency will now be that of a very thick frosting.

Cut one of the cake layers in 8 even wedges.

Line a large bowl (at least 2½ liters or quarts, 10 inches in diameter) with plastic wrap, allowing the plastic to drape generously over the rim.

Out of the second layer of cake cut a small circle, approximately 2 inches in diameter. Place the circle in the bottom of the bowl. Place the wedges of the first layer, points to the circle, around the sides of the bowl, alternating crust side with sponge side against the bowl.

Sprinkle this layer of cake with rum.

Scoop half the almond-chocolate cream into the bowl. Shift the wedges, if necessary, to keep them equidistant. Break the remaining piece of the second cake layer into bite-size pieces, place them on the cream, and press down gently on them to ensure that the cracks between the wedges are all filled with cream. Put the remaining cream in the bowl, spreading it to fill remaining cracks. Place the third layer of cake crust side up over the cream. Sprinkle with the last of the rum.

Fold the plastic wrap back over the bowl to seal the entire *bomba*. Place in the refrigerator overnight or up to 36 hours.

When it is time to serve, unfold the plastic wrap, place a serving plate upside down over the bowl, and turn the bowl and plate over in order to set the *bomba* on the plate. Peel off the last of the plastic. Cut in thin wedges with a very sharp knife. For 20 portions, at least.

Apple and Pomegranate Cake

torta di mele e melagrano

8 tablespoons unsalted butter, softened

¾ cup sugar

grated rind of 1 lemon

2 large eggs at room temperature

1⅛ cup enriched bleached flour

1 teaspoon baking powder

½ teaspoon salt

4 tablespoons milk

2 tart baking apples (Baldwin, Northern Spy, Granny Smith)

2 tablespoons sugar

140 grams (5 ounces) crab-apple or currant jelly

seeds of half a pomegranate

Heat the oven to 200° C (400° F).

Butter and flour a 9-inch spring-form pan.

Cream butter and sugar together with lemon rind until smooth and lightly textured, using a food processor or an electric mixer.

Beat in the eggs one by one.

Put the flour, baking powder, and salt into a sifter and sift into the butter-egg mixture a third at a time; beat each addition until well blended.

Beat in the milk

Spoon the dough into the pan, leveling the top.

Peel, core, and slice the apples and place the slices on the cake, starting with the outside rim and working around and in until the cake is covered. Sprinkle with the extra sugar.

Bake 15 minutes in a hot (200° C, 400° F) oven, then reduce heat to 190° C (375° F), and continue baking for approximately 30 minutes or until a cake tester comes out clean and the apples are slightly golden.

Remove the rim of the pan.

Heat the jelly until completely melted and bubbling. Brush the apples with the jelly. Sprinkle pomegranate seeds over everything and let cool. For 10.

Corn Meal Cake

zaletto

2 cups milk

1 cup sugar

1 teaspoon salt

1 cup finest corn flour

2 cups all-purpose unbleached flour

½ cup (¼ pound) unsalted butter

3 large eggs at room temperature

1 cup mixed seedless golden and dark raisins, plumped in 2 cups hot water

1 cup *pignoli* or slivered almonds

grated rinds of 2 lemons

1 teaspoon vanilla extract

1 tablespoon baking powder

3 tablespoons confectioners' sugar

Preheat oven to 177° C (350° F).

In a large saucepan, scald the milk over medium heat. Add the sugar and salt to the milk, stirring with a wooden spoon until dissolved.

Sift the two flours directly into the scalding milk, stirring constantly and quickly until all the flour is in and the mixture has thickened (if any lumps have formed, beat with a handheld electric beater until smooth).

Remove the pan from the heat, add the butter, and stir until melted. Stir in the eggs one at a time, making sure each is absorbed before the next is added.

Drain the raisins thoroughly, squeeze them dry in a paper towel, and add them with the nuts and lemon rind to the batter. Stir in the vanilla. Sift the baking powder into the batter and mix well.

Pour into a buttered and floured Bundt pan. Bake in a moderate (177° C, 350° F) oven for 50 minutes or until the cake has risen and is a golden brown on top and a cake tester comes out clean.

Turn the *zaletto* upside down and, when it is cool enough to come out of the pan, sprinkle it with powdered sugar forced through a fine sieve. Cool thoroughly before cutting. For at least 12.

Duck Egg Cake

torta grande

4 duck eggs

1⅔ cups sugar

4 cups all-purpose un-
bleached flour, sifted

1 teaspoon salt

2 cups milk

1 cup vegetable oil

4 teaspoons baking powder

2 teaspoons almond ex-
tract

½ cup slivered almonds

Preheat oven to 177° C (350° F).

Beat the eggs well. Add the sugar, and beat until the texture of frosting. Add the flour and salt a bit at a time, stirring well after each addition.

Add the milk and oil, and mix thoroughly. Add the baking powder and, when that is well stirred in, mix in the almond extract.

Butter an 11-inch cake or spring-form pan, dust it with sugar, and pour in the batter. Sprinkle evenly with almonds.

Bake at 177° C (350° F) at least an hour or until a cake tester comes out clean when inserted. Cool thoroughly before cutting. For 16 at least.

Paradise Cake

torta paradiso

1 cup + 2 tablespoons un-
salted butter, softened
1⅓ cups superfine granu-
lated sugar
5 large egg yolks at room
temperature
5 large eggs at room tem-
perature
1⅔ cups all-purpose un-
bleached flour
1½ cups potato starch flour
1 teaspoon baking powder
½ teaspoon salt
grated rind of 1½ lemons
grated rind of ½ orange
1 teaspoon vanilla extract
confectioners' sugar

Preheat oven to 177° C (350° F).

Cream the butter and granulated sugar to-gether until soft and fluffy.

Beat the egg yolks until light in color. Add the whole eggs, and beat for at least 10 minutes with the electric mixer or 20, with a whisk, as the final texture of the cake depends on long beating.

Add the beaten eggs, about a tablespoon at a time, to the butter and sugar. Mix in with a spoon.

When all the eggs are incorporated in the butter-sugar mixture, sift the flours and baking powder and salt three times; then add them to the egg mixture about ½ cup at a time, folding in with a spoon or spatula after each addition.

Add the fruit rind and vanilla.

Butter a 12-inch spring-form pan, cut a circle of waxed paper to line the bottom, and butter it once it is in place. Pour the batter into the pan, tilting the pan to make sure of even distribu-tion.

Bake in a moderate (177° C, 350° F) oven for about 1 hour or until the cake is risen high and is golden brown on top and a cake tester comes out clean.

Allow to cool in pan, then turn out on a serv-ing plate, peel off the waxed paper, and sprinkle generously with sifted or sieved confectioners' sugar. Or you may make patterns on the top of the cake by cutting out designs in waxed paper to fit the top, then sprinkling sugar over all, and then lifting away the waxed paper. For 12 or 24 servings, depending on the width of your slices.

Paradise cake is excellent with a dessert wine or champagne. It keeps superbly, and its flavor approaches its best 24 hours after baking.

Imperial Sponge

spongata imperiale

6 large eggs at room temperature, separated

½ teaspoon salt

1½ cups sugar

¼ cup water

1 cup all-purpose unbleached flour

½ teaspoon cream of tartar

1 tablespoon grated lemon rind

1 teaspoon lemon extract

confectioners' sugar (optional)

Preheat oven to 177° C (350° F).

In a large (three-liter or three-quart) bowl, preferably copper, beat the egg whites until stiff, adding salt slowly as you beat. In a smaller bowl, beat the egg yolks until very pale in color.

Boil the sugar with the water in a small saucepan until it spins a thread.

Pour the boiled sugar in a slow stream into the egg whites, beating constantly. Continue to beat, and add the egg yolks to the whites. Beat until well mixed.

Sift the flour 3 times with the cream of tartar, then sift it into the eggs, folding in a bit at a time. Add the lemon rind and flavoring.

Pour into an unbuttered 10-inch tube pan.

Bake in a moderate (177° C, 350° F) oven until risen high and very toasty on top, about 40 minutes. Let cool upside down before removing from pan.

Serve with or without a sprinkling of confectioners' sugar. For 10 to 12.

Panettone

Years ago, when we first moved from Italy to the United States, few stores were importing Italy's famous Christmas bread, *panettone:* so, with the courage of pioneers, we set out to perfect a recipe that might come close to duplicating Milan's famous industrially produced perfection. *Panettone* is very close to a big brioche, and over the years since our first attempts we have tinkered with the recipe a dozen times. Instead of 7 to 8 risings, we have got it down to a modest 2 to make 4 *panettone,* each large enough for 6 people for breakfast on Christmas day, or for dessert any time, or just for plain wine sipping.

3 tablespoons (3 packets) active dry yeast
¾ cup warm (40° C, 105° F) water
1¾ cups sugar
¾ cup milk
¾ cup + 2 tablespoons unsalted butter
2½ teaspoons salt
grated rinds of 3 large lemons
4 teaspoons vanilla extract
8 cups all-purpose unbleached flour (approximate)
6 large eggs at room temperature
2 teaspoons vegetable oil
⅔ cup seedless golden raisins
½ cup citron, cut in slivers
1 teaspoon sugar, mixed with 1 teaspoon water

Proof the yeast in the warm water in a quart measure, along with 2 tablespoons of the sugar and let it stand in a warm place for 10 minutes (the oven of a gas stove with its pilot and its light on is perfect) until it has nearly tripled its original bulk.

Scald the milk, and add ½ cup of the butter. Stir until the butter is melted, then add the salt and the rest of the sugar. Transfer the milk-butter mixture to a large bowl. Stir in the lemon rind and the vanilla, and let cool a few moments.

Beat in, with a handheld electric mixer or a dough hook, 2 cups of the flour. Beat in the proofed yeast. Beat in 2 more cups flour, 5 of the eggs, one by one, and the white of the sixth egg. Beat until smooth.

If not using a dough hook, put aside the mixer and begin working with a wooden spoon. Add 3 more cups of flour, and mix until the dough becomes unwieldy.

Flour the counter, scoop the dough out onto

it, and add ½ cup of flour. Knead with your hands, adding more flour until all the flour is absorbed. The dough will now be soft, elastic, smooth, and still a bit sticky.

Place the oil in a large (three-liter or three-quart) bowl, add the dough, and twirl it around until both dough and bowl glisten with oil.

Cover the bowl with a dry dish towel and place in a warm corner until nearly 3 times its original size (3 to 4 hours, possibly longer, depending on climate).

Put the raisins in a 2-cup measure, cover with hot water, and let plump up for about 20 minutes to ½ hour. Drain and squeeze dry.

When the dough has risen sufficiently, punch it down and knead in the raisins and the slivered citron. Cut the dough into 4 equal parts.

Butter 4 pint-size casseroles or soufflé dishes (straight-sided charlotte pans or molds will do). Fix a collar of double folded and buttered aluminum foil around the inside of each dish. Put a piece of dough in each pan, mark a cross in the center of the dough with a sharp knife, and put the pans back into the warm place or oven. Cover all four pans with a dish towel. Let rise until more than double in size (a little more than an hour should do).

If you let the dough rise in the oven, remove when risen and cover with 2 or 3 more towels until the oven has been heated up to 200° C (400° F). If the dough is rising outside the oven, preheat to 200° C (400° F) during the last half hour of rising.

Mix the yolk of the last egg with the sugar and water solution until smooth. Brush the tops of the *panettone* with the egg-sugar-water mixture.

Bake 10 minutes at 200 ° C (400 ° F), put ½ tablespoon of butter in the center of each cross, and put the pans back in the oven.

Lower the heat to 190 ° C (375 ° F) for 10 minutes, then lower the heat to 177 ° C (350 ° F), and bake 30 minutes longer or until the *panettone* are crusty and golden brown on top and a cake tester comes out clean after being inserted in the center of the loaves.

Cool completely before removing from pans. Let stand 1 day before cutting.

Makes 4 *panettone*.

Panettone for Food Processor

3 cups cake flour

90 grams (⅕ pound) unsalted butter

1 egg plus 2 yolks

6 tablespoons sugar

½ teaspoon salt

1 cup milk

1 teaspoon lemon extract

1 teaspoon cream of tartar

½ teaspoon baking soda

⅔ cup seedless golden raisins, plumped in 2 cups warm water

2 tablespoons minced citron

grated rind of 1 lemon

1 egg white, lightly beaten

1 to 2 tablespoons sugar

Preheat oven to 200° C (400° F).

Place the flour and butter in the food-processor bowl and process with a steel blade until very well blended.

Add the egg and egg yolks and process on/off until well amalgamated.

Add sugar and salt, and process on/off as before.

Immediately add the milk and lemon extract and continue processing until very smooth (3 to 4 minutes).

Sift the cream of tartar and baking soda into the bowl and process on/off.

Drain the raisins, squeeze them dry in a paper towel, and add to the bowl along with the citron and lemon rind. Process on/off.

Pour the dough into a buttered charlotte pan (or any similar pan with sides higher than bottom is wide), and bake 10 minutes at 200° C (400° F). Lower the heat to 190° C (375° F), and bake 10 more minutes. Lower heat again to 177° C (350° F), and continue baking for about 30 minutes or until a cake tester inserted in the center of the cake comes out clean.

During the early checking of the cake, brush the top with egg white and, when a crust has formed, sprinkle with sugar.

Cool completely before cutting. Serves 8 to 10, depending on the meal. Serve at breakfast with coffee or at dinner with wine.

Veronese Sweet Bread

pandoro di Verona

2 cups + 1 tablespoon all-
purpose unbleached flour

1 scant tablespoon (1
packet) active dry yeast
or 1 cake yeast

1 heaping tablespoon
sugar

2 large eggs at room tem-
perature

3 egg yolks at room tem-
perature

12 tablespoons unsalted
butter

1½ teaspoons vanilla ex-
tract

½ teaspoon salt

confectioners' sugar (op-
tional)

Put 1 heaping tablespoon flour in a cup. Add
the yeast, breaking it up if it is cake yeast. Add 1
tablespoon warm water, and stir with a fork
until a small ball of dough has formed. Let sit in
a warm place for about 20 minutes or until
double in size.

Place ½ cup flour in the food-processor bowl
(or in a small bowl if mixing by hand). Add the
sugar, 1 egg, 1 egg yolk, 1 tablespoon of melted
butter, and the risen ball of dough. Process 10
seconds, scrape the dough down, and process
another 20 seconds; or mix by hand until well
amalgamated. You should now have a batter-
like dough. Cover the bowl with a plate, and
put it in a warm, draft-free place. Let the dough
rise 1 hour; it will fill the bowl of a food processor completely.

To the risen dough add 1 more egg and 2
more yolks, the vanilla, the salt, 2 more tablespoons of melted butter, and 1 cup of flour. Process or mix by hand until all the new ingredients are well incorporated.

Flour your counter or pastry board, place the
risen and mixed dough on it, and start to knead.
As you knead, add ½ cup more flour, a bit at a
time, and, when the flour is all in, continue to
knead for 10 minutes. By now the dough should
be smooth, elastic, and non-sticky.

Put a bit of melted butter in the bottom of a
large bowl, and swirl the ball of dough around
in it to butter the entire surface lightly. Cover
the bowl with plastic wrap and let rise again,
this time for 3 hours.

Soften the remaining 9 tablespoons of butter
and cut into ¼- to ½-inch pieces.

Punch the risen dough down and roll it out
with a rolling pin on a floured surface until you

have a piece of dough about 10 inches square.

Sprinkle the bits of butter over the center of the dough in one layer. Fold the corners of the dough to the center, barely overlapping the edges so that all the butter is enclosed. (This is very like the puff-pastry technique, pages 320 to 323.)

Roll the dough ever so lightly until it is back to its original size of about 10 × 10 inches. Fold a third of the dough to cover the next third. Fold the last third to cover the first two. You now have 3 layers of dough enclosing the butter. Roll out again to its original size, and fold again in thirds. Let sit for 20 minutes. Repeat the folding and rolling twice, and let rest another 20 minutes. Now roll the dough gently with one hand around and around until a ball of dough has formed with no piece of butter protruding. If butter does emerge, reroll the dough with a rolling pin, let it rest, and make a ball a second time.

Butter and sugar a tall, tubeless sponge-cake pan or charlotte pan, the taller the better. Place the dough in it and let rise in a warm place at least an hour until it doubles in size. If you do not have a tall pan, the bottom of which is narrower than its top, make a collar of double aluminum foil for the pan you have, butter and sugar the collar, and let the dough rise in that.

When the cake has risen, keep it covered and warm while you preheat the oven to 230° C (450° F).

Bake the cake at 230° C for 15 minutes, reduce the heat to 190° C (375° F), and continue baking for ½ to ¾ of an hour.

Let the cake cool before removing from its pan. Serve with a sprinkling of confectioners' sugar or with *zabaglione* (page 332). For 10 to 12.

Cakes and Pastry

Puff Pastry

pasta sfogliata

No matter what country of the western world provides the recipe for puff pastry, it is without doubt the most delicate and delightful of all the pastry doughs. There are no real shortcuts in the making of this pastry, which involves rolling, folding, turning, and resting the dough. Each set of these operations is called a turn; and six such turns are involved before the pastry is ready for use. Variations on the methods (such as different times for chilling ingredients or different amounts of an ingredient) can occur from region to region.

In Italy, a tablespoon or two of *acquavite* is added to the water for the dough. In England and in America, a tablespoon of lemon juice is added. Most cooks prefer an equal balance of butter and flour, but some prefer just a bit less butter than flour. An ancient Italian recipe for quick puff pastry uses a combination of lard, butter, yeast, and egg with the flour.

In today's kitchen, with freezers at hand and food processors available to do some of the mixing and in light of the fact that a double recipe takes little longer than a single one, a big batch of puff pastry is the thing to aim for. You can use as much as you want, and freeze the rest.

Before starting, here are a few time-honored rules to make the mixing and rolling more easy:

Chill everything: the flour in its measuring container, the water in its cup, the butter, the rolling pin, and, if possible, the pastry board.

Chill the dough thoroughly after the first mixing and again after each subsequent two turns.

When puff-pastry dough has been cut to the shape and size you desire, chill it again on its cookie sheet or pie pan before baking. It can be kept a day or two in the refrigerator.

The dough can be frozen for weeks. Label the packages of dough by date and weight or cut and freeze them according to a planned recipe.

When thawing frozen puff-pastry dough, put it on the least cold shelf of the refrigerator. Give thawed dough two turns, finishing by rolling to the size and shape needed, and chill again before putting it into the oven.

Do not be put off making puff pastry because of the time involved or the long list of rules. Once you have made it and your hands are familiar with the texture and the turning, you will begin to know the joy of using it in many ways, including in creations of your own. Puff pastry is as creative as egg pasta; there is no end to the combinations and inventions to which it can be put. Now, make a turn or two.

4 cups chilled all-purpose unbleached flour
2 cups chilled unsalted butter
1 teaspoon salt
⅞ cup ice water
2 tablespoons *acquavite* or vodka

Put 3½ cups flour in the bowl of a food processor fitted with the steel blade. Add 4 tablespoons of chilled butter cut into ¼-inch cubes. Add salt. Process on/off until the butter is thoroughly cut into the flour. Turn the machine on and slowly pour the ice water into the flour. Add the *acquavite,* and continue to process until a ball of soft dough forms at one end of the blade. Remove the dough and knead it briefly on a floured, chilled pastry board until smooth and elastic. Wrap in plastic wrap or wax paper and chill ½ hour.

Cut the remaining butter into ¼-inch cubes and place them in the food-processor bowl (you do not have to wash blade or bowl from previous use). Sprinkle in the last of the flour. Process on/off until the entire mixture is cut into tiny beads and ready to be amalgamated with your hands.

Turn the mixture out between two pieces of plastic wrap or heavy waxed paper on the pastry board and work it with your fingers until it is pressed into a 3″ × 8″ × 1½″ brick. Wrap in wax paper or plastic wrap and chill 20 to 25 minutes.

When both mixtures are chilled (they should be of the same firmness), roll out the flour mixture to approximately 10″ × 18″. Place the butter mixture in the center of the upper two-thirds of the flour dough. Bring up the lower (uncovered) third of the flour dough and cover half the butter mixture. Fold the upper third of flour dough (covered with butter mixture) down over the lower, already folded, third. Seal the two ends with a good pinch of the fingers. You now have a packet of dough, with three layers of flour dough separated by two layers of butter dough.

Turn the rectangle with the seam side facing right, with a narrow end toward you. Bang the dough lightly with a rolling pin up and down the length of the dough. Then roll the dough away from you until it is about ½-inch thick and approximately its original length and width.

Fold the narrow ends to meet in the middle, and then fold the new ends to meet each other. You now have a book of four layers of dough. If, during this first rolling out, any butter breaks through, do not despair: repair the hole with a bit of dough broken off one end, dampened, and placed over the escaping butter. Wrap and chill the dough for ½ hour.

Remove the dough from the refrigerator and

again place it on the chilled and lightly floured pastry board. Roll out to its 10″ × 18″ original dimensions, fold the ends to the middle, and fold again. Roll again, fold again, and chill ½ hour.

Roll out as above, fold and roll, and fold again, and chill at least 2 hours. Overnight is even better.

Roll the dough out twice more before cutting, and chill after cutting and before baking for best results.

Makes 1 kilogram, 350 grams (3 pounds). Puff pastry may be frozen for months or refrigerated about a week. Unbleached flour may gray slightly after 3 or 4 days in the refrigerator, but it means nothing and goes back to proper color on baking.

For convenience, pack your dough in easily rolled pieces such as 225 grams (½ pound).

Puff Pastry with Apples

sfogliata alle mele

225 grams (½ pound) puff pastry (pages 320 to 323)

2 Golden Delicious apples

4 tablespoons sugar

¼ teaspoon ground cinnamon

¼ teaspoon freshly grated nutmeg

1 egg, slightly beaten

4 tablespoons crab-apple or currant jelly

Preheat oven to 220° C (425° F).

Roll puff pastry to an ⅛-inch thickness. Cut in equal rectangular pieces, approximately 6″ × 8″.

Peel, slice, and core the apples, and place an equal number of slices in the center of each rectangle. Sprinkle the apple slices with equal amounts of sugar, cinnamon, and nutmeg.

Brush with egg the area of the puff pastry not covered by apple.

Bake 15 minutes in a hot (220° C, 425° F) oven; then lower the heat to 177° C (350° F) and continue baking another 10 to 15 minutes or until the pastry is puffed and browned.

In a small pan, bring the jelly to a boil over moderate heat. When it is completely melted and bubbly, pour it over the apple slices. Allow the pastry to cool before serving. For 4.

Cookies

Meringues
meringhe

Meringhe are a staple of the Italian sweet collection. They were once the exclusive territory of the pastry shops; now, with home freezers (to store casually collected egg whites) and reliable ovens, more and more cooks are making *meringhe* firm and pretty enough to compete with those of any *pasticcere*.

Meringhe are used with cream, in pies between crust and filling, and in layers to make *semifreddi*.

This recipe makes individual *meringhe*, shells, or layers. It doubles easily and lends itself to flavoring in different ways; and the final product stores well in a closed cookie tin or casserole.

cold butter for the cookie
sheets
1 teaspoon (approximate)
cornstarch
½ cup egg whites (approximately 4 large egg
whites) at room tempera-
ture
¼ teaspoon cream of tartar
¼ teaspoon salt
1 cup superfine sugar
1 teaspoon vanilla extract

Butter two cookie sheets lightly and wipe them with paper toweling to remove any excess. Sieve the cornstarch over the tins and shake them well to distribute the cornstarch. Shake off any excess.

Place the egg whites, cream of tartar, and salt in a large bowl (copper, if you have one). Beat with an electric beater, working first at low speed then up to high speed, until the whites hold a shape and all the bubbles are uniform. Turn to low speed again, and start adding the sugar a tablespoon at a time.

When about half the sugar has been beaten in, add the vanilla and continue beating at low speed, adding the rest of the sugar until it all has been mixed in. Continue beating the mixture for about 5 more minutes or until it is really stiff and very glossy and keeps its swirls and peaks like a perfect frosting.

If you are making individual *meringhe* (this recipe makes about 40), you may use a pastry bag with a large plain tip and squeeze and whirl the *meringhe* mixture onto the cookie sheets in rounds 1 to 2 inches in diameter. Or you may use 2 tablespoons (which is more expeditious), dipping with one and pushing the batter out onto the sheets with the other. Just be careful the tails of batter fall back onto the *meringhe* and not the sheet.

If you wish *meringhe* shells, draw two even circles on each of the two cookie sheets. Scoop half the batter into one circle, half into the other. Smooth to the edges of the circle with a spatula, forming the *meringhe* about ½ inch deep in the center, double around the edge. Or you may make a spiral, using the pastry bag with its plain tip: start at the center of the circle and go around and around until you reach the outside edge, which should be done twice for thickness.

If you wish *meringhe* layers, trace 4 circles about 8 inches in diameter (2 on each sheet) and evenly spread the *meringhe* about ⅓ of an inch deep with no border.

Bake small individual *meringhe* at 120° C (250° F) for 1½ hours, turn off the heat, and let the cookies cool at least a half hour in the closed oven. Two-inch *meringhe* should bake 2 hours and cool ½ hour.

Shells and layers also require 2-hour baking and ½-hour cooling.

Variations:

To make chocolate flavored *meringhe,* beat in 1 rounded tablespoon unsweetened cocoa after all the sugar has been beaten in.

To make decorated *meringhe,* sprinkle with chocolate bits (jimmies) or multicolor nonpareils or sugar trims.

Meringhe are served alone as cookies or they can be paired, with 2 to 3 tablespoons whipped cream, or vanilla or chocolate ice cream, or another filling of your choice, between them.

Shells are frequently filled with fresh fruits — strawberries, raspberries, peaches, blueberries, or apricots — and smothered with whipped cream.

Layers are frequently spread with whipped cream and placed in the freezer until the cream is frozen.

Odd pieces of *meringhe* are used crushed in apple tarts (pages 296 to 298).

Almond Meringues

meringhe alle mandorle

cold butter for the cookie sheets

1 teaspoon (approximate) cornstarch

1 cup egg whites (approximately 8 large egg whites)

½ teaspoon cream of tartar

½ teaspoon salt

2 cups superfine sugar

¼ cup ground toasted almonds

1 teaspoon almond extract

This is a big recipe for using up lots of egg whites and a nice variation on the *meringhe* theme. The mixture may be made in layers or shells or dropped in cookie sizes.

Butter three cookie sheets lightly, wiping off any excess with a paper towel. Sieve the cornstarch onto the pans, shake to distribute, and discard any excess.

Place the egg whites, cream of tartar, and salt in a three- or four-quart bowl (copper, if possible). With a handheld electric beater at low speed, begin to beat the egg whites. Gradually raise the speed to the highest point, beating until the whites hold peaks and the bubbles are small and uniform. Reduce the speed to low, and begin to add the sugar, a tablespoon at a time.

When about half the sugar has been beaten in, add the ground almonds mixed with an equal amount of sugar, tablespoon by tablespoon. When all the almonds are in, continue adding the last of the sugar and beating until all the mixture is really thickened, glossy, and stiff and holds its swirls as you beat.

The mixture may be poured in layers (round or rectangular), shaped into shells, or dropped as small egg-size cookies by the dozen. (See pages 325 to 327 for complete *meringhe* instructions.)

Bake at 120° C (250° F) for 1½ hours, a little longer for the larger of layers or shells.

Meringhe are done when they lift off the pan easily. We must admit it is easier to make *meringhe* when the humidity is down, but, in spite of climate, *meringhe* will cook to a hard and dry texture if you just leave them long enough in the oven, with a pilot light on (if you have one) but the heat off, after the baking time is up.

For 6 rectangular layers, 6 round layers or shells, or about 6 dozen small meringues. You may store cookies and layers or shells for literally months, provided you use a tightly sealed container such as a good tin or large covered casserole.

Wine Sipping Cookies *alla Romagnola*

biscottini alla romagnola

1½ cups unsalted butter
1 cup milk
1 egg, beaten
2 cups all-purpose un-bleached flour
4 cups finest corn flour
¾ teaspoon salt
¾ cup granulated sugar
1 teaspoon vanilla extract
¼ cup seedless golden rai-sins, plumped in 1 cup warm water
⅓ cup *pignoli* or slivered almonds

Preheat oven to 200 ° C (400 ° F).

Melt the butter over low heat and let it cool slightly. Mix together the milk and the beaten egg.

Sift the two flours together with the salt onto a pastry board or smooth, clean counter. Make a well in the center of the flour, and pour in the melted butter, sugar, and vanilla. Work with your fingers, adding a bit of the egg-milk mixture as you work.

When all the milk is used, drain the raisins, squeeze them dry in a paper towel, add them and the *pignoli* or almonds to the dough, and work some more until a solid, even dough has been achieved.

Take pieces of dough, about a teaspoon at a time, and roll them into little balls about the size of a cherry tomato. Place the balls on buttered cookie sheets and press each one down to flatten it slightly.

Bake in a hot (200 ° C, 400 ° F) oven for about 20 minutes or until light toast in color. Makes about 3 dozen extremely rich cookies (which keep very well in a sealed cookie tin).

Salted *Brigidini* (or *Cialde* or *Pizzelle*)

brigidini salati

2 tablespoons margarine
(*not* butter)
1 egg
2 tablespoons instant
mashed potato
2 tablespoons potato
starch flour
½ cup water
½ teaspoon salt
1 tablespoon vegetable oil

This recipe has been worked out for the electric *pizzelle* machine found in cookware departments and Italian specialty stores. It has also been adapted for those who desire a salty, crisp wafer with their wine instead of the sweet, traditional *brigidini* or *cialde,* the original wafers used to make cones for ice cream. *Cialde* or *brigidini* are also called *pizzelle,* especially in America.

Heat the electric *pizzelle* machine.

Place all the ingredients in the bowl of a food processor with the dough or steel blade in place. Mix on/off briefly until a dough has formed.

Open the heated *pizzelle* machine, drop about a tablespoonful of dough in the center of each form, close the machine, and cook 30 seconds.

The first two wafers (*brigidini, cialde, pizzelle*) may have to be discarded, serving only for temperature and time control. Once you establish those for your machine, just continue making the wafers. Place cooked wafers on waxed paper to cool. Makes 10 to 12 wafers.

Sweet *Brigidini*

brigidini alla franca

1 cup all-purpose un-
   bleached flour

3 tablespoons sugar

1 large egg

2 tablespoons unsalted
   butter, melted and
   cooled

pinch of salt

¼ teaspoon almond, va-
   nilla, or anise extract

¾ cup dry white wine

Put the flour in a mound on your pastry board
or clean counter. Make a well in the center, and
add the sugar, egg, butter, and salt.

With a small whisk mix the egg and butter together, picking up sugar and flour as you mix.
Add the extract, and continue working with the
whisk. Add the wine, a bit at a time, and continue whisking until a smooth, homogeneous
dough is reached.

Heat the *pizelle/brigidini* iron. Drop a tablespoon of dough in the center of each *brigidini*
form, close the iron tightly, and cook for 30 seconds or so until golden brown. Makes about 15.

Brigidini may be cooled flat on waxed paper
or aluminum foil or they may be rolled up like a
cannolo while still very warm on the open iron.
Serve with wine.

Zabaglione

6 egg yolks
6 tablespoons superfine
    granulated sugar
12 tablespoons Marsala

It would be unfair to close this chapter on desserts without including *zabaglione,* one of Italy's most famous and favorite sweets. Usually served by itself in delicate glasses at the end of a sumptuous meal, *zabaglione* is also served with sponge cakes or Veronese sweet bread to make a spectacular finish for parties.

If you have a large copper bowl, use it as the upper part of a double boiler. Or use a stainless-steel double boiler.

Place the egg yolks in the copper bowl or the upper part of the double boiler, add the sugar, and beat with a whisk or handheld electric beater until pale yellow and very fluffy. Place over hot but not boiling water. Continue beating as the egg mixture warms. Add the Marsala, a little at a time, and continue the beating until the mixture thickens to the consistency of a light, fluffy batter.

Remove from heat, and beat about 3 minutes longer. Pour into dessert glasses or use to top a *pan di Spagna* (pages 302 to 303) or *pandoro di Verona* (pages 318 to 319). *Zabaglione* may be served lukewarm or cold. For 6 individual servings or, if used with cake, for 12.

On Italian Wines

Five centuries before Christ, Sophocles stated that "Italy is the land chosen by Bacchus," but then, the land of the Italian people was also known as *Enotria,* "Land of Wine." This is to prove, if need be, that Italy and wine share a long and rich past. The sobriquet, "Land of Wine," still rightfully applies to today's Italy: the country is the largest wine producer in the world. It is true that quantity does not necessarily imply quality; but when it comes to Italian wine, the strict new laws implemented since 1963 for the production of wine are assuring both quantity and high quality.

"If the quantity is phenomenal," Burton Anderson, wine expert and writer, told us, "the variety of good Italian wines is astounding." Indeed, the variety is such that we leave their full listing and description to those who seem capable of considering wines in the abstract. We, who prefer to consider them in the context of food, will say that Italian wines go beautifully with Italian food, province for province. We are also convinced that many of these wines can stand up to comparison with the aristocracy of wines of other countries.

As for the choice of Italian wine, we go along, up to a point, with the basic rules: full-bodied, deep-tasting wines go best with rich, hearty food, lighter wines with lighter fare. Hence the whites, generally light, go with fish, and the reds, generally heavier, go with red meats. Between the lightest and the most full-bodied wines there is a full spectrum of gradations: if you enjoy learning the subtle differences among wines, you will find that it does not pay to be a stickler for the rules. Many times, to the horror of experts, we have broken the rules and found delight. As always, your taste should decide.

Following is a brief listing of Italian wines grouped by their basic characteristics, as a suggestion for a choice. For a more in-depth and comprehensive study of Italian wines, we recommend reading the new book, *Vino,* by Burton Anderson, published by Little, Brown and Company in association with the Atlantic Monthly Press.

White Wines

Dry, light-bodied

    Albano
    Asprinio
    Corvo Bianco
    Est! Est! Est!
    Frascati
    Lugana
    Marino
    Pinot Bianco
    Pinto Grigio
    Sanguinella
    Torgiano

Dry, medium-bodied

    Castel del Monte
    Cinqueterre
    Cortese di Gavi
    Falerno
    Lacrima Christi
    Montecarlo
    Morasco Cinqueterre
    Orvieto Secco
    Soave
    Terlano
    Tocai
    Trebbiano di Romagna
    Vernaccia di San Gimigniano
    Verdicchio

Mellow

    Aleatico dell'Elba
    Frascati abboccato
    Moscato d'Asti
    Orvieto abboccato
    Procanico
    Prosecco

Red Wines

Dry, light-bodied
- Bardolino
- Lago di Caldaro

Dry, medium-bodied
- Cabernet
- Castel del Monte, Rosso
- Chianti
- Dolcetto
- Grignolino
- Grumello
- Inferno
- Merlot Rosso
- Montepulciano d'Abruzzo
- Nebbiolo
- Sangiovese di Romagna
- Sassella
- Torgiano Rosso
- Valpolicella

Robust
- Amarone
- Barbaresco
- Barbera d'Asti
- Barolo
- Brunello di Montalcino
- Carema
- Chianti Riserva
- Corvo Rosso
- Gattinara
- Ghemme
- Vino Nobile di Montepulciano

Dessert Wines

Marsala
Moscato di Pantelleria

Sparkling Wines

Asti Spumante
Lambrusco
Nebbiolo Spumante
Prosecco Spumante
Spumante Brut

Wines *Vini*

Index

Abbachio. See Lamb
Acciuga. See Anchovy/Anchovies
Agnello. See also Lamb
  arrosto (Roast Baby [New Zealand]
    Lamb), 176–177
  al Barolo (Lamb with Barolo), 180
  brasato (Braised Leg of Lamb), 181
  fritto dorato (Golden-Fried Lamb Steaks),
    183
Agnolotti
  conserving, 99
  cutting, 98
Almond(s)
  -Chocolate Cream Cake (*La Bomba mocha*),
    307–308
  Duck with (*Anitra alle mandorle*), 212–213
  Filled Peaches (*Pesche ripiene alle mandorle*),
    290
  Meringues (*Meringhe alle mandorle*),
    328–329
  -Prune Stuffing, Rock Cornish Hen with
    (*Galletto ripieno alle mandorle e prugne*),
    185–186
  in *Risotto* with Chestnuts and Almonds
    (*Risotto alle castagne e mandorle*), 139
Anchovy/Anchovies
  in general, 4
  Dressing, Artichokes with (*Carciofi con salsa
    d'acciuga*), 55
  Roasted Sweet Peppers with (*Peperoni
    all'acciughe*), 58
  Sauce, Avocado with (*Avocado in salsa d'ac-
    ciuga*), 53

Anchovy paste, 4
Anelli di mele e cipolle (Apple and Onion
  Rings), 256
Anguille. See also Eels
  marinate (Marinated Eels), 235–236
Anitra (Duck)
  alla griglia (Grilled Duckling), 211–212
  alle mandorle (Duck with Almonds),
    212–213
Antipasti. See Appetizers
Antipasto
  di mare (Seafood Cocktail), 61
  Pepper-Celery-Olive (*Peperoni, sedani, ed
    olive*), 59
Appetizers (*Antipasti*), 49–76
  in general, 51–52
  Artichokes with Anchovy Dressing (*Car-
    ciofi con salsa d'acciuga*), 55
  Artichokes, Jewish Style (*Carciofi alla Giu-
    dia*), 53–55
  Avocado with Anchovy Sauce (*Avocado in
    salsa d'acciuga*), 53
  Batter-Fried *Mozzarella* (*Mozzarella fritta*),
    56
  Broiled Stuffed Tomatoes (*Pomodori ripieni
    alla griglia*), 60
  Broiled Stuffed Tomatoes with Ham and
    Cheese (*Pomodori ripieni con prosciutto cotto
    e formaggio*), 59
  Cheese-and-Spinach Turnovers (*Sfogliatine
    di spinaci e formaggio*), 70
  Chicken Liver Mousse in Aspic (*Spuma di
    fegatini in gelatina*), 75–76

Appetizers (*Continued*)
Crab Meat Filling for Tartlets (*Barchette di granchio*), 63
Crab Meat, Venetian Style (*Granzeola alla veneziana*), 55
Grilled Stuffed Mushrooms (*Funghi ripieni alla griglia*), 57
Little Pizzas (*Pizzette*), 66–69
Marinated Mushrooms (*Funghi marinati*), 57
Mozzarella, Batter-Fried (*Mozzarella fritta*), 56
Mushrooms, Grilled Stuffed (*Funghi ripieni alla griglia*), 57
Mushrooms, Marinated (*Funghetti marinati*), 57
Mussels in Piquant Sauce (*Cozze in salsa piccante*), 56
Pâté, Venetian (*Pâté alla veneziana*), 74–75
Pepper-Celery-Olive *Antipasto* (*Peperoni, sedani, ed olive*), 59
Peppers, Roasted, with Anchovies (*Peperoni all'acciughe*), 58
Pizzas, Little (*Pizzette*), 66–69
Pizzette with Mushrooms and *Mozzarella* (*Pizzette con funghi e mozzarella*), 69
Pizzette with Tomatoes and *Mozzarella* (*Pizzette con pomodori e mozzarella*), 69
Puff Pastries with Ham and *Ricotta* (*Sfogliatine con prosciutto e ricotta*), 72
Puff Pastries with Tomato and *Mozzarella* (*Sfogliatine*), 71
Roasted Sweet Peppers with Anchovies (*Peperoni all'acciughe*), 58
Russian Salad (*Insalata russa*), 64
Salty Pastry for Tartlets (*Pasta salata per tartellette*), 62–63
Savory Squid (*Calamari all'appetitosa*), 65
Seafood Cocktail (*Antipasto di mare*), 61
Squid, Savory (*Calamari all'appetitosa*), 65
Sweet Peppers, Roasted, with Anchovies (*Peperoni all'acciughe*), 58
Tartlets (*Tartellette*), 62–63
Tomatoes, Broiled Stuffed (*Pomodori ripieni alla griglia*), 60
Tomatoes, Broiled Stuffed, with Ham and Cheese (*Pomodori ripieni con prosciutto cotto e formaggio*), 59
Tuna Mousse (*Spuma di tonno*), 73
Venetian Pâté (*Pâté alla veneziana*), 74–75
Apple(s)
and Onion Rings (*Anelli di mele e cipolle*), 256
and Pomegranate Cake (*Torta di mele e melagrano*), 309
Puff Pastry with (*Sfogliata alle mele*), 324
Tart I (*Crostata di mele I*), 296

Tart II (*Crostata di mele II*), 297
Tart, Imperial (*Crostata imperiale di mele*), 298
Aragosta. See also Lobster
lessa (Boiled Lobster), 241–242
Arancie. See Orange
Aromi (Flavorings). *See* Flavorings, herbs, and ingredients
Arrosto d'agnello (Lamb Roast, Umbrian Style), 182
Artichoke(s)
boiling, 5
deep-frying, 53–55
in general, 4–5
with Anchovy Dressing (*Carciofi con salsa d'acciuga*), 55
in Avocado, Asparagus and Artichoke Salad (*Insalata di avocado, asparagi, e carciofi*), 262
Casserole (*Parmigiana di carciofi*), 258
Golden-Fried (*Carciofi fritti dorati*), 257; in Artichoke Casserole (*Parmigiana di carciofi*), 258
Jewish Style (*Carciofi alla Giudia*), 53–55
Pasta with (*Pasta ai carciofi*), 119
with Peas (*Carciofi con piselli*), 257
Pie (*Torta di carciofi*), 259–260
Risotto with (*Risotto ai carciofi*), 138
Soup (*Minestra di carciofi*), 82
Asparagus
in Avocado, Asparagus, and Artichoke Salad (*Insalata di avocado, asparagi, e carciofi*), 262
Pie (or Easter Pie; *Torta di pasqua*), 261–262
Rice with (*Riso con asparagi*), 138
and Rice Salad (*Insalata di riso ed asparagi*), 272
Aspic
Chicken-Beef Broth for (*Brodo di pollo e manzo per gelatina e zuppe*), 45–46
Chicken Liver Mousse in (*Spuma di fegatini in gelatina*), 75–76
Rolled Stuffed Turkey Breast in (*Rollato di tacchino ripieno in galantina*), 200–202
Avocado
with Anchovy Sauce (*Avocado in salsa d'acciuga*), 53
Asparagus, and Artichoke Salad (*Insalata di avocado, asparagi, e carciofi*), 262
Avocado in salsa d'acciuga (Avocado with Anchovy Sauce), 53

Baby Clam Sauce, Sicilian Style (*Salsa con vongole alla siciliana*), 105
Baccalà (Dried salt cod), 221, 232

Bacon
  in general, 11–12
  in *Risotto* with Mushrooms, Sausages, and
    Bacon (*Risotto ai funghi, salsiccie, e pan-
    cetta affumicata*), 144
Balsamella (*Besciamella*). *See* White Sauce
Barchette di granchio (Crab Meat Filling for
    Tartlets), 63
Barolo, Lamb with (*Agnello al Barolo*), 180
Basic Sauces (*Salse*), 30–42
  Bolognese Meat (*Ragù alla bolognese*),
    35–36
  Green (*Salsa verde*), 33–34
  Mayonnaise (*Maionese*), 30–32
  Pesto, 36–39
  Tomato (*Salsa di pomodoro*), 40
  Tomato and Basil (*Salsa di pomodoro e basi-
    lico*), 40
  White (*Besciamella/Balsamella*), 41–42
Basil
  in general, 5–6
  in *Risotto* with Tomatoes and Basil (*Risotto
    al pomodoro fresco e basilico*), 148
  in Tomato and Basil Sauce (*Salsa di pomo-
    doro e basilico*), 40
Bass. *See* Sea Bass
Batter I (Yeast; *Pastella con lievito*), 25–26
  deep-frying with, 26–27
  in Batter-Fried Chicken (*Pollo fritto*), 207
  in Deep-Fried Cod Filets (*Filetti di baccalà
    fritti*), 232
Batter II (Egg; *Pastella semplice*), 27
  in Batter-Fried *Mozzarella* (*Mozzarella
    fritta*), 56
  in Fried Scallops (*Conchiglie di San Giacomo
    fritte*), 245
Batter-Fried
  Chicken (*Pollo fritto*), 207
  Mozzarella (*Mozzarella fritta*), 56
Batteria di cucina. See Equipment
Batters (*Pastelle*), 25–27
Battuto (Mince), 3
Bean(s)
  and Celery Salad (*Insalata di fagioli e se-
    dano*), 268
  Green, Florentine Style (*Fagiolini alla
    fiorentina*), 268
  Lima, Tuscan Style (*Fave alla toscana*), 269
  in Pasta and Bean Soup (*Pasta e fagioli*),
    86–88
Beef (*Manzo*). *See also* Beef Broth
  Broth, Chicken-, for Aspic and Soups
    (*Brodo di pollo e manzo per gelatina e
    zuppe*), 45–46
  Corned, and Cabbage, Italian Style (*Bol-
    lito irlandese all'italiana*), 168

and Pork Meat Loaf (*Polpettone di manzo e
    maiale*), 159
  Pot Roast for the Pressure Cooker (*Stufato
    di manzo per la pentola a pressione*), 161
  Roast Tenderloin of (*Filetto di manzo ar-
    rosto*), 162
  Rolls (*Involtini di manzo*), 157–158
  Tenderloin of, Marco Polo (*Filetto alla
    Marco Polo*), 163
  Tenderloin of, Roast (*Filetto di manzo ar-
    rosto*), 162
  and Turkey Croquettes (*Polpette di tacchino
    e manzo*), 194
Beef Broth (*Brodo di carne*), 43
  in aspic, 75
  in Braised Leg of Lamb (*Agnello brasato*),
    181
  in Lamb with Barolo (*Agnello al Barolo*),
    180
  in Mixed Spring Vegetables (*Padellata pri-
    maverile*), 275
  in *risotto*, 139, 143, 151
Belgian Endive–Cress Salad (*Insalata d'indi-
    via belga e crescione*), 263
Besciamella (*Balsamella*). *See* White Sauce
Beurre manié. See Floured Butter
Bianco: in bianco (poached) fish, 221–222
Bisato e bisi (Venetian Eels and Peas), 235
Biscottini alla romagnola (Wine Sipping Cook-
    ies *alla Romagnola*), 329
Blender
  for Mayonnaise (*Maionese*), 31
  for *Pesto*, 38
Boiled Lobster (*Aragosta lessa*), 241–242
Bollito
  irlandese all'italiana (Corned Beef and Cab-
    bage, Italian Style), 168
  misto, 33
Bolognese Meat Sauce (*Ragù alla bolognese*),
    35–36
  Lasagne with (*Lasagne al ragù*), 131
Bomba mocha, La (Almond-Chocolate Cream
    Cake), 307–308
Boneless Pork Loin with Orange Sauce
    (*Lombo di maiale all'arancia*), 171–172
Bonito (*Tonnetto al cartoccio*), 231
Bouillon cubes, 6
Braised Leg of Lamb (*Agnello brasato*), 181
Branzino. See also Sea Bass
  al forno (Baked Sea Bass), 248
Bread
  in general, 6
  Sweet, Veronese (*Pandoro di Verona*),
    318–319
Bread dough, commercially frozen, 68–69
Breadcrumbs, 6–7

Breaded Pork Cutlets, Herbed (*Cotolette di maiale all'erbe*), 173
Breast of Veal
  Rolled, for the Pressure Cooker (*Rollato di vitello per la pentola a pressione*), 165
  Stuffed (*Petto di vitello ripieno*), 166
Breasts of Chicken, Stuffed (*Petti di pollo farciti*), 205
Brigidini
  alla franca (Sweet *Brigidini*), 331
  salati (Salted *Brigidini*), 330
  Salted (*Brigidini salati*), 330
  Sweet (*Brigidini alla franca*), 331
Brodi. See Broths
Brodo
  di carne (Beef Broth), 43
  di pesce (Fish Broth), 47
  di pollo (Chicken Broth), 44
  di pollo e manzo per gelatina e zuppe (Chicken-Beef Broth for Aspic and Soups), 45–46
  di tacchino per la pentola a pressione (Turkey Broth for the Pressure Cooker), 89
  di verdure (Vegetable Broth), 46
Broths (*Brodi*), 43–47. *See also* Soups
  clarifying, 44
  for *risotto*, 137
  Beef (*Brodo di carne*), 43. *See also* Beef Broth
  Chicken (*Brodo di pollo*), 44. *See also* Chicken Broth
  Chicken-Beef, for Aspics and Soups (*Brodo di pollo e manzo per gelatina e zuppe*), 45–46; in Stuffed Cabbage (*Cavolo ripieno*), 264–265
  Fish (*Brodo di pesce*), 47. *See also* Fish Broth
  Turkey, for the Pressure Cooker (*Brodo di tacchino per la pentola a pressione*), 89
  Vegetable (*Brodo di verdure*), 46; in *risotto*, 138, 146
Brussels Sprouts and Onions (*Cavolini di Bruxelles e cipolline*), 263
Burro (Butter)
  ai caperi (Caper Butter for Fish), 28
  maneggiato (Floured Butter), 28, 29
  saporito per pesce (Herbed Butter for Fish), 28
  verde (Parsley Butter), 29
Butter
  in general, 7
  Caper, for Fish (*Burro ai caperi*), 28
  Floured (*Burro maneggiato*), 28, 29
  Herbed, for Fish (*Burro saporito per pesce*), 28
  Parsley (*Burro verde*), 29; with Broiled Turbot (*Rombo alla griglia*), 254

Cabbage
  Corned Beef and, Italian Style (*Bollito irlandese all'italiana*), 168
  Stuffed (*Cavolo ripieno*), 264–265
Cake
  Almond-Chocolate Cream (*La Bomba mocha*), 307–308
  Apple and Pomegranate (*Torta di mele e melagrano*), 309
  Corn Meal (*Zaletto*), 310
  Duck Egg (*Torta grande*), 311
  Imperial Sponge (*Spongata imperiale*), 313
  Italian Chocolate Layer, 301
  Italian Pound, 300; in Italian Chocolate Layer Cake, 301
  Margherita (*Torta Margherita*), 306. *See also* Margherita Cake
  Paradise (*Torta paradiso*), 312
  Sponge (*Pan di Spagna*), 302–303. *See also* Sponge Cake
Calamari. See also Squid
  all'appetitosa (Savory Squid), 65
  fritti (Fried Squid), 252
Cannelloni
  conserving, 99
  cutting, 98
  rolling, 96
  del curato (Saint's Day *Cannelloni*), 127–128
  Pork-Veal-Ham Filling for (*Ripieno per cappelletti o cannelloni*), 122–123
  ripieno per (Pork-Veal-Ham Filling for *Capelletti* or *Cannelloni*), 122–123
  Saint's Day (*Cannelloni del curato*), 127–128
Cape sante. See Scallops
Caper(s)
  in general, 4, 7
  Butter for Fish (*Burro ai caperi*), 28
Cappelletti
  conserving, 99
  cutting, 98
  filling, 120–121
  rolling, 96
  in Cream Sauce (*Cappelletti alla panna*), 124
  alla panna (*Cappelletti* in Cream Sauce), 124
  Pork-Veal-Ham Filling for (*Ripieno per cappelletti o cannelloni*), 122–123
  ripieno per (Pork-Veal-Ham Filling for *Cappelletti* or *Cannelloni*), 122–123
Carciofi. See also Artichoke(s)
  fritti dorati (Golden-Fried Artichokes), 257
  alla Giudia (Artichokes, Jewish Style), 53–55
  con piselli (Artichokes with Peas), 257
  con salsa d'acciuga (Artichokes with Anchovy Dressing), 55

Carote e funghi (Carrots and Mushrooms), 265

Carrots and Mushrooms (*Carote e funghi*), 265

Cartoccio: al cartoccio (roasted) fish, 222–223

Casserole
Artichoke (*Parmigiana di carciofi*), 258
Pepper (*Peperoni in casseruola*), 271

Castagne. See Chestnuts

Cavolini di Bruxelles e cipolline (Brussels Sprouts and Onions), 263

Cavolo ripieno (Stuffed Cabbage), 264–265

Celery
and Bean Salad (*Insalata di fagioli e sedano*), 268
-Olive-Pepper *Antipasto* (*Peperoni, sedani, ed olive*), 59

Charcoal Makers' Style Spaghetti (*Spaghetti alla carbonara*), 111

Cheese(s). *See also* Mozzarella; Parmesan and Parmigiana; Pecorino (*Romano*), Ricotta
in Broiled Stuffed Tomatoes with Ham and Cheese (*Pomodori ripieni con prosciutto cotto e formaggio*), 59
in Crêpes with Mushrooms, Ham, Cheese (*Crespelle ai funghi, prosciutto, formaggio*), 132–133
Fennel Baked with (*Finocchio ai formaggi*), 267
Omelet (*Frittata al formaggio*), 219
in Pear and Cheese Mold (*Torta di formaggio con le pere*), 292–293
Sauce, Pasta with, 109–110
-and-Spinach Turnovers (*Sfogliatine di spinaci e formaggio*), 70
Three, Omelets with Ham and (*Frittate con prosciutto e tre formaggi*), 219
Three, *Risotto* with Ham and (*Risotto al prosciutto e tre formaggi*), 141

Cherrystone Clam Sauce, Spaghetti with (*Spaghetti mare d'estate*), 104

Chestnuts and Almonds, *Risotto* with (*Risotto alle castagne e mandorle*), 139

Chicken (*Pollo*), 203–210. *See also* Chicken Broth
Baked (*Pollo al forno*), 210
Batter-Fried (*Pollo fritto*), 207
-Beef Broth for Aspic and Soups (*Brodo di pollo e manzo per gelatina e zuppe*), 45–46; in Stuffed Cabbage (*Cavolo ripieno*), 264–265
Breasts, Stuffed (*Petti di pollo farciti*), 205
Hungarian Style (*Pollo all'ungherese*), 208
Legs and Peas (*Coscie di pollo con piselli*), 209
Legs in Wine Sauce (*Coscie di pollo al vino*), 206

Liver Mousse in Aspic (*Spuma di fegatini in gelatina*), 75–76

Livers, Pasta with (*Tagliatelle coi fegatini*), 113

Livers, *Risotto* with (*Risotto coi fegatini*), 140

Marengo (*Pollo alla Marengo*), 203–204

Poor Gypsy's (*Galletto alla povera zingara*), 190–191

Chicken Broth (*Brodo di pollo*), 44
in Artichokes with Peas (*Carciofi con piselli*), 257
in aspic, 75
in Chicken Marengo (*Pollo alla Marengo*), 203–204
in Christmas Turkey with Rice Stuffing (*Tacchino di Natale con ripieno di riso*), 196–197
in Duck with Almonds (*Anitra alle mandorle*), 212
in Lentil and Sausage Soup (*Zuppa di lenticchie e salsicce*), 83
in Peas, Piedmont Style (*Piselli alla piemontese*), 271
in *risotto*, 138, 140, 141, 142, 143, 145, 148, 149, 150
in Rock Cornish Hen with Lemon (*Galletto al limone*), 189
in Turkey *Osso Buco* (*Osso buco di tacchino*), 195
in Venetian Pâté (*Pâté alla veneziana*), 74
in White Sauce (*Besciamella/Balsamella*), 75

Chili con Carne, Roman Style (*Chili con carne alla romana*), 169–170

Chocolate
Cream Mold (*Semifreddo di cioccolato*), 289
Ice Cream (*Gelato al cioccolato*), 282
Layer Cake, Italian, 301
and Orange Tart (*Crostata di arancie e cioccolato*), 299–300

Chops. *See also* Cutlets
Pork, Marinated (*Cotolette di maiale marinate*), 174

Christmas Turkey with Rice Stuffing (*Tacchino di Natale con ripieno di riso*), 196–197

Cialde, Salted (*Cialde salate*), 330

Cioccolato. See Chocolate

Cipolle. See Onion(s)

Cipolline con peperoni (Onions and Peppers), 270

Clam Sauce
Baby, Sicilian Style (*Salsa con vongole alla siciliana*), 105
Cherrystone, Spaghetti with (*Spaghetti mare d'estate*), 104

Clam Sauce (*Continued*)
   Pasta with Tuna and (*Pasta con tonno e von-gole*), 103
Clarifying broth, 44
Cloves, 8
Cocktail, Seafood (*Antipasto di mare*), 61
Cocomero ripieno (Filled Watermelon), 294
Cod
   dried salt (*Baccalà*), 221, 232
   Filets, Deep-Fried (*Filetti di baccalà fritti*), 232
Conchiglie di San Giacomo. See also Scallops
   fritte (Fried Scallops), 245
   con maionese (Poached Scallops with Mayonnaise), 246
Contorni, 256. See also Salads; Vegetables
Cookies
   Almond Meringues (*Meringhe alle mandorle*), 328–329
   Brigidini (*Cialde, Pizelle*), Salted (*Brigidini salati*), 330
   Brigidini, Sweet (*Brigidini alla franca*), 331
   Meringues (*Meringhe*), 325–329
   Salted *Brigidini* (*Cialde, Pizzelle*) (*Brigidini salati*), 330
   Sweet *Brigidini* (*Brigidini alla franca*), 331
   Wine Sipping, *alla Romagnola* (*Biscottini alla romagnola*), 329
Corn Meal Cake (*Zaletto*), 310
Corned Beef and Cabbage, Italian Style (*Bollito irlandese all'italiana*), 168
Coscia d'agnello al gin (Leg of Lamb with Gin), 179
Coscie di pollo
   con piselli (Chicken Legs and Peas), 209
   al riso (Chicken Legs in Wine Sauce), 206
Cotolette di maiale
   all'erbe (Herbed, Breaded Port Cutlets), 173
   marinate (Marinated Pork Chops), 174
Cozze. See also Mussels
   in salsa piccante (Mussels in Piquant Sauce), 56
Crab Meat
   Filling for Tartlets (*Barchette di granchio*), 63
   Sauce, Thin Spaghetti with (*Spaghettini al granchio*), 106
   Venetian Style (*Granzeola alla veneziana*), 55
Cream Sauce, *Cappelletti* in (*Cappelletti alla panna*), 124
Crêpes with Mushrooms, Ham, Cheese (*Crespelle ai funghi, prosciutto, formaggio*), 132–133
Crescione. See Cress
Crespelle
   made with egg substitute, 8

ai funghi, prosciutto, formaggio (Crêpes with Mushrooms, Ham, Cheese), 132–133
Cress and Belgian Endive Salad (*Insalata d'indivia belga e crescione*), 263
Croquettes
   Meat (*Polpette di manzo*), 160
   Pork and Turkey (*Polpette di maiale e tacchino*), 175
   Rice (*Supplì*), 137, 152
   Turkey and Beef (*Polpette di tacchino e manzo*), 194
Crostata
   di arancie e cioccolato (Orange and Chocolate Tart), 299–300
   imperiale di mele (Imperial Apple Tart), 298
   di mele I (Apple Tart I), 296
   di mele II (Apple Tart II), 297
Crostata dough (*Pasta frolla*), 298
   for food processor, 295
Cutlets. *See also* Chops
   Pork, Herbed, Breaded (*Cotolette di maiale all'erbe*), 173

Deep-Fried Cod Filets (*Filetti di baccalà fritti*), 232
Deep-frying with yeast batter, 26–27
Desserts (*Dolci*), 277–332
   in general, 279
   Almond-Chocolate Cream Cake (*La Bomba mocha*), 307–308
   Almond Filled Peaches (*Pesche ripiene alle mandorle*), 290
   Almond Meringues (*Meringhe alle mandorle*), 328–329
   Apple and Pomegranate Cake (*Torta di mele e melagrano*), 309
   Apple Tart I (*Crostata di mele I*), 296
   Apple Tart II (*Crostata di mele II*), 297
   Apple Tart, Imperial (*Crostata imperiale di mele*), 298
   Brigidini (*Cialde, Pizzelle*), Salted (*Brigidini salati*), 330
   Brigidini, Sweet (*Brigidini alla franca*), 331
   Chocolate Cream Mold (*Semifreddo di cioccolato*), 289
   Chocolate Ice Cream (*Gelato al cioccolato*), 282
   Chocolate Layer Cake, Italian, 301
   Corn Meal Cake (*Zaletto*), 310
   Crostata, 295–300
   Duck Egg Cake (*Torta grande*), 311
   Filled Watermelon (*Cocomero ripieno*), 294
   Flamed Peaches (*Pesche al brandy*), 291
   Grapefruit Sherbet with Pomegranate Seeds (*Sorbetto di pompelmo con melagrano*), 283–284

Imperial Apple Tart (*Crostata imperiale di mele*), 298
Imperial Sponge (*Spongata imperiale*), 313
Italian Chocolate Layer Cake, 301
Italian Pound Cake, 300
Lemon Sherbet (*Sorbetto di limone*), 285
Lime Ice (*Granita di limetta*), 287
Margherita Cake (*Torta Margherita*), 306
Melon Ice (*Granita di melone*), 287
Meringues (*Meringhe*), 325–329
Orange and Chocolate Tart (*Crostata di arancie e cioccolato*), 299–300
Panettone, 314–317
Paradise Cake (*Torta paradiso*), 312
Peaches, Almond Filled (*Pesche ripiene alle mandorle*), 290
Peaches, Flamed (*Pesche al brandy*), 291
Pear and Cheese Mold (*Torta di formaggio con le pere*), 292–293
Pears, Stuffed (*Pere ripiene*), 291
Pound Cake, Italian, 300
Puff Pastry (*Pasta sfogliata*), 320–323
Puff Pastry with Apples (*Sfogliata alle mele*), 324
Raspberry Sherbet (*Sorbetto di lampone*), 286
Salted *Brigidini* (*Cialde, Pizzelle*) (*Brigidini salati*), 330
Sponge, Imperial (*Spongata imperiale*), 313
Sponge Cake (*Pan di Spagna*), 302–303
Strawberry Ice (*Granita di fragole*), 288
Stuffed Pears (*Pere ripiene*), 291
Sweet Bread, Veronese (*Pandoro di Verona*), 318–319
Sweet *Brigidini* (*Brigidini alla franca*), 331
Vanilla Ice Cream (*Gelato alla vaniglia*), 281
Veronese Sweet Bread (*Pandoro di Verona*), 318–319
Watermelon, Filled (*Cocomero ripieno*), 294
Wine Sipping Cookies *alla Romagnola* (*Biscottini alla romagnola*), 329
Zabaglione, 332
Zuppa inglese, 304–305
Dolci. See Desserts
Dough
  bread, commercially frozen, 68–69
  Crostata (*Pasta frolla*), 295, 298
  Pizzette, 67–68
Dried salt cod (*Baccalà*), 221, 232
Duck (*Anitra*), 211–213
  with Almonds (*Anitra alle mandorle*), 212–213
Duck Egg Cake (*Torta grande*), 311
Duckling, Grilled (*Anitra alla griglia*), 211–212

Easter Pie (or Asparagus Pie; *Torta di pasqua*), 261–262
Eels (*Anguille*), 233–236
  preparing for cooking, 233–234
  Marinated (*Anguille marinate*), 235–236
  and Peas, Venetian (*Bisato e bisi*), 235
  on Skewers (*Spiedini d'anguille*), 236
Egg(s). *See also* Omelets
  Batter (*Pastelle semplice*), 27
  Pasta. *See* Pasta
  Risotto with (*Risotto all'uovo*), 140
Egg substitutes, 8
Egg whites, 8
Eggplant, Baked (*Melanzane al forno*), 266
Endive, in Belgian Endive–Cress Salad (*Insalata d'indivia belga e crescione*), 263
Equipment (*Batteria di cucina*), 22–24

Fagioli. See Bean(s)
Fagiolini alla fiorentina (Green Beans, Florentine Style), 268
Fave alla toscana (Lima Beans, Tuscan Style), 269
Fegatini. See Chicken Liver(s)
Fennel Baked with Cheese (*Finocchio ai formaggi*), 267
Fettuccine
  conserving, 98–99
  cutting, 97–98
  rolling, 96
  ai funghi e prosciutto (Fettuccine with Mushrooms and Ham), 118
  with Mushrooms and Ham (*Fettuccine ai funghi e prosciutto*), 118
  sciué-sciué ("Tossed" *Fettuccine*), 109–110
  "Tossed" (*Fettuccine sciué-sciué*), 109–110
Filberts, *Ravioli* with (*Ravioli alle nocciole*), 125–126
  in Squash *Ravioli* (*Ravioli alla zucca*), 129
Filets
  Cod, Deep-Fried (*Filetti di baccalà fritti*), 232
  Fish, Baked (*Filetti di pesce al forno*), 226
  Fish, Poached (*Filetti di pesce in bianco*), 227
Filetti
  di baccalà fritti (Deep-Fried Cod Fillets), 232
  di pesce in bianco (Poached Fish Filets), 227
  di pesce al forno (Baked Fish Filets), 226
Filetto
  di manzo arrosto (Roast Tenderloin of Beef), 162
  alla Marco Polo (Tenderloin of Beef, Marco Polo), 163
Filled
  Pasta. *See* Pasta, filled, layered, rolled
  Watermelon (*Cocomero ripieno*), 294

Finocchio ai formaggi (Fennel Baked with Cheese), 267

Fish. *See also* Fish Broth; Fish Sauces; Seafood
  methods of preparing, 221–223
  Caper Butter for (*Burro ai caperi*), 28
  Filets, Baked (*Filetti di pesce al forno*), 226
  Filets, Poached (*Filetti di pesce in bianco*), 227
  Herbed Butter for (*Burro saporito per pesce*), 28
  Soup (*Zuppa di pesce*), 228–230

Fish Broth (*Brodo di pesce*), 47
  in Fish Soup (*Zuppa di pesce*), 228–230
  in Lobster Soup (*Zuppa di aragosta*), 84
  in Poached Scallops with Mayonnaise (*Conchiglie di San Giacomo con maionese*), 246
  in *Risotto* with Shrimp and Mussels (*Risotto ai gamberetti e cozze*), 147
  in Seafood Cocktail (*Antipasto di mare*), 61

Fish Sauces, Pasta with, 102–108
  Baby Clam, Sicilian Style (*Salsa con vongole alla siciliana*), 105
  Cherrystone Clam, Spaghetti with (*Spaghetti mare d'estate*), 104
  Crab Meat, Thin Spaghetti with (*Spaghettini al granchio*), 106
  Salmon and Peas (*Pasta al salmone e piselli*), 102
  alla Sarah Caldwell, 108
  Shrimp and Fresh Tomatoes, Spaghetti with (*Spaghetti agli scampi e pomodori*), 107
  Tuna and Clam (*Pasta con tonno e vongole*), 103

Flamed Peaches (*Pesche al brandy*), 291

Flavorings, herbs, and ingredients (*Aromi, spezie, ed ingrediente*), 3–18

Florentine Style
  Green Beans (*Fagiolini alla fiorentina*), 268
  Scallops (*Pellegrine alla fiorentina*), 247–248

Flour, 8

Floured Butter (*Burro maneggiato*), 28, 29

Food processor
  in general, 23
  for *Crostata* Dough (*Pasta frolla*), 295
  for Green Pasta (*Pasta verde*), 100
  for Green Sauce (*Salsa verde*), 34
  for Mayonnaise (*Maionese*), 31–32
  for *Panettone*, 317
  for Pasta, 97, 100
  for *Pesto*, 39
  for *Pizzette* Dough, 68
  for *Salsa verde* (Green Sauce), 34

Formaggio. See also Cheese(s)
  grana, 12

Forno: al forno (baked) fish, 223

Fragole. See Strawberry

Fresh Tomatoes
  Spaghetti with Shrimp and (*Spaghetti agli scampi e pomodori*), 107
  Ziti with (*Ziti con pomodori freschi*), 117

Fried. *See also* Batter-Fried; Deep-Fried; Golden-Fried
  Scallops (*Conchiglie di San Giacomo fritte*), 245
  Squid (*Calamari fritti*), 252

Frittata
  al formaggio (Cheese Omelet), 219
  di zucchine (Zucchini Omelet), 217

Frittate. See also Omelets
  con prosciutto e tre formaggi (Omelets with Ham and Three Cheeses), 219

Frittatine al sugo (Little Omelets with Sauce), 218

Fruit (*Frutta*), 290–294. *See also* Desserts
  Almond Filled Peaches (*Pesche ripiene alle mandorle*), 290
  Filled Watermelon (*Cocomero ripieno*), 294
  Flamed Peaches (*Pesche al brandy*), 291
  Peaches, Almond Filled (*Pesche ripiene alle mandorle*), 290
  Peaches, Flamed (*Pesche al brandy*), 291
  Pear and Cheese Mold (*Torta di formaggio con le pere*), 292
  Pears, Stuffed (*Pere ripiene*), 291
  Stuffed Pears (*Pere ripiene*), 291
  Watermelon, Filled (*Cocomero ripieno*), 294

Frutta. See Fruit

Frying, deep, with yeast batter, 26–27

Funghetti marinati (Marinated Mushrooms), 57

Funghi. See also Mushroom(s)
  ripieni alla griglia (Grilled Stuffed Mushrooms), 57
  secchi (Dried mushrooms), 10

Galletto
  alla grappa (Rock Cornish Hen with Grappa), 188–189
  al limone (Rock Cornish Hen with Lemon), 189
  alla povera zingara (Poor Gypsy's Chicken), 190–191
  ripieno ai funghi e salsiccia (Rock Cornish Hen Stuffed with Mushrooms and Sausage), 187
  ripieno alle mandorle e prugne (Rock Cornish Hen with Almond-Prune Stuffing), 185–186

Gamberetti. See Shrimp

Gamberi. See also Shrimp
  e cape sante (Shrimp and Scallops), 249

Garlic, 8–9
Gelatina. See Aspic
Gelato
    al cioccolato (Chocolate Ice Cream), 282
    alla vaniglia (Vanilla Ice Cream), 281
Genoa Style
    Minestrone (*Minestrone genovese*), 85
    Red Mullet (*Triglia alla genovese*), 243
Gin, Leg of Lamb with (*Coscia d'agnello al gin*), 179
Golden-Fried
    Artichokes (*Carciofi fritti dorati*), 257; in Artichoke Casserole (*Parmigiana di carciofi*), 258
    Lamb Steaks (*Agnello fritto dorato*), 183
Granchio. See Crab Meat
Granita
    di fragole (Strawberry Ice), 288
    di limetta (Lime Ice), 287
    di melone (Melon Ice), 287
Granzeola alla veneziana (Crab Meat, Venetian Style), 55
Grapefruit Sherbet with Pomegranate Seeds (*Sorbetto di pompelmo con melagrano*), 283–284
Grappa, Rock Cornish Hen with (*Galletto alla grappa*), 188–189
Green Beans, Florentine Style (*Fagiolini alla fiorentina*), 268
Green Pasta (*Pasta verde*), 99–100
Green Sauce (*Salsa verde*), 33–34
    with Poached Fish Filets (*Filetti di pesce in bianco*), 227
    with Poached Sea Bass (*Spigola in bianco*), 249
Griglia: alla griglia (grilled) fish, 222
Grilled
    Duckling (*Anitra alla griglia*), 211–212
    Salmon Steaks (*Salmone alla griglia*), 244
    Stuffed Mushrooms (*Funghi ripieni alla griglia*), 57
    Swordfish (*Pescespada alla griglia*), 253
Grouper
    Baked (*Scorfano al forno*), 237
    with Tomato Sauce (*Scorfano coi pomodori*), 238

Haddock, Baked Stuffed (*Merluzzo ripieno*), 239–240
Ham. *See also Prosciutto*
    in general, 13, 14
    and Cheese, Broiled Stuffed Tomatoes with (*Pomodori ripieni con prosciutto cotto e formaggio*), 59
    in Crêpes with Mushrooms, Ham, Cheese (*Crespelle ai funghi, prosciutto, formaggio*), 132–133
    in *Fettuccine* with Mushrooms and Ham (*Fettuccine ai funghi e prosciutto*), 118
    in Pork-Veal-Ham Filling for *Cappelletti* or *Cannelloni* (*Ripieno per cappelletti o cannelloni*), 122–123
    and *Ricotta*, Puff Pastries with (*Sfogliatine con prosciutto e ricotta*), 72
    and Three Cheeses, Omelets with (*Frittate con prosciutto e tre formaggi*), 219
    and Three Cheeses, *Risotto* with (*Risotto al prosciutto e tre formaggi*), 141
Handmade
    Green Pasta (*Pasta verde*), 100
    Green Sauce (*Salsa verde*), 33
    Mayonnaise (*Maionese*), 30–31
    Pasta, 95–96, 100
    Pizzette dough, 67–68
    Salsa verde (Green Sauce), 33
Hen. *See* Rock Cornish Hen
Herbed
    Breaded Pork Cutlets (*Cotolette di maiale all'erbe*), 173
    Butter for Fish (*Burro saporito per pesce*), 28
Herbs. *See* Flavorings, herbs, and ingredients
Homemade pasta (*Pasta fatta in casa*), 93–101
Hot pepper sauce, 14
Hungarian Style Chicken (*Pollo all'ungherese*), 208

Ice Cream (*Gelati*). *See also* Ices; Sherbet
    in general, 280
    Chocolate (*Gelato al cioccolato*), 282
    Vanilla (*Gelato alla vaniglia*), 281
Ices (*Granite*). *See also* Ice Cream; Sherbet
    Lime (*Granita di limetta*), 287
    Melon (*Granita di melone*), 287
    Strawberry (*Granita di fragole*), 288
Imperial Apple Tart (*Crostata imperiale di mele*), 298
Imperial Sponge (*Spongata imperiale*), 313
Indivia belga. See Belgian Endive
Ingredients. *See* Flavorings, herbs, and ingredients
Insalata
    di avocado, asparagi, e carciofi (Avocado, Asparagus, and Artichoke Salad), 262
    di fagioli e sedano (Bean and Celery Salad), 268
    d'indivia belga e crescione (Belgian Endive–Cress Salad), 263
    di riso ed asparagi (Rice and Asparagus Salad), 272
    russa (Russian Salad), 64
Involtini
    di manzo (Beef Rolls), 157–158
    di vitello e prosciutto (Veal and *Prosciutto* Birds), 164

Italian Chocolate Layer Cake, 301
Italian Pound Cake, 300
  in Italian Chocolate Layer Cake, 301
Italian Style Corned Beef and Cabbage
  (*Bollito irlandese all'italiana*), 168
Italian wines, 333–339

Jewish Style Artichokes (*Carciofi alla Giudia*),
  53–55

Kidneys, Veal, and Mushrooms with Rice
  (*Riso con rognoni e funghi*), 151

Lamb (*Agnello*), 176–184
  with Barolo (*Agnello al Barolo*), 180
  Braised Leg of (*Agnello brasato*), 181
  Leg of, with Gin (*Coscia d'agnello al gin*),
    179
  Roast Baby (New Zealand) (*Agnello ar-
    rosto*), 176–177
  Roast, Umbrian Style (*Arrosto d'agnello*),
    182
  on Skewers (*Spiedini d'agnello*), 178–179
  Steaks, Golden-Fried (*Agnello fritto dorato*),
    183
  Stew (*Spezzatino d'agnello*), 184
Lampone. See Raspberry
Lasagne
  cutting, 98
  rolling, 96
  with Bolognese Meat Sauce (*Lasagne al
    ragù*), 131
  with Mushroom Sauce (*Lasagne al sugo di
    funghi*), 130–131
  al ragù (*Lasagne* with Bolognese Meat
    Sauce), 131
  al sugo di funghi (*Lasagne* with Mushroom
    Sauce), 130–131
Layer, Cake, Italian Chocolate, 301
Layered pasta. *See* Pasta, filled, layered,
    rolled
Leg of Lamb
  Braised (*Agnello brasato*), 181
  with Gin (*Coscia d'agnello al gin*), 179
Lemon(s)
  in general, 9
  Risotto with (*Risotto al limone*), 141
  Rock Cornish Hen with (*Galletto al limone*),
    189
  Sauce, Spaghetti with (*Spaghetti al limone*),
    117
  Sherbet (*Sorbetto di limone*), 285
Lenticchie. See also Lentil(s)
  del primo d'anno (New Year's Day Lentils),
    270
Lentil(s)
  New Year's Day (*Lenticchie del primo
    d'anno*), 270

and Sausage Soup (*Zuppa di lenticchie e sal-
    siccie*), 83
Lima Beans, Tuscan Style (*Fave alla toscana*),
    269
Lime Ice (*Granita di limetta*), 287
Limone. See Lemon(s)
Little Omelets with Sauce (*Frittatine al sugo*),
    218
Little Pizzas (*Pizzette*), 66–69
Liver. *See* Chicken Liver(s)
Lobster
  Boiled (*Aragosta lessa*), 241–242
  Risotto with (*Risotto all'aragosta*), 142
  Soup (*Zuppa di aragosta*), 84
Lombo di maiale all'arancia (Boneless Pork
  Loin with Orange Sauce), 171–172

Macaroni with Summer Sauce (*Maccheroni al
  sugo d'estate*), 116
Maccheroni al sugo d'estate (Macaroni with
  Summer Sauce), 116
Maiale. See also Pork
  arrosto alla senape (Roast Pork with Mus-
    tard), 174
Maionese. See Mayonnaise
Mandorle. See Almond(s)
Manzo. See Beef
Marengo, Chicken (*Pollo alla Marengo*),
    203–204
Margherita Cake (*Torta Margherita*), 306
  in Almond-Chocolate Cream Cake (*La
    Bomba mocha*), 307–308
  in Chocolate Cream Mold (*Semifreddo di
    cioccolato*), 289
Marinated
  Eels (*Anguille marinate*), 235–236
  Mushrooms (*Funghetti marinati*), 57
  Pork Chops (*Cotolette di maiale marinate*),
    174
Marjoram, 9
Mayonnaise (*Maionese*)
  blender, 31
  food-processor, 31–32
  in general, 11
  handmade, 30–31
  with Boiled Lobster (*Aragosta lessa*),
    241–242
  with Poached Fish Filets (*Filetti di pesce in
    bianco*), 227
  with Poached Salmon (*Salmone in bianco*),
    243
  Poached Scallops with (*Conchiglie di San
    Giacomo con maionese*), 246
  with Poached Sea Bass (*Spigola in bianco*),
    249
  in Russian Salad (*Insalata russa*), 64
  in Salmon Trout with Rice and Shrimp

(*Trota salmonata con riso e gamberi*), 244–245
Measures. *See* Weights and measures
Meat Croquettes (*Polpette di manzo*), 160
Meat Loaf, Beef and Pork (*Polpettone di manzo e maiale*), 159
Meat Sauce, Bolognese (*Ragù alla bolognese*), 35–36
  Lasagne with (*Lasagne al ragù*), 131
Meat Sauces, Pasta with, 111–113
  Charcoal Makers' Style Spaghetti (*Spaghetti alla carbonara*), 111
  Chicken Livers (*Tagliatelle coi fegatini*), 113
    alla Paolo, 112
  Sausages and Mushrooms, *Rigatoni* with (*Rigatoni, salsiccie, e funghi*), 113
Meats, 157–184
  Beef and Pork Meat Loaf (*Polpettone di manzo e maiale*), 159
  Beef Rolls (*Involtini di manzo*), 157–158
  Beef, Roast Tenderloin of (*Filetto di manzo arrosto*), 162
  Beef, Tenderloin of, Marco Polo (*Filetto alla Marco Polo*), 163
  Boneless Pork Loin with Orange Sauce (*Lombo di maiale all'arancia*), 171–172
  Braised Leg of Lamb (*Agnello brasato*), 181
  Chili con Carne, Roman Style (*Chili con carne alla romana*), 169–170
  Corned Beef and Cabbage, Italian Style (*Bollito irlandese all'italiana*), 168
  Golden-Fried Lamb Steaks (*Agnello fritto dorato*), 183
  Herbed, Breaded Pork Cutlets (*Cotolette di maiale all'erbe*), 173
  Lamb with Barolo (*Agnello al Barolo*), 180
  Lamb, Braised Leg of (*Agnello brasato*), 181
  Lamb, Leg of, with Gin (*Coscia d'agnello al gin*), 179
  Lamb, Roast Baby (New Zealand) (*Agnello arrosto*), 176–177
  Lamb Roast, Umbrian Style (*Arrosto d'agnello*), 182
  Lamb on Skewers (*Spiedini d'agnello*), 178–179
  Lamb Steaks, Golden-Fried (*Agnello fritto dorato*), 183
  Lamb Stew (*Spezzatino d'agnello*), 184
  Marinated Pork Chops (*Cotolette di maiale marinate*), 174
  Pork Chops, Marinated (*Cotolette di maiale marinate*), 174
  Pork Cutlets, Herbed, Breaded (*Cotolette di maiale all'erbe*), 173
  Pork Loin, Boneless, with Orange Sauce (*Lombo di maiale all'arancia*), 171–172
  Pork, Roast, with Mustard (*Maiale arrosto alla senape*), 174

Pork Roast, Tipsy (*Porchetta umbriaca*), 173
Pork and Turkey Croquettes (*Polpette di maiale e tacchino*), 175
Pot Roast for the Pressure Cooker (*Stufato di manzo per la pentola a pressione*), 161
Roast Baby (New Zealand) Lamb (*Agnello arrosto*), 176–177
Roast Pork with Mustard (*Maiale arrosto alla senape*), 174
Roast Tenderloin of Beef (*Filetto di manzo arrosto*), 162
Rolled Breast of Veal for the Pressure Cooker (*Rollato di vitello per la pentola a pressione*), 165
Stuffed Veal Breast (*Petto di vitello ripieno*), 166
Tenderloin of Beef, Marco Polo (*Filetto alla Marco Polo*), 163
Tipsy Pork Roast (*Porchetta umbriaca*), 173
Veal and *Prosciutto* Birds (*Involtini di vitello e prosciutto*), 164
Veal, Rolled Breast of, for the Pressure Cooker (*Rollato di vitello per la pentola a pressione*), 165
Veal on Skewers, Sicilian Style (*Spiedini alla siciliana*), 167
Veal, Stuffed Breast of (*Petto di vitello ripieno*), 166
Melagrano. See Pomegranate
Melanzane al forno (Baked Eggplant), 266
Mele. See Apple(s)
Melon Ice (*Granita di melone*), 287
Meringhe. See also Meringues
  alle mandorle (Almond Meringues), 328–329
Meringues (*Meringhe*), 325–329
  Almond (*Meringhe alle mandorle*), 328–329
  in Apple Tart I (*Crostata di mele I*), 296
  in Apple Tart II (*Crostata di mele II*), 297
  chocolate-flavored, 327
Merluzzo ripieno (Baked Stuffed Haddock), 239–240
Milanese *Risotto* (*Risotto alla milanese*), 143
Mince (*Battuto*), 3
Minestra di carciofi (Artichoke Soup), 82
Minestre. See Soups
Minestrone, Genoa Style (*Minestrone genovese*), 85
Mixed Spring Vegetables (*Padellata primaverile*), 275
Mold
  Chocolate Cream (*Semifreddo di cioccolato*), 289
  Pear and Cheese (*Torta di formaggio con le pere*), 292–293
  Russian Salad (*Insalata russa*), 64
Mollusks. See Seafood

Monkfish, Mushrooms, and Tomatoes, Skewers of (*Spiedini di rana pescatrice*), 242

Mortar and pestle *pesto*, 37–38

Mostarda di Cremona, 174

Mousse
Chicken Liver, in Aspic (*Spuma di fegatini in gelatina*), 75–76
Tuna (*Spuma di tonno*), 73

Mozzarella
in general, 9–10
Batter-Fried (*Mozzarella fritta*), 56
fritta (Batter-Fried *Mozzarella*), 56
Pizzette with Mushrooms and (*Pizzette con funghi e mozzarella*), 69
Pizzette with Tomatoes and (*Pizzette con pomodori e mozzarella*), 69
Puff Pastries with Tomato and (*Sfogliatine*), 71

Mullet, Red, Genoa Style (*Triglia alla genovese*), 243

Mushroom(s)
in general, 10
Carrots and (*Carote e funghi*), 265
in Crêpes with Mushrooms, Ham, Cheese (*Crespelle ai funghi, prosciutto, formaggio*), 132–133
Grilled Stuffed (*Funghi ripieni alla griglia*), 57
and Ham, *Fettuccine* with (*Fettuccine ai funghi e prosciutto*), 118
Marinated (*Funghetti marinati*), 57
and *Mozzarella*, *Pizzette* with (*Pizzette con funghi e mozzarella*), 69
in Rice with Shrimp and Mushrooms (*Riso con gamberetti e funghi*), 146
Rice with Veal Kidneys and (*Riso con rognoni e funghi*), 151
in *Rigatoni* with Sausages and Mushrooms (*Rigatoni, salsiccie, e funghi*), 113
Risotto with (*Risotto ai funghi*), 143
in *Risotto* with Mushrooms, Sausages, and Bacon (*Risotto ai funghi, salsiccie, e pancetta affumicata*), 144
Sauce, *Lasagne* with (*Lasagne al sugo di funghi*), 130–131
Sauce, Pasta with (*Tonnarelli ai funghi*), 115
and Sausage, Rock Cornish Hen Stuffed with (*Galletto ripieno ai funghi e salsiccia*), 187
in Skewers of Monkfish, Mushrooms, and Tomatoes (*Spiedini di rana pescatrice*), 242

Mussels
in Piquant Sauce (*Cozze in salsa piccante*), 56
in *Risotto* with Shrimp and Mussels (*Risotto ai gamberetti e cozze*), 147

Mustard, Roast Pork with (*Maiale arrosto alla senape*), 174

New Year's Day Lentils (*Lenticchie del primo d'anno*), 270

Nocciole. See Filberts

Nutmeg, 10

Oil, cooking, 11

Olive oil, 11

Olive-Pepper-Celery *Antipasto* (*Peperoni, sedani, ed olive*), 59

Omelets (*Frittate*), 214–219
in general, 214–216
Cheese (*Frittata al formaggio*), 219
with Ham and Three Cheeses (*Frittate con prosciutto e tre formaggi*), 219
Little, with Sauce (*Frittatine al sugo*), 218
Zucchini (*Frittata di zucchine*), 217

Onion(s)
Brussels Sprouts and (*Cavolini di Bruxelles e cipolline*), 263
and Peppers (*Cipolline con peperoni*), 270
Rings, Apple and (*Anelli di mele e cipolle*), 256

Orange
and Chocolate Tart (*Crostata di arancie e cioccolato*), 299–300
Sauce, Boneless Pork Loin with (*Lombo di maiale all'arancia*), 171–172

Oregano, 9

Osso buco, 137
di tacchino (Turkey *Osso Buco*), 195

Padella: in padella (pan-cooked) fish, 221

Padellata primaverile (Mixed Spring Vegetables), 275

Pan di Spagna (Sponge Cake), 302–303
in Almond-Chocolate Cream Cake (*La Bomba mocha*), 307–308
in Chocolate Cream Mold (*Semifreddo di ciaccolato*), 289
in *Zuppa inglese*, 304

Pancetta. See Bacon

Pandoro di Verona (Veronese Sweet Bread), 318–319

Pane a cassetta. See Bread

Panettone, 314–317
for food processor, 317

Paradise Cake (*Torta paradiso*), 312

Parmesan cheese, 12

Parmigiana di carciofi (Artichoke Casserole), 258

Parsley, 12

Parsley Butter (*Burro verde*), 29
with Broiled Turbot (*Rombo alla griglia*), 254

Pasta, 91–133
conserving, 98–99
cooking, 100–101
cutting, 97–98
al dente, 92
fatta in casa (homemade), 93–101
food-processor, 97
in general, 91–92
handmade, 95–96
homemade (*Pasta fatta in casa*), 93–101
with Artichokes (*Pasta ai carciofi*), 119
with Baby Clam Sauce, Sicilian Style
  (*Salsa con vongole alla siciliana*), 105
and Bean Soup (*Pasta e fagioli*), 86–88
Cannelloni, Saint's Day (*Cannelloni del
  curato*), 127–128
Cappelletti, 120–121
Cappelletti in Cream Sauce (*Cappelletti alla
  panna*), 124
di carciofi (Pasta with Artichokes), 119
with Cheese Sauce, 109–110
with Chicken Livers (*Tagliatelle coi fegatini*), 113
Crêpes with Mushrooms, Ham, Cheese
  (*Crespelle ai funghi, prosciutto, formaggio*),
  132–133
e fagioli (Pasta and Bean Soup), 86–88
Fettuccine with Mushrooms and Ham (*Fettuccine ai funghi e prosciutto*), 118
Fettuccine, "Tossed" (*Fettuccine sciué-sciué*),
  109–110
filled, layered, rolled, 120–133
with Fish Sauces, 102–108
Green (*Pasta verde*), 99–100
Lasagne with Bolognese Meat Sauce (*Lasagne al ragù*), 131
Lasagne with Mushroom Sauce (*Lasagne al
  sugo di funghi*), 130–131
Macaroni with Summer Sauce (*Maccheroni
  al sugo d'estate*), 116
with Meat Sauces, 111–113
with Mushroom Sauce (*Tonnarelli ai
  funghi*), 115
Pork-Veal-Ham Filling for *Cappelletti* or
  Cannelloni (*Ripieno per cappelletti o cannelloni*), 122–123
Ravioli with Filberts (*Ravioli alle nocciole*),
  125–126; in Squash *Ravioli* (*Ravioli alla
  zucca*), 129
Ravioli, Squash (*Ravioli alla zucca*), 129
Rigatoni with Sausages and Mushrooms
  (*Rigatoni, salsiccie, e funghi*), 113
Saint's Day *Cannelloni* (*Cannelloni del
  curato*), 127–128
with Salmon and Peas (*Pasta al salmone e
  piselli*), 102

al salmone e piselli (Pasta with Salmon and
  Peas), 102
alla Sarah Caldwell, 108
Spaghetti, Charcoal Makers' Style (*Spa-
  ghetti alla carbonara*), 111
Spaghetti with Cherrystone Clam Sauce
  (*Spaghetti mare d'estate*), 104
Spaghetti with Lemon Sauce (*Spaghetti al
  limone*), 117
Spaghetti *alla Paolo*, 112
Spaghetti with Shrimp and Fresh Toma-
  toes (*Spaghetti agli scampi e pomodori*), 107
Spaghetti with Sweet-Pepper Sauce (*Spa-
  ghetti ai peperoni*), 118
Squash *Ravioli* (*Ravioli alla zucca*), 129
Thin Spaghetti with Crab Meat Sauce
  (*Spaghettini al granchio*), 106
con tonno e vongole (Pasta with Tuna and
  Clam Sauce), 103
"Tossed" *Fettuccine* (*Fettuccine sciué-sciué*),
  109–110
with Tuna and Clam Sauce (*Pasta con
  tonno e vongole*), 103
with Vegetable Sauces, 114–119
verde (Green Pasta), 99–100
Vermicelli with Super-Quick Tomato
  Sauce (*Vermicelli al pomodoro rapidissimi*),
  114
Ziti with Fresh Tomatoes (*Ziti con pomodori
  freschi*), 117
Pasta frolla (Crostata dough), 295, 298
Pasta machine, 23
in rolling pasta, 96
Pasta pot, 23
Pasta salata per tartellette (Salty Pastry for
  tartlets), 62–63
Pasta sfogliata (Puff Pastry), 320–323
Pastella
  con lievito (Batter I [Yeast]), 25–26
  semplice (Batter II [Egg]), 27
Pastry. *See also* Puff Pastry/Pastries
  Apple Tart I (*Crostata di mele I*), 296
  Apple Tart II (*Crostata di mele II*), 297
  Apple Tart, Imperial (*Crostata imperiale di
    mele*), 298
  Crostata dough, 295, 298
  Imperial Apple Tart (*Crostata imperiale di
    mele*), 298
  Orange and Chocolate Tart (*Crostata di
    arancie e cioccolato*), 299–300
  Panettone, 314–317
  Salty, for Tartlets (*Pasta salata per tartel-
    lette*), 62–63
  Veronese Sweet Bread (*Pandoro di Verona*),
    318–319
Pastry Cream, 304

Patate. See also Potatoes
  araganate (Roast Potatoes and Tomatoes), 273
  rosse al forno (Roast Red Potatoes), 273
Pâté, Venetian (*Pâté alla veneziana*), 74–75
Peaches
  Almond Filled (*Pesche ripiene alle mandorle*), 290
  Flamed (*Pesche al brandy*), 291
Peanut oil, 11
Pear(s)
  and Cheese Mold (*Torta di formaggio con le pere*), 292–293
  Stuffed (*Pere ripiene*), 291
Peas
  Artichokes with (*Carciofi con piselli*), 257
  Chicken Legs and (*Coscie di pollo con piselli*), 209
  in Pasta with Salmon and Peas (*Pasta al salmone e piselli*), 102
  Piedmont Style (*Piselli alla piemontese*), 271
  Venetian Eels and (*Bisato e bisi*), 235
Pecorino cheese, 13
Pellegrine. See also Scallops
  alla fiorentina (Scallops, Florentine Style), 247–248
Peperoncino. See Red Pepper
Peperoni. See also Pepper(s)
  all'acciughe (Roasted Sweet Peppers with Anchovies), 58
  in casseruola (Pepper Casserole), 271
  sedani, ed olive (Pepper-Celery-Olive *Antipasto*), 59
Pepper (ground), 13
Pepper(s)
  Casserole (*Peperoni in casseruola*), 271
  -Celery-Olive *Antipasto* (*Peperoni, sedani, ed olive*), 59
  Onions and (*Cipolline con peperoni*), 270
  red. *See* Red pepper
  Sweet, Roasted with Anchovies (*Peperoni all'acciughe*), 58
  Sweet-, Spaghetti Sauce (*Spaghetti ai peperoni*), 118
Pere. See also Pear(s)
  ripiene (Stuffed Pears), 291
Pesce. See also Seafood
  al forno (Baked Red Snapper), 250
Pescespada
  al forno con patate (Baked Swordfish with Potatoes), 253
  alla griglia (Grilled Swordfish), 253
  in padella (Sautéed Swordfish), 254
Pesche
  al brandy (Flamed Peaches), 291
  ripiene alle mandorle (Almond Filled Peaches), 290

Pesto
  blender, 38
  conserving, 39
  food-processor, 39
  in general, 5–6, 36–37
  mortar and pestle, 37–38
  in Minestrone, Genoa Style (*Minestrone genovese*), 85
  in Red Mullet, Genoa Style (*Triglia alla genovese*), 243
Petti di pollo farciti (Stuffed Chicken Breasts), 205
Petto di vitello ripieno (Stuffed Veal Breast), 166
Pie
  Artichoke (*Torta di carciofi*), 259–260
  Asparagus (or Easter; *Torta di pasqua*), 261–262
  Piedmont Style Peas (*Piselli alla piemontese*), 271
  Piquant Sauce, Mussels in (*Cozze in salsa piccante*), 56
Piselli. See also Peas
  alla piemontese (Peas, Piedmont Style), 271
Pizzas, Little (*Pizzette*), 66–69
Pizzelle, Salted (*Pizzelle salate*), 330
Pizzette (Little Pizzas), 66–69
  con funghi e mozzarella (*Pizzette* with Mushrooms and *Mozzarella*), 69
  with Mushrooms and *Mozzarella* (*Pizzette con funghi e mozzarella*), 69
  con pomodori e mozzarella (*Pizzette* with Tomatoes and *Mozzarella*), 69
  with Tomatoes and *Mozzarella* (*Pizzette con pomodori e mozzarella*), 69
Pizzette dough
  food-processor, 68
  handmade, 67–68
Plum tomatoes, 16–18
Poached
  Fish Filets (*Filetti di pesce in bianco*), 227
  Salmon (*Salmone in bianco*), 243
  Scallops with Mayonnaise (*Conchiglie di San Giacomo con maionese*), 246
  Sea Bass (*Spigola in bianco*), 249
Pollame. See Poultry
Pollo. See also Chicken
  al forno (Baked Chicken), 210
  fritto (Batter-Fried Chicken), 207
  alla Marengo (Chicken Marengo), 203–204
  all'ungherese (Chicken, Hungarian Style), 208
Polpette
  di maiale e tacchino (Pork and Turkey Croquettes), 175
  di manzo (Meat Croquettes), 160

di tacchino e manzo (Turkey and Beef Croquettes), 194
Polpettone di manzo e maiale (Beef and Pork Meat Loaf), 159
Pomegranate, in Apple and Pomegranate Cake (*Torta di mele e melagrano*), 309
Pomodori. See also Tomato(es)
  ripieni alla griglia (Broiled Stuffed Tomatoes), 60
  ripieni e patate arroste (Stuffed Tomatoes with Roast Potatoes), 274
  ripieni con prosciutto cotto e formaggio (Broiled Stuffed Tomatoes with Ham and Cheese), 59
Pompelmo. See Grapefruit
Poor Gypsy's Chicken (*Galletto alla povera zingara*), 190–191
Porchetta umbriaca (Tipsy Pork Roast), 173
Pork (*Maiale*), 171–175. *See also* Salt pork
  and Beef Meat Loaf (*Polpettone di manzo e maiale*), 159
  Chops, Marinated (*Cotolette di maiale marinate*), 174
  Cutlets, Herbed, Breaded (*Cotolette di maiale all'erbe*), 173
  Loin, Boneless, with Orange Sauce (*Lombo di maiale all'arancia*), 171–172
  Roast, with Mustard (*Maiale arrosto alla senape*), 174
  Roast, Tipsy (*Porchetta umbriaca*), 173
  and Turkey Croquettes (*Polpette di maiale e tacchino*), 175
  -Veal-Ham Filling for *Cappelletti* or *Cannelloni* (*Ripieno per cappelletti o cannelloni*), 122–123
Pot Roast for the Pressure Cooker (*Stufato di manzo per la pentola a pressione*), 161
Potatoes
  Baked Swordfish with (*Pescespada al forno con patate*), 253
  Roast Red (*Patate rosse al forno*), 273
  Roast, with Stuffed Tomatoes (*Pomodori ripieni e patate arroste*), 274
  and Tomatoes, Roast (*Patate araganate*), 273
Poultry (*Pollame*), 185–213
  Baked Chicken (*Pollo al forno*), 210
  Batter-Fried Chicken (*Pollo fritto*), 207
  Chicken, Baked (*Pollo al forno*), 210
  Chicken, Batter-Fried (*Pollo fritto*), 207
  Chicken Breasts, Stuffed (*Petti di pollo farciti*), 205
  Chicken, Hungarian Style (*Pollo all'ungherese*), 208
  Chicken Legs and Peas (*Coscie di pollo con piselli*), 209

Chicken Legs in Wine Sauce (*Coscie di pollo al vino*), 206
Chicken Marengo (*Pollo alla Marengo*), 203–204
Chicken, Poor Gypsy's (*Galletto alla povera zingara*), 190–191
Christmas Turkey with Rice Stuffing (*Tacchino di Natale con ripieno di riso*), 196–197
Duck with Almonds (*Anitra alle mandorle*), 212–213
Duckling, Grilled (*Anitra alla griglia*), 211–212
Poor Gypsy's Chicken (*Galletto alla povera zingara*), 190–191
Rock Cornish Hen with Almond-Prune Stuffing (*Galletto ripieno alle mandorle e prugne*), 185–186
Rock Cornish Hen with *Grappa* (*Galletto alla grappa*), 188–189
Rock Cornish Hen with Lemon (*Galletto al limone*), 189
Rock Cornish Hen Stuffed with Mushrooms and Sausage (*Galletto ripieno ai funghi e salsiccia*), 187
Rolled Stuffed Turkey Breast in Aspic (*Rollato di tacchino ripieno in galantina*), 200–202
Stuffed Chicken Breasts (*Petti di pollo farciti*), 205
Turkey and Beef Croquettes (*Polpette di tacchino e manzo*), 194
Turkey Breast, Rolled Stuffed, in Aspic (*Rollato di tacchino ripieno in galantina*), 200–202
Turkey, Christmas, with Rice Stuffing (*Tacchino di Natale con ripieno di riso*), 197–198
Turkey *Osso Buco* (*Osso buco di tacchino*), 195
Turkey with Sausage Stuffing (*Tacchino ripieno con salsicce*), 198–199
Turkey Slices with *Prosciutto* (*Saltimbocca di tacchino*), 193
Pound Cake, Italian, 300
Pressure cooker, 24
  for Beef Broth (*Brodo di carne*), 43
  for Beef Rolls (*Involtini di manzo*), 157–158
  for Bolognese Meat Sauce (*Ragù alla bolognese*), 35–36
  for Boneless Pork Loin with Orange Sauce (*Lombo di maiale all'arancia*), 171–172
  for Chicken Broth (*Brodo di pollo*), 44
  for Chicken, Hungarian Style (*Pollo all'ungherese*), 208

Pressure cooker (*continued*)
  for Chicken Legs in Wine Sauce (*Coscie di pollo al vino*), 206
  for Chili con Carne, Roman Style (*Chili con carne alla romana*), 169–170
  for Corned Beef and Cabbage, Italian Style (*Bollito irlandese all'italiana*), 168
  for Fish Broth (*Brodo di pesce*), 47
  for Lamb with Barolo (*Agnello al Barolo*), 180
  for Lentil and Sausage Soup (*Zuppa di lenticchie e salsiccie*), 83
  for Lima Beans, Tuscan Style (*Fave alla toscana*), 269
  for Minestrone, Genoa Style (*Minestrone genovese*), 85
  for Pasta and Bean Soup (*Pasta e fagioli*), 87
  for Pot Roast (*Stufato di manzo per la pentola a pressione*), 161
  for *risotto*, 135, 136, 138–144, 146–151
  for Rock Cornish Hen with Almond-Prune Stuffing (*Galletto ripieno alle mandorle e prugne*), 185–186
  for Rock Cornish Hen with *Grappa* (*Galletto alla grappa*), 188–189
  for Rolled Breast of Veal (*Rollato di vitello per la pentola a pressione*), 165
  for Turkey Broth (*Brodo di tacchino per la pentola a pressione*), 89
  for Turkey *Osso Buco* (*Osso buco di tacchino*), 195
  for Turkey with Sausage Stuffing (*Tacchino ripieno con salsiccie*), 198–199
  for Vegetable Broth (*Brodo di verdure*), 46
Prosciutto. *See also* Ham
  in general, 13–14
  Risotto with (*Risotto al prosciutto*), 145
  in *Risotto* with Tomatoes and *Prosciutto* (*Risotto al pomodoro e prosciutto*), 149
  Turkey Slices with (*Saltimbocca di tacchino*), 193
  and Veal Birds (*Involtini di vitello e prosciutto*), 164
Prunes, in Almond-Prune Stuffing, Rock Cornish Hen with (*Galletto ripieno alle mandorle e prugne*), 185–186
Puff Pastry/Pastries (*Pasta sfogliata*), 320–323
  with Apples (*Sfogliata alle mele*), 324
  in Artichoke Pie (*Torta di carciofi*), 259
  in Asparagus or Easter Pie (*Torta di pasqua*), 261
  in Cheese-and-Spinach Turnovers (*Sfogliatine di spinaci e formaggio*), 70
  with Ham and *Ricotta* (*Sfogliatine con prosciutto e ricotta*), 72

  with Tomato and *Mozzarella* (*Sfogliatine*), 71

Ragù alla bolognese (Bolognese Meat Sauce), 35–36
Raspberry Sherbet (*Sorbetto di lampone*), 286
Ravioli
  conserving, 99
  cutting, 98
  rolling, 96
  with Filberts (*Ravioli alle nocciole*), 125–126; in Squash *Ravioli* (*Ravioli alla zucca*), 129
  alle nocciole (*Ravioli* with Filberts), 125–126
  Squash (*Ravioli alla zucca*), 129
  alla zucca (Squash *Ravioli*), 129
Red Mullet, Genoa Style (*Triglia alla genovese*), 243
Red pepper (*Peperoncino*), 14–15
Red Potatoes, Roast (*Potate rosse al forno*), 273
Red Snapper, Baked (*Pesce al forno*), 250
Rice (*Riso*), 134–152
  available brands of, 135–136
  in general, 15, 134–137
  in the pressure cooker, 135, 136
  with Artichokes (*Risotto ai carciofi*), 138
  with Asparagus (*Riso con asparagi*), 138
  and Asparagus Salad (*Insalata di riso ed asparagi*), 272
  with Chestnuts and Almonds (*Risotto alle castagne e mandorle*), 139
  with Chicken Livers (*Risotto coi fegatini*), 140
  Croquettes (*Supplì*), 137, 152
  with Eggs (*Risotto all'uovo*), 140
  with Ham and Three Cheeses (*Risotto al prosciutto e tre formaggi*), 141
  with Lemon (*Risotto al limone*), 141
  with Lobster (*Risotto all'aragosta*), 142
  Milanese (*Risotto alla milanese*), 143
  with Mushrooms (*Risotto ai funghi*), 143
  with Mushrooms, Sausages, and Bacon (*Risotto ai funghi, salsiccie, e pancetta affumicata*), 144
  with *Prosciutto* (*Risotto al prosciutto*), 145
  in Salmon Trout with Rice and Shrimp (*Trota salmonata con riso e gamberi*), 244–245
  with Shrimp and Mushrooms (*Riso con gamberetti e funghi*), 146
  with Shrimp and Mussels (*Risotto ai gamberetti e cozze*), 147
  Stuffing, Christmas Turkey with (*Tacchino di Natale con ripieno di riso*), 196–197
  with Tomatoes and Basil (*Risotto al pomodoro fresco e basilico*), 148

with Tomatoes and *Prosciutto* (*Risotto al pomodoro e prosciutto*), 149
with Turkey (*Risotto col tacchino*), 150
with Veal Kidneys and Mushrooms (*Riso con rognoni e funghi*), 151
Ricotta
in general, 15
Puff Pastries with Ham and (*Sfogliatine con prosciutto e ricotta*), 72
Rigatoni with Sausages and Mushrooms (*Rigatoni, salsicce, e funghi*), 113
Ripieno per cappelletti o cannelloni (Pork-Veal-Ham Filling for *Cappelletti* or *Cannelloni*), 122–123
Riso. See also Rice
con asparagi (Rice with Asparagus), 138
con gamberetti e funghi (Rice with Shrimp and Mushrooms), 146
con rognoni e funghi (Rice with Veal Kidneys and Mushrooms), 151
Risotto. See also Rice
broth for, 137
in general, 134–137
for *Supplì* (Croquettes), 140, 141, 143, 152
all'aragosta (*Risotto* with Lobster), 142
ai carciofi (*Risotto* with Artichokes), 138
alle castagne e mandorle (*Risotto* with Chestnuts and Almonds), 139
coi fegatini (*Risotto* with Chicken Livers), 140
ai funghi (*Risotto* with Mushrooms), 143
ai funghi, salsicce, e pancetta affumicata (*Risotto* with Mushrooms, Sausages, and Bacon), 144
ai gamberetti e cozze (*Risotto* with Shrimp and Mussels), 147
al·limone (*Risotto* with Lemon), 141
alla milanese (*Risotto* Milanese), 136–137, 143
al pomodoro fresco e basilico (*Risotto* with Tomatoes and Basil), 148
al pomodoro e prosciutto (*Risotto* with Tomatoes and *Prosciutto*), 149
al prosciutto (*Risotto* with *Prosciutto*), 145
al prosciutto e tre formaggi (*Risotto* with Ham and Three Cheeses), 141
al ragù, 137
col tacchino (*Risotto* with Turkey), 150
all'uovo (*Risotto* with Eggs), 140
Roasted Sweet Peppers with Anchovies (*Peperoni all'acciughe*), 58
Rock Cornish Hen, 185–191
with Almond-Prune Stuffing (*Galletto ripieno alle mandorle e prugne*), 185–186
with *Grappa* (*Galletto alla grappa*), 188–189
with Lemon (*Galletto al limone*), 189

Poor Gypsy's Chicken (*Galletto alla povera zingara*), 190–191
Stuffed with Mushrooms and Sausage (*Galletto ripieno ai funghi e salsiccia*), 187
Rognoni. See Veal Kidneys
Rollato
di tacchino ripieno in galantina (Rolled Stuffed Turkey Breast in Aspic), 200–202
di vitello per la pentola a pressione (Rolled Breast of Veal for the Pressure Cooker), 165
Rolled Breast of Veal for the Pressure Cooker (*Rollato di vitello per la pentola a pressione*), 165
Rolled pasta. *See* Pasta, filled, layered, rolled
Rolled Stuffed Turkey Breast in Aspic (*Rollato di tacchino ripieno in galantina*), 200–202
Rolls, Beef (*Involtini di manzo*), 157–158
Romagnola, Wine Sipping Cookies *alla* (*Biscottini alla romagnola*), 329
Roman Style Chili con Carne (*Chili con carne alla romana*), 169–170
Romano cheese, 13
Rombo alla griglia (Broiled Turbot), 254
Rosemary, 15
Russian Salad (*Insalata russa*), 64

Safflower oil, 11
Saffron, 16
Sage, 16
Saint's Day *Cannelloni* (*Cannelloni del curato*), 127–128
Salads (*Insalate*). *See also* Vegetable(s)
Avocado, Asparagus, and Artichoke (*Insalata di avocado, asparagi, e carciofi*), 262
Bean and Celery (*Insalata di fagioli e sedano*), 268
Belgian Endive–Cress (*Insalata d'indivia belga e crescione*), 263
Rice and Asparagus (*Insalata di riso ed asparagi*), 272
Russian (*Insalata russa*), 64
Salmon
and Peas, Pasta with (*Pasta al salmone e piselli*), 102
Poached (*Salmone in bianco*), 243
Steaks, Grilled (*Salmone alla griglia*), 244
Salmon Trout with Rice and Shrimp (*Trota salmonata con riso e gamberi*), 244–245
Salmone. See also Salmon
in bianco (Poached Salmon), 243
alla griglia (Grilled Salmon Steaks), 244

Salsa. See also Sauces
  di pomodoro (Tomato Sauce), 40. *See also*
    Tomato Sauce
  di pomodoro e basilico (Tomato and Basil
    Sauce), 40. *See also* Tomato and Basil
    Sauce
  verde (Green Sauce), 33–34; *see also* Green
    Sauce
  con vongole alla siciliana (Baby Clam Sauce,
    Sicilian Style), 105
Salse. See also Sauces
  vellutate, 41
Salsiccie. See Sausage(s)
Salt cod, dried (*Baccalà*), 221, 232
Salt pork, 12
Salted *Brigidini* (*Cialde, Pizzelle*) (*Brigidini sa-
  lati*), 330
Saltimbocca di tacchino (Turkey Slices with
  Prosciutto), 193
Salty Pastry for Tartlets (*Pasta salata per tar-
  tellette*), 62–63
Sauces (*Salse*)
  Baby Clam, Sicilian Style (*Salsa con vongole
    alla siciliana*), 105
  Basic, 30–42
  Bolognese Meat (*Ragù alla bolognese*),
    35–36; *Lasagne* with (*Lasagne al ragù*),
    131
  Cheese, Pasta with, 109–110
  Cherrystone Clam, Spaghetti with (*Spa-
    ghetti mare d'estate*), 104
  Clam, Baby, Sicilian Style (*Salsa con von-
    gole alla siciliana*), 105
  Clam, Pasta with Tuna and (*Pasta con
    tonno e vongole*), 103
  Crab Meat, Thin Spaghetti with (*Spaghet-
    tini al granchio*), 106
  Cream, *Cappelletti* in (*Cappelletti alla
    panna*), 124
  Fish, Pasta with, 102–108
  Green. *See* Green Sauce
  Lemon, Spaghetti with (*Spaghetti al li-
    mone*), 117
  Little Omelets with (*Frittatine al sugo*), 218
  Mayonnaise. *See* Mayonnaise
  Meat, Pasta with, 111–113
  Mushroom, *Lasagne* with (*Lasagne al sugo
    di funghi*), 130–131
  Mushroom, Pasta with (*Tonnarelli ai
    funghi*), 115
  Orange, Boneless Pork Loin with (*Lombo
    di maiale all'arancia*), 171–172
  Pesto. See Pesto
  Summer, Macaroni with (*Maccheroni al
    sugo d'estate*), 116
  Super-Quick Tomato, *Vermicelli* with (*Ver-
    micelli al pomodoro rapidissimi*), 114

Sweet Pepper, Spaghetti with (*Spaghetti ai
    peperoni*), 118
  Tomato. *See* Tomato Sauce
  Tomato and Basil. *See* Tomato and Basil
    Sauce
  Vegetable, Pasta with, 114–119
  White. *See* White Sauce
  Wine, Chicken Legs in (*Coscie di pollo al
    vino*), 206
Sausage(s)
  in Lentil and Sausage Soup (*Zuppa di len-
    ticchie e salsiccie*), 83
  and Mushrooms, *Rigatone* with (*Rigatoni,
    salsiccie, e funghi*), 113
  in *Risotto* with Mushrooms, Sausages, and
    Bacon (*Risotto ai funghi, salsiccie, e pan-
    cetta affumicata*), 144
  in Rock Cornish Hen Stuffed with Mush-
    rooms and Sausage (*Galletto ripieno ai
    funghi e salsiccia*), 187
  Stuffing, Turkey with (*Tacchino ripieno con
    salsiccie*), 198–199
Savory Squid (*Calamari all'appetitosa*), 65
Scallops
  Florentine Style (*Pellegrine alla fiorentina*),
    247–248
  Fried (*Conchiglie di San Giacomo fritte*), 245
  Poached, with Mayonnaise (*Conchiglie di
    San Giacomo con maionese*), 246
  Shrimp and (*Gamberi e cape sante*), 249
Scampi. See Shrimp
Scorfano
  al forno (Baked Grouper), 237
  coi pomodori (Grouper with Tomato
    Sauce), 238
Sea Bass
  Baked (*Branzino al forno*), 248
  Poached (*Spigola in bianco*), 249
Seafood (*Pesce*), 220–254
  in general, 220–225
  guide to, 223–225
  Baked Fish Filets (*Filetti di pesce al forno*),
    226
  Baked Grouper (*Scorfano al forno*), 237
  Baked Red Snapper (*Pesce al forno*), 250
  Baked Sea Bass (*Branzino al forno*), 248
  Baked Stuffed Haddock (*Merluzzo ripieno*),
    239–240
  Baked Swordfish with Potatoes (*Pescespada
    al forno con patate*), 253
  Boiled Lobster (*Aragosta lessa*), 241–242
  Bonito (*Tonnetto al cartoccio*), 231
  Broiled Turbot (*Rombo alla griglia*), 254
  Cocktail (*Antipasto di mare*), 61
  Cod Filets, Deep-Fried (*Filetti di baccalà
    fritti*), 232

Deep-Fried Cod Filets (*Filetti di baccalà fritti*), 232
Eels, Marinated (*Anguille marinate*), 235–236
Eels and Peas, Venetian (*Bisato e bisi*), 235
Eels on Skewers (*Spiedini d'anguille*), 236
Fish Filets, Baked (*Filetti di pesce al forno*), 226
Fish Filets, Poached (*Filetti di pesce in bianco*), 227
Fish Soup (*Zuppa di pesce*), 228–230
Fried Scallops (*Conchiglie di San Giacomo fritte*), 245
Fried Squid (*Calamari fritti*), 252
Grilled Salmon Steaks (*Salmone alla griglia*), 244
Grilled Swordfish (*Pescespada alla griglia*), 253
Grouper, Baked (*Scorfano al forno*), 237
Grouper with Tomato Sauce (*Scorfano coi pomodori*), 238
Haddock, Baked Stuffed (*Merluzzo ripieno*), 239–240
Lobster, Boiled (*Aragosta lessa*), 241–242
Marinated Eels (*Anguille marinate*), 235–236
Monkfish, Mushrooms, and Tomatoes, Skewers of (*Spiedini di rana pescatrice*), 242
Poached Fish Filets (*Filetti di pesce in bianco*), 227
Poached Salmon (*Salmone in bianco*), 243
Poached Scallops with Mayonnaise (*Conchiglie di San Giacomo con maionese*), 246
Poached Sea Bass (*Spigola in bianco*), 249
Red Mullet, Genoa Style (*Triglia alla genovese*), 243
Red Snapper, Baked (*Pesce al forno*), 250
Salmon, Poached (*Salmone in bianco*), 243
Salmon Steaks, Grilled (*Salmone alla griglia*), 244
Salmon Trout with Rice and Shrimp (*Trota salmonata con riso e gamberi*), 244–245
Sautéed Swordfish (*Pescespada in padella*), 254
Scallops, Florentine Style (*Pellegrine alla fiorentina*), 247–248
Scallops, Fried (*Conchiglie di San Giacomo fritte*), 245
Scallops, Poached, with Mayonnaise (*Conchiglie di San Giacomo con maionese*), 246
Sea Bass, Baked (*Branzino al forno*), 248
Sea Bass, Poached (*Spigola in bianco*), 249
Shrimp and Scallops (*Gamberi e cape sante*), 249
Skewers of Monkfish, Mushrooms, and Tomatoes (*Spiedini di rana pescatrice*), 242
Squid, Fried (*Calamari fritti*), 252

Squid, Venetian Style (*Seppie alla veneziana*), 252
Swordfish, Baked, with Potatoes (*Pescespada al forno con patate*), 253
Swordfish, Grilled (*Pescespada alla griglia*), 253
Swordfish, Sautéed (*Pescespada in padella*), 254
Turbot, Broiled (*Rombo alla griglia*), 254
Venetian Eels and Peas (*Bisato e bisi*), 235
Seasonings. *See* Flavorings, herbs, and ingredients
Sedani. See Celery
Semifreddo di cioccolato (Chocolate Cream Mold), 289
Senape. See Mustard
Seppie. See also Squid
   alla veneziana (Squid, Venetian Style), 252
Sfogliata alle mele (Puff Pastry with Apples), 324
Sfogliatine (Puff Pastries with Tomato and Mozzarella), 71
   con prosciutto e ricotta (Puff Pastries with Ham and Ricotta), 72
   di spinaci e formaggio (Cheese-and-Spinach Turnovers), 70
Shellfish. *See* Seafood
Sherbet (*Sorbetti*). *See also* Ice Cream; Ices
   Grapefruit, with Pomegranate Seeds (*Sorbetto di pompelmo con melagrano*), 283–284
   Lemon (*Sorbetto di limone*), 285
   Raspberry (*Sorbetto di lampone*), 286
Shrimp
   and Fresh Tomatoes, Spaghetti with (*Spaghetti agli scampi e pomodori*), 107
   and Mushrooms, Rice with (*Riso con gamberetti e funghi*), 146
   and Mussels, Risotto with (*Risotto ai gamberetti e cozze*), 147
   in Salmon Trout with Rice and Shrimp (*Trota salmonata con riso e gamberi*), 244–245
   and Scallops (*Gamberi e cape sante*), 249
Sicilian Style
   Baby Clam Sauce (*Salsa con vongole alla siciliana*), 105
   Veal on Skewers (*Spiedini alla siciliana*), 167
Skewers
   Eels on (*Spiedini d'anguille*), 236
   Lamb on (*Spiedini d'agnello*), 178–179
   of Monkfish, Mushrooms, and Tomatoes (*Spiedini di rana pescatrice*), 242
   Veal on, Sicilian Style (*Spiedini alla siciliana*), 167
Sorbetto
   di lampone (Raspberry Sherbet), 286
   di limone (Lemon Sherbet), 285

Sorbetto (continued)
  di pompelmo con melagrano (Grapefruit Sherbet with Pomegranate Seeds), 283–284
Soups (Minestre), 81–90. See also Broths
  in general, 81–82
  Artichoke (Minestra di carciofi), 82
  Fish (Zuppa di pesce), 228–230
  Lentil and Sausage (Zuppa di lenticchie e salsiccie), 83
  Lobster (Zuppa di aragosta), 84
  Minestrone, Genoa Style (Minestrone genovese), 85
  Pasta and Bean (Pasta e fagioli), 86–88
  Vegetable (Zuppa di verdure), 90
Spaghetti
  alla carbonara (Charcoal Makers' Style), 111
  Charcoal Makers' Style (Spaghetti alla carbonara), 111
  with Cherrystone Clam Sauce (Spaghetti mare d'estate), 104
  with Lemon Sauce (Spaghetti al limone), 117
  al limone (Spaghetti with Lemon Sauce), 117
  mare d'estate (Spaghetti with Cherrystone Clam Sauce), 104
  alla Paolo, 112
  ai peperoni (Spaghetti with Sweet-Pepper Sauce), 118
  agli scampi e pomodori (Spaghetti with Shrimp and Fresh Tomatoes), 107
  with Shrimp and Fresh Tomatoes (Spaghetti agli scampi e pomodori), 107
  with Sweet-Pepper Sauce (Spaghetti ai peperoni), 118
  Thin, with Crab Meat Sauce (Spaghettini al granchio), 106
Spaghettini al granchio (Thin Spaghetti with Crab Meat Sauce), 106
Spezie (Herbs). See Flavorings, herbs, and ingredients
Spezzatino d'agnello (Lamb Stew), 184
Spiedini
  d'agnello (Lamb on Skewers), 178–179
  d'anguille (Eels on Skewers), 236
  di rana pescatrice (Skewers of Monkfish, Mushrooms, and Tomatoes), 242
  alla siciliana (Veal on Skewers, Sicilian Style), 167
Spigola. See also Sea Bass
  in bianco (Poached Sea Bass), 249
Spinach, in Cheese-and-Spinach Turnovers (Sfogliatine di spinaci e formaggio), 70
Spongata imperiale (Imperial Sponge), 313
Sponge, Imperial (Spongata imperiale), 313
Sponge Cake (Pan di Spagna), 302–303

  in Almond-Chocolate Cream Cake (La Bomba mocha), 307–308
  in Chocolate Cream Mold (Semifreddo di cioccolato), 289
  in Zuppa inglese, 304
Spring Vegetables, Mixed (Padellata primaverile), 275
Spuma
  di fegatini in gelatina (Chicken Liver Mousse in Aspic), 75–76
  di tonno (Tuna Mousse), 73
Squash Ravioli (Ravioli alla zucca), 129
Squid (Calamari)
  preparing for cooking, 251–252
  Fried (Calamari fritti), 252
  Savory (Calamari all'appetitosa), 65
  Venetian Style (Seppie alla veneziana), 252
Steaks
  Lamb, Golden-Fried (Agnello fritto dorato), 183
  Salmon, Grilled (Salmone alla griglia), 244
Stew, Lamb (Spezzatino d'agnello), 184
Strawberry Ice (Granita di fragole), 288
Stufato di manzo per la pentola a pressione (Pot Roast for the Pressure Cooker), 161
Stuffed
  Cabbage (Cavolo ripieno), 264–265
  Chicken Breasts (Petti di pollo farciti), 205
  Haddock, Baked (Merluzzo ripieno), 239–240
  Mushrooms, Grilled (Funghi ripieni alla griglia), 57
  Pears (Pere ripiene), 291
  Tomatoes, Broiled (Pomodori ripieni alla griglia), 60
  Tomatoes, Broiled, with Ham and Cheese (Pomodori ripieni con prosciutto cotto e formaggio), 59
  Tomatoes with Roast Potatoes (Pomodori ripieni e patate arroste), 274
  Turkey Breast, Rolled, in Aspic (Rollato di tacchino ripieno in galantina), 200–202
  Veal Breast (Petto di vitello ripieno), 166
Stuffing
  Almond-Prune, Rock Cornish Hen with (Galletto ripieno alle mandorle e prugne), 185–186
  Rice, Christmas Turkey with (Tacchino di Natale con ripieno di riso), 196–197
  Sausage, Turkey with (Tacchino ripieno con salsiccie), 198–199
Sugo. See Sauces
Summer Sauce, Macaroni with (Maccheroni al sugo d'estate), 116
Super-Quick Tomato Sauce, Vermicelli with (Vermicelli al pomodoro rapidissimi), 114
Supplì (Rice Croquettes), 137, 152

Sweet Bread, Veronese (*Pandoro di Verona*), 318–319
Sweet *Brigidini* (*Brigidini alla franca*), 331
Sweet Peppers. *See* Pepper(s)
Swordfish
  Baked, with Potatoes (*Pescespada al forno con patate*), 253
  Grilled (*Pescespada alla griglia*), 253
  Sautéed (*Pescespada in padella*), 254

Tabasco sauce, 14
Tacchino. See also Turkey
  di Natale con ripieno di riso (Christmas Turkey with Rice Stuffing), 196–197
  ripieno con salsiccie (Turkey with Sausage Stuffing), 198–199
Tagliatelle coi fegatini (Pasta with Chicken Livers), 113
Tart
  Apple, I (*Crostata di mele I*), 296
  Apple, II (*Crostata di mele II*), 297
  Imperial Apple (*Crostata imperiale di mele*), 298
  Orange and Chocolate (*Crostata di arancie e cioccolato*), 299–300
Tartlets
  Crab Meat Filling for (*Barchette di granchio*), 63
  Salty Pastry for (*Pasta salata per tartellette*), 62–63
Temperatures, 20–21
Tenderloin of Beef
  Marco Polo (*Filetto alla Marco Polo*), 163
  Roast (*Filetto di manzo arrosto*), 162
Thin Spaghetti with Crab Meat Sauce (*Spaghettini al granchio*), 106
Tipsy Pork Roast (*Porchetta umbriaca*), 173
Tomato(es). *See also* Tomato and Basil Sauce; Tomato Sauce
  fresh, 17
  in general, 16–18
  ground, 17
  and Basil, *Risotto* with (*Risotto al pomodoro fresco e basilico*), 148
  Broiled Stuffed (*Pomodori ripieni alla griglia*), 60
  Broiled Stuffed, with Ham and Cheese (*Pomodori ripieni con prosciutto cotto e formaggio*), 59
  Fresh, in Spaghetti with Shrimp and Fresh Tomatoes (*Spaghetti agli scampi e pomodori*), 107
  Fresh, *Ziti* with (*Ziti con pomodori freschi*), 117
  and *Mozzarella*, *Pizzette* with (*Pizzette con pomodori e mozzarella*), 69
  and *Mozzarella*, Puff Pastry with (*Sfogliatine*), 71
  and *Prosciutto*, *Risotto* with (*Risotto al pomodoro e prosciutto*), 149
  and Roast Potatoes (*Patate araganate*), 273
  in Skewers of Monkfish, Mushrooms, and Tomatoes (*Spiedini di rana pescatrice*), 242
  Stuffed, with Roast Potatoes (*Pomodori ripieni e patate arroste*), 274
Tomato and Basil Sauce (*Salsa di pomodoro e basilico*), 40
  in Little Omelets with Sauce (*Frittatine al sugo*), 218
Tomato juice, 18
Tomato paste, 17, 18
Tomato puree, 17
Tomato Sauce (*Salsa di pomodoro*), 40
  in Chicken, Hungarian Style (*Pollo all'ungherese*), 208
  Grouper with (*Scorfano coi pomodori*), 238
  in Puff Pastries with Tomato and *Mozzarella* (*Sfogliatine*), 71
  Super-Quick, *Vermicelli* with (*Vermicelli al pomodoro rapidissimi*), 114
Tonnarelli
  conserving, 99
  cutting, 98
  rolling, 96
  ai funghi (Pasta with Mushroom Sauce), 115
Tonnetto al cartoccio (Bonito), 231
Tonno. See Tuna
Torta. See also Cake
  di carciofi (Artichoke Pie), 259–260
  di formaggio con le pere (Pear and Cheese Mold), 292–293
  grande (Duck Egg Cake), 311
  Margherita (Margherita Cake), 306. *See also* Margherita Cake
  di mele e melagrano (Apple and Pomegranate Cake), 309
  paradiso (Paradise Cake), 312
  di pasqua (Asparagus or Easter Pie), 261–262
"Tossed" *Fettuccine* (*Fettuccine sciué-sciué*), 109–110
Triglia alla genovese (Red Mullet, Genoa Style), 243
Trota salmonata con riso e gamberi (Salmon Trout with Rice and Shrimp), 244–245
Trout, Salmon, with Rice and Shrimp (*Trota salmonata con riso e gamberi*), 244–245
Tuna
  in general, 18
  and Clam Sauce, Pasta with (*Pasta con tonno e vongole*), 103
  Mousse (*Spuma di tonno*), 73

Turbot, Broiled (*Rombo alla griglia*), 254
Turkey (*Tacchino*), 192–202
  in general, 192
  and Beef Croquettes (*Polpette di tacchino e manzo*), 194
  Breast, Rolled Stuffed, in Aspic (*Rollato di tacchino ripieno in galantina*), 200–202
  Broth for the Pressure Cooker (*Brodo di tacchino per la pentola a pressione*), 89
  Christmas, with Rice Stuffing (*Tacchino di Natale con ripieno di riso*), 196–197
  Osso Buco (*Osso buco di tacchino*), 195
  and Pork Croquettes (*Polpette di maiale e tacchino*), 175
  Risotto with (*Risotto col tacchino*), 150
  with Sausage Stuffing (*Tacchino ripieno con salsiccie*), 198–199
  Slices with *Prosciutto* (*Saltimbocca di tacchino*), 193
Turnovers, Cheese-and-Spinach (*Sfogliatine di spinaci e formaggio*), 70
Tuscan Style Lima Beans (*Fave alla toscana*), 269

Umbrian Style Lamb Roast (*Arrosto d'agnello*), 182
Uovo. See Eggs

Vanilla Ice Cream (*Gelato alla vaniglia*), 281
Veal (*Vitello*)
  Breast, Stuffed (*Petto di vitello ripieno*), 166
  Kidneys and Mushrooms, Rice with (*Riso con rognoni e funghi*), 151
  in Pork-Veal-Ham Filling for *Cappelletti* or *Cannelloni* (*Ripieno per cappelletti o cannelloni*), 122–123
  and *Prosciutto* Birds (*Involtini di vitello e prosciutto*), 164
  Rolled Breast of, for the Pressure Cooker (*Rollato di vitello per la pentola a pressione*), 165
  on Skewers, Sicilian Style (*Spiedini alla siciliana*), 167
Vegetable(s) (*Verdure*). *See also* Salads; Vegetable Broth; Vegetable Sauces
  in general, 255–256
  Apple and Onion Rings (*Anelli di mele e cipolle*), 256
  Artichoke Casserole (*Parmigiana di carciofi*), 258
  Artichoke Pie (*Torta di carciofi*), 259–260
  Artichokes, Golden-Fried (*Carciofi fritti dorati*), 257; in Artichoke Casserole (*Parmigiana di carciofi*), 258
  Artichokes with Peas (*Carciofi con piselli*), 257

Asparagus or Easter Pie (*Torta di pasqua*), 261–262
Baked Eggplant (*Melanzane al forno*), 266
Brussels Sprouts and Onions (*Cavolini di Bruxelles e cipolline*), 263
Cabbage, Stuffed (*Cavolo ripieno*), 264–265
Carrots and Mushrooms (*Carote e funghi*), 265
Eggplant, Baked (*Melanzane al forno*), 266
Fennel Baked with Cheese (*Finocchio ai formaggi*), 267
Golden-Fried Artichokes (*Carciofi fritti dorati*), 257; in Artichoke Casserole (*Parmigiana di carciofi*), 258
Green Beans, Florentine Style (*Fagiolini alla fiorentina*), 268
Lentils, New Year's Day (*Lenticchie del primo d'anno*), 270
Lima Beans, Tuscan Style (*Fave alla toscana*), 269
Mixed Spring (*Padellata primaverile*), 275
New Year's Day Lentils (*Lenticchie del primo d'anno*), 270
Onions and Peppers (*Cipolline con peperoni*), 270
Peas, Piedmont Style (*Piselli alla piemontese*), 271
Pepper Casserole (*Peperoni in casseruola*), 271
Platter (*Verdure all'agro*), 276
Potatoes, Red, Roast (*Patate rosse al forno*), 273
Potatoes, Roast, and Tomatoes (*Patate araganate*), 273
Roast Potatoes and Tomatoes (*Patate araganate*), 273
Roast Red Potatoes (*Patate rosse al forno*), 273
Soup (*Zuppa di verdure*), 90
Stuffed Cabbage (*Cavolo ripieno*), 264–265
Stuffed Tomatoes with Roast Potatoes (*Pomodori ripieni e patate arroste*), 274
Tomatoes, Stuffed, with Roast Potatoes (*Pomodori ripieni e patate arroste*), 274
Vegetable Broth (*Brodo di verdure*), 46
  in *risotto*, 138, 146
Vegetable oils, 11
Vegetable Sauces, Pasta with, 114–119
  Artichokes (*Pasta ai carciofi*), 119
  Fresh Tomatoes, *Ziti* with (*Ziti con pomodori freschi*), 117
  Lemon, Spaghetti with (*Spaghetti al limone*), 117
  Mushroom (*Tonnarelli ai funghi*), 115
  Mushrooms and Ham, *Fettuccine* with (*Fettuccine ai funghi e prosciutto*), 118

Summer, Macaroni with (*Maccheroni al sugo d'estate*), 116
Super-Quick Tomato, *Vermicelli* with (*Vermicelli al pomodoro rapidissimi*), 114
Sweet Pepper, Spaghetti with (*Spaghetti ai peperoni*), 118
Tomato, Super-Quick, *Vermicelli* with (*Vermicelli al pomodoro rapidissimi*), 114
Tomatoes, Fresh, *Ziti* with (*Ziti con pomodori freschi*), 117
Venetian
  Crab Meat (*Granzeola alla veneziana*), 55
  Eels and Peas (*Bisato e bisi*), 235
  Pâté (*Pâté alla veneziana*), 74–75
  Squid (*Seppie alla veneziana*), 252
Verdure. See also Vegetable(s)
  all'agro (Vegetable Platter), 276
Vermicelli with Super-Quick Tomato Sauce (*Vermicelli al pomodoro rapidissimi*), 114
Veronese Sweet Bread (*Pandoro di Verona*), 318–319
Vitello. See Veal
Vongole. See Clam Sauce

Watermelon, Filled (*Cocomero ripieno*), 294
Weights and measures, 19–20
White Sauce (*Besciamella/Balsamella*), 41–42, 75
  in Fennel Baked with Cheese (*Finocchio ai formaggi*), 267

in *Lasagne* with Bolognese Meat Sauce (*Lasagne al ragù*), 131
in *Lasagne* with Mushroom Sauce (*Lasagne al sugo di funghi*), 130
in Pork-Veal-Ham Filling for *Cappelletti* or *Cannelloni* (*Ripieno per cappelletti o cannelloni*), 122–123
in Stuffed Cabbage (*Cavolo ripieno*), 264–265
Wine Sauce, Chicken Legs in (*Coscie di pollo al vino*), 206
Wine Sipping Cookies *alla Romagnola* (*Biscottini alla romagnola*), 329
Wines, Italian, 333–339

Yeast Batter (*Pastella con lievito*), 25–26

Zabaglione, 332
Zaletto (Corn Meal Cake), 310
Ziti with Fresh Tomatoes (*Ziti con pomodori freschi*), 117
Zucca. See Squash
Zucchini Omelet (*Frittata di zucchine*), 217
Zuppa. See also Soups
  di aragosta (Lobster Soup), 84
  inglese, 304–305
  di lenticchie e salsiccie (Lentil and Sausage Soup), 83
  di pesce (Fish Soup), 228–230
  di verdure (Vegetable Soup), 90